REIMAGINING LIVELIHOODS

Diverse Economies and Livable Worlds

Series Editors J. K. GIBSON-GRAHAM, MALIHA SAFRI,
KEVIN ST. MARTIN, STEPHEN HEALY

REIMAGINING LIVELIHOODS

Life beyond Economy, Society, and
Environment

ETHAN MILLER

Diverse Economies and Livable Worlds

University of Minnesota Press

Minneapolis

London

Portions of the Introduction and chapters 1, 2, 3, 5, 7, and 9 were previously published as "Economization and Beyond: (Re)composing Livelihoods in Maine, USA," *Environment and Planning A* 46, no. 11 (2014): 2735–51; copyright 2014 by Pion and its Licensors; reprinted by permission of SAGE Publications, Ltd. Portions of chapter 9 have been published as Ethan Miller and J. K. Gibson-Graham, "From Economy/Ecology to Ecological Livelihoods," in *Thinking in the World*, edited by Jill Bennett and Mary Zourazni (London: Bloomsbury, 2019).

Published by the University of Minnesota Press
111 Third Avenue South, Suite 290
Minneapolis, MN 55401-2520
http://www.upress.umn.edu

Printed on acid-free paper

The University of Minnesota is an equal-opportunity educator and employer.

Library of Congress Cataloging-in-Publication Data
Names: Miller, Ethan, author.
Title: Reimagining livelihoods : life beyond economy, society, and environment / Ethan Miller.
Description: Minneapolis : University of Minnesota Press, [2019] | Series: Diverse economies and livable worlds | Includes bibliographical references and index.
Identifiers: LCCN 2018037442 (print) | ISBN 978-1-5179-0431-9 (hc) | ISBN 978-1-5179-0432-6 (pb)
Subjects: LCSH: Economic development—Environmental aspects. | Economic development—Social aspects.
Classification: LCC HD75.6 .M558 2019 (print) | DDC 338.9—dc23
LC record available at https://lccn.loc.gov/2018037442

For Julie and Kath

CONTENTS

INTRODUCTION

Troubling Economy, Society,
and Environment in Maine

RICK AND THERESA live in rural northern Maine with their three children.[1] For nearly thirty years, Rick worked in a sawmill owned by an ever-changing sequence of multinational firms. He cut Maine trees into the lumber that fed the U.S. housing construction bubble, making what for his part of the world was a decent wage—that is, until the mill's corporate managers decided that it was no longer adequately profitable, shut down the mill, and sold off its equipment. Rick is now unemployed, along with 150 other people in his small rural community. There are no other mills, and few decent jobs to speak of in the nearby area. His wife, Theresa, works part-time as a housecleaner while also taking primary responsibility for childcare, and her income plus Rick's unemployment benefits and some food stamps are now the only financial support for them and their three children.

Rick is angry: no way of sustaining his family, now "on the goddamn dole like one of those lazy parasites who just *take and take* from hard-working Americans." His family has been in this part of Maine for five generations—it's the only place he knows, and it's *home*. Now he might have to leave, but to where? "Illegal immigrants are taking the jobs everywhere," he says, "and a hard-working man can't make an honest living anymore." Meanwhile, "a bunch of rich yuppie environmentalists" are coming up here and proposing to turn these woods into a National Park. "These are the same people," thinks Rick, "whose regulations sent my job packing to places with a better business climate, and now they want to lock up the resource for good so they can have their spiritual experiences in the so-called 'wilderness' that my people have been working in, hunting in, and managing for more than a hundred years!"

Maine media outlets have reported that the mill closed due to "market pressures," and that the company was responding to the "economic reality" of an increasingly competitive "global marketplace." Rick is a casualty of this "inevitable" response. Experts are now studying and discussing what (if anything) can be done to ensure an "economic recovery," to encourage "much-needed economic growth" in this "hard-hit" area. Economists and economic developers rally to proclaim that Maine needs less red tape, new job-training programs, a more hospitable "business climate," and a revolution of "innovation" that will create new products for people like Rick to manufacture.

Meanwhile, a host of social workers are mobilizing to help Rick "get back on his feet," to help him cultivate "social capital" and ensure that he becomes an "asset" to the region. He and Theresa get letters in the mail almost weekly from the cruelly named Maine Office of Family Independence telling them what they must do in order to keep getting benefits. Theresa despairs about their situation, fearing the worst and feeling little but spiteful judgment from the institutional landscape that now overtly sustains her family. The message is loud and clear, and it only reinforces resentment and despair: When you cease to have a job, when you are no longer able to be part of "the economy," you become a parasite, a liability to your "society," someone who needs help. And this "help" comes primarily in the form of pushing you to become—as one Maine Community Action Program mission statement puts it—"self-sufficient." What this means in practice is: "no longer dependent on a handout," "employable," "competitive," "appropriately skilled," and "adaptable" for the "dynamic" (i.e., perpetually volatile) economy of the future. Rick and Theresa's whole community and region have effectively become target zones for economic developers and social workers, all concerned to adjust, adapt, and discipline the population into conformity with the economic imperatives of the times. This is not an ill-intentioned conspiracy; it is, for those earnestly involved, a necessary response to crisis.

The shifting fortune of Maine workers, however, is not the only crisis unfolding in northern Maine. Environmentalists are also raising urgent concerns: the abundant trees of this heavily forested region are the "lungs of the world" and are needed for carbon sequestration to mitigate climate change; this landscape is filled with endangered and threatened species who need our help; humans need "wild places" to be sane and healthy, and we're losing them everywhere. In short, there is something called "the environment" that needs saving, and Rick and Theresa live amid this environment but are not part of it. Perhaps they are its enemies; unless, of course (the message from environmentalists goes), they support the National Park and accept that ecotourism jobs can transform the seeming "trade-offs" between economy and environment into a "win-win" situation of renewed (presumably capitalist, and probably low-paid) wage work. Most often, however, it would seem that Rick, Theresa, and so many others must simply choose (if it is a choice at all) between "economy" and "environment." When the children are at risk of going hungry, and "the economy" has captured so many of the means of livelihood via an enforced dependence on monetary exchange and employment, the choice is rarely difficult to make.

The characters in this story are caught up in what can be called a "hegemonic assemblage" of *economy*, *society*, and *environment*. In Maine, as in so many other places around the world, these three categories and their associated materialities constitute a particular space of common sense within which struggles over life and livelihood unfold. Whether we are asked to choose between inevitable trade-offs, seek balances, harmonize efforts, or forge new connections, economy, society, and environment stand as pervasive—indeed, obligatory—articulations of the structure of reality. Yet these terms of engagement are neither innocent nor inevitable. This trio is a contingent, historically produced configuration, born from the throes of capitalist industrialism and colonialism. Its distinctions do not simply describe domains of reality with(in) which we must contend; they work to *produce* these distinctions while covering over their own contingency in the name of objective explanation.

Multiple relations of power are differentially actualized here: divisions between nature and culture, oscillations between dynamics of state governmentality and capital accumulation, and a linear movement of "development" pushing toward endless growth and a never-achieved Promised Land. Whether due to the ways that these distinctions isolate certain relations of sustenance ("the economy") into a reified domain of depoliticized, asocial, and anti-ecological inevitability, or to the ways in which they reproduce divisions between a "human" sociality and a nonhuman "environment," this trio functions to reinforce multiple ethical and political patterns that undermine possibilities for human and more-than-human flourishing. In Maine, where the empirical work of this book is situated, this has entailed the naturalization of capitalist employment and monetary exchange as the only legitimate mode of sustenance; the autonomous (isolated), self-sufficient (employed) individual as the normative model of humanity; a reinforcement of separations between humans and the more-than-human living world; and an obligation to subordinate all other concerns to the demands of these articulations. This book begins from the intuition that our ability to distinguish among entities called "economy," "society," and "environment" is a problematic symptom of a mode of collective organization and thought that must be radically and creatively transformed.

Troubling the Trio

My own concerns about this trio and its politics began to crystallize during my participation in the struggle over the Plum Creek company's "concept plan" for a major resort development on the shores of Moosehead Lake in northern Maine. A real estate investment trust based in Seattle, Washington, Plum Creek purchased 905,000 acres of Maine forestland from the South African paper company Sappi in 1998. This land had been zoned for timber management by the region's Land Use Regulation Commission (LURC), and Plum Creek requested the rezoning of approximately 17,000 acres to enable the development of 975 single-family vacation residences and two high-amenity, shoreline luxury resorts comprising 1,050 total residential units. For those in favor of the plan, Plum Creek's proposed development was "an ideal balance of planned development and conservation that will help revitalize the area as a destination for nature-based tourism, and fulfill a demonstrated need for economic development" (Fichtner 2007).[2] For many of those opposed, it was a dangerous and poorly aimed response to such a need, undermining the very ecotourist potentials it claimed to enhance and ultimately despoiling one of the largest remaining undeveloped forestlands in the eastern United States (Carley 2007). After nearly five years, three hundred hours of hearings, reams of testimony and cross-examination by twenty-eight intervening parties, multiple acts of anonymous sabotage targeting Plum Creek, nonviolent civil disobedience, and an appeal taken all the way to the Maine Supreme Court, the investment trust prevailed.[3]

For all the heated debate and struggle, however, much of the conflict unfolded on—and, in fact, served to *affirm*—a distinctly shared terrain. There was something called "the environment," and specific concerns that could be labeled "environmental," which pertained to a nonhuman world of aesthetically pleasing landscapes, a "heritage" of "unspoiled" places, and exotic organisms inhabiting ecosystems in which (certain) humans could exercise "primitive recreation opportunities" (Didisheim and De Wan 2006; Spalding 2007). There was, on the other hand, an "economy," and forces or demands designated as "economic." Here, an undisputed need for increased numbers of jobs and "opportunities" for local people was positioned in a wider context of "economic forces" that affirmed regional subordination to inevitable competitive demands. Torn or pinched between these two domains were regional "communities," constituted simultaneously as sites of organic unity and legitimacy whose "voices" were to be determinate in the deliberation process and as sites of deficiency or lack—desperate collectivities with little choice but to accept the only viable option for economic salvation that was offered to them (Fish 2006; Bowley 2007). "Environment" and "society" were expressed as important concerns by parties on both sides of the conflict, but most often amid affirmation that legitimate or politically effective expressions of these values could be articulated only in quantitative *economic* terms—as numbers of jobs, volumes of monetary transactions, or market valuations of recreation, open space, and "ecosystem services." The actual debate, for the mainstream parties, was effectively over whether regional underdevelopment should be addressed via a (low-wage, seasonal) tourism industry built on luxury resorts and second homes or on (low-wage, seasonal) "sustainable" ecotourism and protected recreation lands. Where was the space for radical, creative alternatives?

The eclectic group of activists with whom I was working, positioned outside the mainstream of either set of groups yet adamantly opposed to Plum Creek's proposal, attempted to open up a different space of contestation and possibility. Inspired by the work of J. K. Gibson-Graham and the Community Economies Collective, as well as by numerous emerging "solidarity economy" organizing efforts around the world, we challenged the core framing of the issue. This was not about which strategy would most effectively "balance" the demands of economic laws with the need for a protected "environment," but rather about how to craft forms of collective life in northern Maine communities that refuse to make such a distinction and that actively resist institutions and patterns of power that produce these apparent trade-offs. "True 'development,'" we wrote in our final submitted testimony to LURC, "is the development of the capacity of individuals and communities to be active, healthy, and empowered participants in family and community life, and the maintenance of the capacity of ecosystems to sustain themselves and we who depend on them" (Native Forest Network 2008, 72). But it was too little, too late. Our perspectives on the struggle not only were up against a tremendous volume of organized money and institutional capacity, but also ran counter to a hegemonic assemblage of "reality" itself. With the world divided into particular, seemingly inevitable articulations of economy, society, and environment, and with people on all sides of the debate continually affirming this world as the only viable space for contestation, our "alternative visions for North Woods communities" (2008, 66) would appear not only unviable and unreasonable, but also *unintelligible*. With well-being measured in dollars and "the environment" appearing as a special interest of elites "from away" (as they say in northern Maine), Plum Creek was a shoo-in. As one local person depicted in a 2008 Plum Creek television advertisement, put it: "It may not be the best plan, but it's the only plan we've got."[4]

My concerns about the trio came to a conceptual head one year later as I was presenting an introductory workshop at the U.S. Solidarity Economy Forum in Amherst, Massachusetts. I was uncomfortable with the narrow implications of the term "economy" in the phrase "solidarity economy," since many organizing efforts identified by this name are clearly oriented well beyond economistic framings, seeking to construct wider articulations of human and more-than-human flourishing.[5] I showed, therefore, a slide depicting a simple triangle: at each point was written, respectively, "economic solidarity," "social solidarity," and "environmental solidarity," their triangulation indicating that one must keep all three in play while building transformative movements. As I described this framework to my audience, I could hear another voice speaking inside me: "What are you *saying*? What, really, are the differences between these three points? Isn't this just a problematic patch-job trying to cover over the fact that the very distinctions themselves must be taken as a problem?" While I may have reminded my fellow activists that a solidarity *economy* was not alone sufficient, I participated in reproducing a division that I could not defend. In what sense are the economic and the social not always already "environmental"? In what sense can an "economy" be isolated—even for strategic or analytical purposes—from a domain of sociality? Don't these distinctions—regardless of the precision of their definitions—in fact reproduce an ethico-political habitat in which capitalist economism, human exceptionalism, and multiple forms of colonial domination can continue to thrive? Is this not the very structure of thought that rendered alternatives to the framing of the Plum Creek struggle nonviable?

Significant critical scholarly work in philosophy, political theory, science studies, and critical geography has focused on each of the three categories in turn, challenging the ways in which their presumed distinction, objectivity, systematicity, and hierarchization variously function to cover over radical difference, support assertions of necessity, limit imagination, and render a politics of the categories themselves invisible. From Bruno Latour's (2005) critique of the "social" and J. K. Gibson-Graham's deconstruction of "the economy" (Cameron and Gibson-Graham 2003; Gibson-Graham 2006c) to the multiple challenges mounted against concepts of "nature" and "environment" (e.g., Soper 1995; Braun and Castree 1998; Latour 2004a), each term increasingly appears as a contingent, historically produced articulation loaded with problematic ethical and political implications. Additionally, a host of scholarship has located itself at various sites of pairing between the categories, seeking to interrogate and often reconfigure their relationships: *economy-society*, *society-environment*, and *economy-environment*. Hybrid disciplines (e.g., environmental sociology, environmental economics, and social ecology) have emerged at these intersections, questioning conventional relations between the terms.

Surprisingly little critical work, however, has engaged economy, society, and environment *as a trio* outside common rhetoric about "trade-offs," "balances," and "triple bottom lines."[6] It is as if only two balls can be juggled at one time, or only two categories deconstructed simultaneously—as if one of the three fields must remain tacitly stabilized as a foundation for thought or as the ground from which the others can be challenged. It is admittedly unsettling to confront the limits of all three world-constitutive articulations simultaneously. Where are we left standing? But this work cannot ultimately be avoided. Economy, society, and environment are intimately interrelated, even co-constituted, on numerous levels. As I will describe further in chapter 1, this trio was born from the same historical formation, and the stability of each category relies on the others. One does not simply encounter (much less resolve) a conflict between an "economy," a "society," and an "environment"; these terms *co-construct the very context within which such conflicts appear.* They cannot be critically engaged in isolation, but must be challenged together, as a single assemblage.

Such a challenge can be posed, of course, only if one refuses to accept these categories as simply *given.* To a widely circulating common sense, this refusal might seem absurd. What do economists *do* if not identify the specific mechanics of an economy that they encounter "out there" in the world? How can sociologists study "society" if it isn't already present for them to engage with? The environment, surely, is the very *opposite* of a "social construction," confronting humans with multiple demands and limits that clearly exist independently of any discourse about them. Yet these are precisely the kinds of assumptions that threads of poststructuralist and "new materialist" theory have called into question. In various ways, writers such as Michel Foucault, Gilles Deleuze, Judith Butler, Donna Haraway, and Bruno Latour (among many others) have argued that the categories with which we organize the world are not simply neutral descriptions of objective realities awaiting elucidation, but rather are *technologies of world-making,* "performative" articulations that participate in the composition of that which they purport only to describe. While one can clearly say that human beings have always participated in processes of production and transaction, an "economy" emerges only via a historically specific configuration of discursive practices and constructed material relations. Sociality may be present in multiple forms across human and more-than-human communities, but it takes a specific set of contingent, material-semiotic interventions to produce a distinct domain that can be marked off as "society" or "the social." And though all living beings can be said to subsist within a web of ecological relations, these become an "environment" only when made so by particular practices of representation and material construction. Economy, society, and environment are neither inevitable realities nor neutral descriptions.

As this book argues, there are politics at play not only in the definitions of these categories and their relations, but also in their very *production* as operative, world-changing distinctions. These are not politics in the conventional sense of public deliberations about rules and distributions, but rather *ontological politics* that entail struggles over the composition of the terms of reality itself, or as Annemarie Mol puts it, "the way in which 'the real' is implicated in the 'political' and vice versa" (1998, 74). Such an approach asks of any given articulation: What are its effects? What does it open and what does it foreclose? What relations of power does it affirm and express? How does it *fail* to become the singular shape of reality (always remaining one partial articulation among others)? What multiplicity does it express beyond its hegemonic forms? What are its "lines of flight" (Deleuze and Guattari 1987, 203) that unravel it toward other becomings? What other worlds are clamoring, beyond its reach, to be born?

Situated Engagements

This book emerges from a process of thinking-in-place. While it is, in many ways, a "theory book," engaging threads of postdevelopment, posthumanist, and new materialist thought, it is born from and rooted in my commitment to the place I have called home for the past twenty years: the state of Maine, in the northeasternmost corner of the United States (Figure 1).[7] Driven by a long-term commitment to transformative work in this place, and informed by years of participation in grassroots efforts around alter-globalization, immigrant and worker rights, racial justice, land protection, and cooperative livelihood in the state, my theoretical work in these pages is inextricably bound together with the landscapes and communities it seeks to engage. I view theory as a tool for challenging fixed modes of thought, opening up new possibilities, and enabling transformative action in the world, and I practice it here as a process of experimentation and provocation. In one sense, then, I mobilize it in this book to explore possibilities for a different kind of politics *in* Maine, composing concepts that might do real work when translated from this text into other forms of practice. In another sense, I hope that by thinking with theory in Maine, I might spark productive "transpositions" (Braidotti 2006) for and by people working in other places. I write *from* and *in* my place for those here and elsewhere whom this thinking might generatively spark and incite.

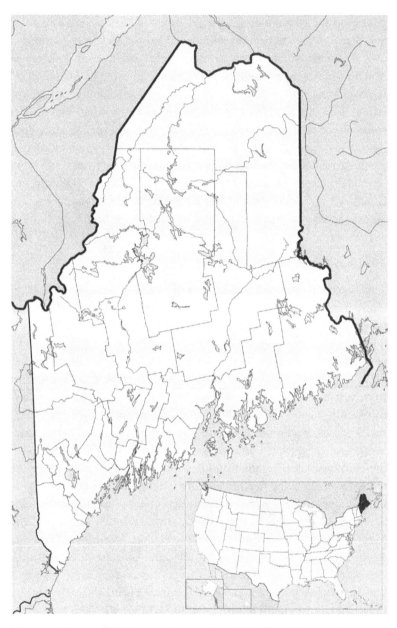

Figure 1. The state of Maine and its location in the United States. Images by Alexrk2 and TUBS, Wikimedia Commons.

Maine: "The Way Life Should Be"

Maine is a particularly good place to think with when it comes to economy, society, and environment.[8] Widely known for its harsh winters, rocky coastlines, extensive forests, and wild lakes, not to mention the lobsters and moose whose images adorn much of the state's tourist propaganda, human livelihoods in the state of Maine have long been bound together with the living abundance of land and waters. Waves of European settlers usurped much (though not all) of this abundance from the Wabanaki people beginning in the late seventeenth century, constructing multiple, overlapping cultures of subsistence and commercial extraction around forestry, farming, and fishing (MacDougall 2004; Rolde 2004). Formerly a hinterland of Massachusetts, Maine has functioned for centuries as a kind of internal colony (Osborn 1974) with all the complexity that this entails. As a peripheral site for resource extraction to serve the "core," Maine supplied timber, food, and low-cost labor to the capitalists of Boston. As a celebrated site of "wild" and "pristine" landscapes (Judd and Beach 2003), Maine has served as a recreational escape for the wealthy whose industrial endeavors have made their own places less livable. As a "frontier" space, somewhat removed from the influence of dominant (urban) U.S. cultural trends, the state has developed proud, independent-minded, sufficiency-oriented rural cultures and communities. These communities, at the same time, have continually failed to achieve the standards of living determined by conventional measures to be viable or desirable. Maine has, in this way, been constituted as *underdeveloped*, in need of more "economic" activity to generate a higher standard of living. These multiple dimensions produce a web of tension and conflict. Over the past five decades, in particular, shifting extractive resource practices and changes in industry configurations have increasingly collided with heightened concerns for the well-being of nonhuman species and ecosystems, and Maine has emerged as a significant site of conflict over how "we"—the very definition of which is at stake—should live together on a shared earth.[9] It is the perfect setup for a constellation of tensions among an economy, a society, and an environment.

Amid such conflict, Maine is also an excellent "living laboratory" in which to experiment with alternative forms of political articulation. A large and significantly rural state with a relatively small population

(1.5 million people, the lowest population density of any state in the eastern United States), Maine is home to a complex and variously interconnected patchwork of indigenous communities, working-class settler families with deep generational roots, wealthy seasonal residents, baby boomer "back-to-the-landers," East African refugees, and young aspiring organic farmers (among many others). A longstanding set of cultural and political traditions, including the informal mutual-aid of rural "neighborliness" and the direct democracy forum of the New England town meeting (Palmer et al. 2009), create unusual potential for interactions across difference, even as these traditions also continue to constitute sites of significant exclusion.[10] This extends to many of Maine's institutions as well. The state is known to have a relatively informal and accessible political culture, which enables comparatively high degrees of interaction between policymakers and citizens.[11] One can imagine, in Maine more than many other states, effectively inserting new forms of political articulation into the wider field of public contestation and institution. Whether they "work" or not is a matter of active experimentation.

Finally, Maine is articulated around a set of internal and external self-images that render it particularly fertile for this kind of work. The state's widely held self-image as "a place apart" (Palmer et al. 2009, 5), unique from the rest of the United States, may contribute to a collective sense that Maine is willing to break with certain dominant significations of "typical" American places. It is less strange in Maine, compared to many other more "developed" places in the United States, to speak about living off the land, surviving by nonmonetary trade, creating a life from multiple forms of work and income, or relying on nonfamily relationships for crucial dimensions of sustenance. At the same time, Maine has crafted—via no small effort in advertising over the past hundred years—a wider public image as a place where life is slower, healthier, and more connected. Visitors driving into Maine on Interstate 95 are greeted with the state's publicity motto: "Maine: The Way Life Should Be." While this phrase rings hollow for many people struggling to make ends meet, it nonetheless exceeds its utility as a mere marketing slogan. It stands as an aspiration or even normative demand toward something not yet achieved, yet still possible. It is an open question: How *should* life be? Who decides? And how might we produce the conditions under which these questions can grow into viable new experiments in living?

Provocative Conversations

The empirical research upon which this book is based consists of a series of in-depth interviews with Maine professionals working in economic development, social service, and environmental advocacy, plus close readings of publications associated with their work.[12] I could have taken any number of approaches to a critical and generative engagement with this trio in Maine, but I have opted for one that is quite literal: I have gone directly to those people whose daily paid work is ostensibly oriented around the ongoing articulation of one of the three categories. Why this choice? On a personal level, I wanted to extend myself beyond the activist and "alternative" milieu of which I have been a part for the past two decades. As a founding member of a cooperative subsistence farm and community land trust in central Maine and a long-time advocate and practitioner of "postcapitalist politics" (Gibson-Graham 2006a), I might all-too-easily remain ensconced in a world outside of a mainstream that must be engaged. On a wider political level, I sought to take these hegemonic articulations "head-on": Can I find, even in the heart of what might seem to be the places of their greatest strength and collective investment, openings toward another kind of politics beyond economy, society, and environment? With a commitment, in particular, to generating useful tools for thought and action, I *needed* my research to engage with people, institutions, and practices of articulation that would challenge me to make this work as connective and relevant as possible even in the most conventional institutional worlds.

My style of interviewing, as well as my practices of interpretation, reflect this commitment to transformation. A conventional (one might even say "hegemonic") notion of the interview tends to present the interviewer as a detached observer, asking questions so as to "maximize the flow of valid, reliable information while minimizing distortions of what the respondent knows" (Holstein and Gubrium 2003, 67). Pursuing such an approach, I would have engaged my interviewees with as little prompting and interference as possible, seeking to uncover what they "really" think or how they "really" talk about their realities even in my absence. In contrast, and following in the footsteps of a variety of critical, feminist, and action research traditions that view fieldwork as an active, situated process of intervention in the world, I pursued these interviews as dynamic and potentially transformative mutual encounters. I have engaged my interviewees not as sources to be mined for data, but rather as collaborators and co-thinkers in multi-layered, "non-innocent conversations" (Haraway 1991, 199)

One might think, at various moments in this book, that I am guilty of "leading" my interviewees to generate the kinds of clear and relevant comments that I describe. But the very notion of "leading the interviewee" must be challenged here. If an interview is a dynamic mutual encounter intended to generate transformations of collective understanding, then the problem of "leading" shifts to one of ethically negotiating languages, matters of concern, and relations of power. How can one *locate* the locus of power in an interview dynamic prior to the specific unfolding of the dynamic itself? We must be wary, as Casper Jensen and Peter Lauritsen (2005) argue, of essentializing power relations and obscuring the ways in which power dynamics can shift and morph in different contexts and at different moments. I could not easily locate the singular source of "power" during the process of my interviews. Who is leading whom? While at times I may have assumed a powerful role as the questioning researcher, most of my interviewees were outspoken leaders in their fields who did not hesitate to take the conversation in new directions—even, in a number of cases, turning the tables to ask questions of *me*. What emerged in these interviews was the outcome of a complex, dynamic negotiation, and this was precisely the point: I am less interested in attempting to gain a "God's eye view" (Haraway 1991) of how things "really" are, or what my interviewees "really" think, than in exploring what might emerge from a different kind of conversation. What might professional practitioners of economy, society, and environment *become* if challenged and enrolled into new discourses and associations?

I begin my interpretive work from the assumption that my interviewees do not speak as simple, unified subjects. If, at one moment, they affirm the hegemony of a problematic divide between economy, society, and environment, they may, at another moment, destabilize this articulation and suggest radically different ways of framing ethical and political negotiations in Maine. This is not a matter of teasing out inconsistencies or contradictions ("What is *really* going on here is . . ."). The conversations I have catalyzed are sites of *multiplicity*, spaces in which myriad conflicting and comingling desires, understandings, and becomings emerge and circulate. Words are never spoken by individuals alone; we speak as participants in worlds of meaning that exceed us, and the things we say have effects well beyond our conscious intentions. Nobody ever really *is*, in fact, the "individual" that a certain commonsense account of reality would have us believe. We each exist at the intersection of many forces, and we negotiate with these forces daily to construct provisional solutions to impossibly complex problems. Some of what we each say, think, and do is inevitably an expression of problematic aspects of a status quo (I say "we" because I, too, am complicit). And yet some of what we say, think, and do is much more complicated and interesting; it continually *escapes* dominant ways of speaking and acting. We find ourselves, or might be found by others, moving beyond conventional categories, challenging habits of thinking, and transgressing boundaries. We are all a *mess*, and out of this mess emerge threads of longing, aspiration, and creativity that (might) carry us toward other—I hope better—modes of being and becoming.

Critique and Creation

There are, then, many ways not only of "reading" the world, but also of participating in its *composition* with the performative amplification of conceptual and analytical practice (Mol 2002; Law 2004; Latour 2010). How, then, to compose? This is an ethical and political choice, and it indicates a key leitmotif that is woven through this book and elaborated in the methodological introductions to each part. If the recognition of economy, society, and environment as contingent historical productions opens up a space for ontological politics, then the question of how we engage with the multiple forms of their possible composition is a matter of ontopolitical *strategy*. There has been intense debate in recent years among left and progressive scholars regarding the nature and place of "critique" in transformative research, and it all too often appears to boil down to a binary choice between *critique* and *creation*. Are economy, society, and environment articulated in a hegemonic form that is complicit with destructive and violent patterns of power? Yes. Do my interviewees express understandings and engage in practices that reproduce these patterns? Yes. Do articulations of the trio also exceed these hegemonic relations, cracking and multiplying into a thousand pieces that cannot be assembled into a simple story of unified power? Yes, indeed. Are other articulations emerging even from "within" the very spaces that appear in one view to be sites of hegemonic oppression? This, too, is true. I refuse to choose between these multiple positions. In the pages that follow, I seek instead to craft an approach capable of simultaneously identifying durable patterns of hegemonic power, acknowledging the limits and performative dangers of this paranoia, diffracting hegemonic formations into excessive and fertile multiplicities, and engaging in generative practices of articulation capable of inspiring productive betrayal and affirming new becomings that are already emerging "between the cracks."

I write in the spirit of what Michael Hardt refers to as a "militant biopolitics" that aspires "to struggle against the life we are given and to make a new life, *against* this world and *for* another" (2010, 34, emphasis added), or perhaps, said differently, *against some becomings* of this world and *for others* that are already present and emerging. While Hardt arrives at the glimmers of such a politics via Foucault's genealogies of ancient Greek "truth-telling" (*parrhesia*), my approach here riffs on the "pragmatics" of Gilles Deleuze and Félix Guattari in *A Thousand Plateaus* (1987). If we shift from an ontological stance focused on singular *being* (reality is *x*) to one attentive to multiple, simultaneous *becomings* (realities are plural and continuously emerging), economy, society, and environment can be understood as a multidimensional *assemblage*, at once powerful and totalizing, incomplete and unstable, and already in the process of being replaced by other world-making articulations. Pragmatics is a transformative approach that iteratively morphs its object from a hegemonic apparatus of capture into a site of "alternatives, jumps, and mutations" (Deleuze and Guattari 1987, 147), a multiplicity of becomings that open toward new modes of being.

My version of pragmatics, composed of four strategic analytical "moments" around which the four parts of the book are organized, takes creative liberties with Deleuze and Guattari's process while retaining many of its core transformative intuitions. I begin, in Part I, with a *problematization* of economy, society, and environment. Drawing on multiple valences of Foucault's (2001) notion of problematization, I describe the trio as constituting a pervasive "problem-space" within which many conflicts Maine and elsewhere are formatted; I briefly sketch a genealogical account of these articulations to clearly establish their contingency and relatively recent (industrial European) origins; and I beckon toward some of the ways in which the categories are shifting from simply *formatting* problems to *becoming* problems themselves. This simultaneous consolidation and unraveling of the hegemonic trio serves as the unstable ground upon which the rest of the book unfolds.

Part II takes up the work of critique, enacting a *tracing* that iden-
tifies ways in which common mobilizations of the three categories often
serve to reproduce capitalist hegemony, nature-culture divisions, democratic demobilization, and the marginalization of more-than-human
living beings and processes. In chapter 2, this critical analysis involves
an examination of the three categories—as constituted via interviews
and Maine policy literature—as *forces* that exceed and determine the
limits of human agency, and as *domains* to be domesticated and governed by professional representatives of a sovereign humanity. Chapter 3 extends this analysis, unpacking multiple ways in which this
configuration is implicated in the ongoing production and domestication of *externalities*—excluded elements upon which each category of
the trio nonetheless relies. My critique reaches its apogee in chapter 4
as I draw on Deleuze's (drawn from Foucault) notion of the "diagram
of power" to broadly describe economy, society, and environment as
effectuations of a set of power-patterns that exceed them. I name these
Nature-Culture, Capital-State, and Development, and suggest a way
to think about them as durable tendencies of hegemonic world-making
without ever rendering them into totalized systems or structures.

The diagram comes unraveled, however, in Part III where the work
of *decomposition* engages interviews and policy literature in ways that
amplify the failures of hegemony to fully capture the spaces it claims.
Maine's policy professionals can be seen to variously resist, evade, or
overflow the very hegemonic articulations they are also captured by,
enacting lines of flight toward other possibilities. Chapter 5 initiates
this decomposition by identifying key moments and sites of hesitation,
uncertainty, and even betrayal relative to the trio in interview encounters. Chapter 6 pushes this destabilization further, multiplying and frac-
turing interviewees' articulations of economy, society, and environment
beyond recognition and generating a "fog bank" of blurred complexity
and interdependence.

This fog bank, which I reframe as a space of radical possibility via
Deleuze and Guattari's (1987) notion of a "body without organs," constitutes a starting point for the final portion of the book, Part IV. Here,
through the necessarily speculative work of *(re)composition*, I aim
to strengthen and consolidate emergent yearnings beyond the trio by
elaborating a series of experimental concepts that both draw on and
transform articulations by interviewees in Maine. Chapter 7 seeks to
constitute an affective and conceptual space for thinking beyond (or

perhaps before) economy, society, and environment through the theorization of "ecopoiesis," derived from the Greek *oikos* (habitat, home) and *poiesis* (creation). This refers to the multifaceted, indeterminate, and ongoing material-semiotic co-composition of *habitats* and their *inhabitants*, and it functions as a conceptual tool for shifting the focus from the *product* of composition (e.g., economy, society, environment) to the continual, open *process* by which current—and, most important, future, *other*—assemblages are made. The trio of economy, society, and environment becomes only one possible actualization of habitat, and space is expanded for others to emerge.

But what are these "others"? How might we imagine replacing articulations of economy, society, and environment while avoiding ungrounded abstractions and remaining attentive to the urgent demand to *make sense* of day-to-day struggles? My experimental proposal in chapter 8 is to speak in terms of "ecological livelihoods," drawing on terms emergent from my interviews while also engaging critically and constructively with other theorizations of livelihood. This is, in many ways, an attempt to transpose Gibson-Graham's (2006a) notion of "community economy" into a more explicitly ecological, and less "economic," key. I argue for a concept of ecological livelihood that includes humans and nonhumans alike, refuses a priori determinations of causal dynamics (such as economic "laws"), offers an expansive, "transversal" notion of interdependence, acknowledges the incommensurability of livelihood values, and reconceives "development" not as a progressive trajectory but as a ruptural *event* that might open possibilities for enacting livelihoods differently.

The final two chapters of the book attempt to flesh out ecological livelihoods as an experimental ethico-political articulation via a series of conceptual and strategic tools. In chapter 9, I develop a framework for thinking about three co-constitutive moments in the process of composing livelihood: *making a living* (autopoiesis), *making livings for others* (alterpoiesis), and *being-made by others* (allopoiesis). We—that is, all living singularities—emerge as active participants in ecopoiesis at the intersection of these three processes, and ecological livelihood can be understood as the ongoing negotiation of their unfolding amid a web of wider habitat relations. I propose that this "livelihoods triad" can be explicitly politicized when viewed through the lens of *commoning* and *uncommoning*, the struggle over whether particular relations of interdependence become sites for explicit ethical negotiation or whether negotiation is closed down or obscured by practices of "anesthetiza-tion" (Stengers 2005b). Such a politics is consolidated and amplified by practices of *trans-commoning* that link multiple sites of common negotiation together in sustaining networks of interdependence.

With these tools in hand, I listen carefully in chapter 10 to the nuances of negotiations and conflicts in Maine previously framed by the hegemonic trio. Gibson-Graham's proposal for replacing economic determinations with "ethical coordinates" (2006a) and Latour's pro-posals for conceptualizing key "tasks" for "composing the common world" (2004a) inspire my elaboration of eight transversal coordinates around which livelihoods—human and nonhuman—are negotiated: constituency, value(s), measurement and comparison, performances of the "whole," knowledge and uncertainty, needs and strategies, sur-plus, and "incentives." These are sites of struggle that cut across and through the trio of economy, society, and environment, and their in-creased visibility might help to render more tangible the multiple forms of interrelation and interdependence that compose our common (and uncommon) worlds and to open up new, experimental terrains for ethico-political articulation, alliance, and transformation.

My tasks in this book are, admittedly, quite ambitious: to enact a situated, critical unworking the hegemonic trio of economy, society, and environment and to contribute toward imagining and enacting more vibrant, viable, and liberatory forms of life beyond it. I can only begin to grapple with such huge challenges in these pages, and I view this book as an experiment that may achieve more in its failures than in its successes. But the task before us all is too urgent to be avoided, however limited our responses may be. We live in a world bursting at the seams with crises born from the vigorous and violent unfold-ings of a mode of life formatted in significant part by the division between something called "the economy," something called "society," and something called "the environment." These articulations need to be challenged to their core, radically rethought, and perhaps even left behind. Writing of the uncertainty presented by climate destabilization of the Anthropocene, ecologist C. S. Holling (2004) proposes that "the only way to approach such a period . . . is not to predict, but to exper-iment and act inventively and exuberantly via diverse adventures in living." I hope, with this book, to make one small contribution toward provoking such generative adventures in Maine and beyond.

Part I. Problematizing the Trio

Critique is not a matter of saying that things are not right as they are. It is a matter of pointing out on what kinds of assumptions, what kinds of familiar, unchallenged, unconsidered modes of thought the practices that we accept rest . . . a matter of flushing out that thought and trying to change it: to show that things are not as self-evident as one believed, to see that what is accepted as self-evident will no longer be accepted as such. Practicing criticism is a matter of making facile gestures difficult.

—Michel Foucault, *Politics, Philosophy, Culture*

"EVERYTHING IS DANGEROUS," Foucault reminds us (1984, 343). Every concept, category, institution, and habit produced by human beings has effects that exceed, and indeed often betray, our intentions. There are no innocent constructions, and the worlds we inhabit—the forms of life that make us and that we, in turn, participate in making—are built upon layers of sedimented patterns that simultaneously offer us ground to stand on and continually unsettle us. One key role of critical scholarship is to call the *givenness* of our realities into question, to productively destabilize our sense that things simply *are* a certain way, and to open up space to imagine that they might be made differently. This is not a matter of exposing "false consciousness" and revealing how things "really" are beneath a surface of illusion, nor is it a matter of constructing a new foundation upon which the flag of judgment may be planted. It is, rather, about rendering contingent that which might otherwise seem inevitable, and about amplifying the instabilities that are already emerging within a particular historical formation. Did we assume something to be eternal that was historically produced? Did we take something for granted that merits careful scrutiny? Did we inadvertently reproduce something that we should have called into question? Is something we have assumed to be stable actually in the midst of unraveling? These are the questions raised by the practice of *problematization* (Foucault 2001; Koopman 2013).

In one sense, problematization is about *making* something a problem—about taking that which is unproblematic and rendering it into something that can no longer go unquestioned. If referring to an economy, a society, and an environment has been a "facile gesture," then my task in the chapter that follows is to render such easy reference more difficult. In another related sense, problematization is about analyzing the historical and contemporary processes by which "certain things (behavior, phenomena, processes)" are made "problems" in specific ways: *economic* problems, *social* problems, *environmental* problems, and, later, problems of their (re)connection or integration. This is what Foucault refers to as "genealogy" (1984, 76), and its effects are powerful: first, to show how particular sets of "solutions" are conditioned by the very terms of the problems they purport to solve; and second, to affirm that if things have been produced in a particular way, shaped by particular forces and conditions, then they can be produced differently—or not at all.

1 CONSTITUTIONAL GEOMETRY

Shapes of Power

The Pervasive Trio

In 2006, GrowSmart Maine commissioned the Brookings Institution to write a strategic report outlining Maine's prospects in the face of wider national and global transformations. *Charting Maine's Future* urges the state's policymakers to recognize that Maine stands at a "critical juncture" amid a rapidly changing world, positioned "within reach of a new prosperity—*if* [the state] takes bold action and focuses its limited resources on a few critical investments" (Brookings Institution 2006, 6). With a dramatic tone oscillating between threatening scarcity and Promethean abundance, the report makes clear that such prosperity must be "sustainable," balancing economic needs with social and environmental concerns: "Economic growth is more and more seen as essential to support environmental and community health, but so are the latter goods recognized as essential to securing the former. . . . This holistic insight, moreover, is widely shared by Maine people" (2006, 6).

Charting Maine's Future may have done for Maine's policy landscape what the famous World Commission on Environment and Development's Brundtland Report did at the level of international policy discourse (WCED 1987b). Sustainability is now a widespread aspiration in Maine. A generalized, if vague, agreement can be found across the literature produced by the state's policy professionals that development must proceed in ways that balance economic, social, and environmental dimensions. Indeed, the opening pages of the Maine Economic Growth Council's annual statistical survey, *Measures of Growth in Focus*, is adorned with a now-familiar image (Figure 2) in discourses of

V I S I O N

A high quality of life for all Maine people.

Achieving this vision requires a vibrant and sustainable economy supported by vital communities and a healthy environment.

Prepared for the Maine Economic Growth Council
by the
MAINE DEVELOPMENT FOUNDATION

Figure 2. The opening page of *Maine Measures of Growth in Focus*. Reprinted courtesy of the Maine Development Foundation.

"sustainable development": three core domains of contemporary life arranged as a Venn diagram and converging to constitute the vague normative space called "quality of life." Effective development policy in Maine, the report's framing suggests, involves making measurable improvements in all three domains with the hope of achieving their optimal combined outcome "for all Maine people" (MEGC 2013).

A familiar and pervasive structure of thought confronts us, with each individual term and its cognates constituting seemingly stable points of reference or categorization. When reporter Matthew Stone (2013) asks, "Is Maine's economy recovering?" he can presume that his object of inquiry is already constituted as a real entity or field, which itself needs no definition. When research biologist Fred Kircheis (2014) proposes in an editorial that "rules to protect Maine's environment are insufficient," this environment can be taken as an uncontroversial object around which various management conflicts might circulate. When Maine governor Paul LePage says that illegal drugs are "tearing at the social fabric of our communities" (qtd. in Hoey 2014), the force of his rhetoric can rely on a notion of a "social" that functions as a kind of relational glue in the background of daily life in Maine. When the legislatively mandated Sustainable Maine report (1996) proposes that "sustainability is three dimensional," no further explanation of these dimensions is needed. *Economic* sustainability assures the viability of "economic" activity, *environmental* sustainability engages key dimensions of "the environment," and *social* sustainability addresses "social relationships" in various ways. Everyone knows what economy, society, and environment mean; or at least these articulations appear so foundational that the question of their meaning rarely arises in public debate.

Maine is positioned as but one participating node in a planetary network of practices and relations that continually produce and affirm this triple distinction (Orenstein and Shach-Pinsley 2017). International bodies such as the United Nations, the Organisation for Economic Co-operation and Development (OECD), the International Labor Organization (ILO), and the World Bank place "economic, social, and environmental" concerns at the core of their policy articulations. The economic, the social, and the environmental domains are the targets of various widely disseminated forms of measurement and quantitative representation that help to give them their shape and "obviousness": the U.S. Bureau of Economic Analysis generates a continual stream of data about "the economy"; the U.S. Environmental Protection Agency (EPA) and a host of nonprofit organizations and academic researchers report on the ever-changing "state of the environment"; and numerous government and nonprofit agencies accumulate "social statistics" to monitor the ongoing health and well-being of "society."[1] Federal and state regulations mandate attention, in various forms and to varying degrees, to "economic, social, and environmental" dimensions of proposed projects and policies. Multiple public and private institutions across overlapping scales appear to manage, protect, develop, support, and struggle over sets of issues, objects, and relationships that are assumed to be of an economic, social, and environmental nature.

Policy professionals in Maine, as in so many places subjected to the demands of "development," encounter the triple distinction again and again in voluminous academic and gray literatures on "sustainable development," "sustainable growth," "triple bottom line accounting," or "corporate social responsibility." Even beyond these specialist domains, references in social science literature to the "economic, social, and environmental dimensions" of x, y, or z are too widespread for citation. Attempts to "bring in the social" to economic analyses, to assess the "environmental dimensions" of social situations, or to examine the "economic factors" at play in particular social conflicts or environmental issues are repeated in ways that most often assume the stability or self-evidence of the categories themselves. Indeed, the disciplines of economics, sociology, and environmental science all have these domains as their presumed objects of study, and even hybrid disciplines presume and affirm something distinctly *economic* about certain dimensions of society (economic sociology) or environment (environmental economics), something specifically *social* about the economy (institutional and social economics), or something *environmental* about aspects of the social (environmental sociology).

In all of these cases, the three categories commonly mark out a space of tension between differing forces, interests, or institutional demands. Maine is one of many places in which something called "the economy" has often appeared to be in conflict with something called "the environment," and in a perhaps more ambiguous relationship with something called "community" or "society." Multiple complex struggles over the past fifty years in Maine have been captured and distilled into the classic formulation of "economy versus environment": the heated "payroll versus pickerel" debates surrounding Maine senator Edmund Muskie's 1972 Clean Water Act; the forest clear-cutting regulation struggles of the late 1990s; and more recent conflicts over private resort development along the largely wild Moosehead Lake and a proposed private east-west highway through the center of the state. At the same time, "community" or "community vitality" in Maine appears to be at once threatened by and in desperate need of a robust "economy." In a common framing, an aging and flat or declining population, rising unemployment, and multiple economic changes threaten to undermine longstanding rural communities and traditions and unravel the "social fabric" of the state. The economy causes this unraveling while at the same time offering the only perceived solution.

Resolutions to these kinds of conflicts are often sought and framed *via* the three terms, as in the "three-legged stool of sustainable development" (Barringer 2004). From the attempt in *Charting Maine's Future* to link economy, community, and environment via "quality of place" to Environment Maine's *Trail Map to Prosperity* (Kelley 2010), advocating for "livable communities" and a "green economy," some version of the trio remains at the heart of political intervention even when the singular rule of any one category is challenged. The strategies may vary. Some seek a common denominator derived from one of the three categories that can bring the others into alignment, as in the concepts of social and natural "capital." If the conflict appears to unfold on ground that cannot be rendered commensurate, then the task shifts to "balancing," "integrating," or "harmonizing" formerly antagonistic spheres. Should this fail (as it often does), a seemingly more radical path often appears: to "rethink" the relationships *among* the categories, repositioning them relative to one another in our conceptual and institutional schemes. In all of these variations, the categories themselves—albeit in different forms and configurations—remain intact as the ground upon which solutions are imagined and enacted. Even the most radical proposals tend to remain in the orbit of the three terms: imagining an *alternative* economy, a *different* set of social relations, and a *new relationship* with the environment.

The force of this entrapment can be found at work when Seth Goodall (2011), former state senator from Maine's 19th District, says that "Maine Democrats believe strongly that the environment is not separate and distinct from the economy, instead it is an important variable in the economic equation that will help Maine grow." Pointedly refusing the distinction between categories, Goodall at the same time *radically reaffirms it* and ultimately renders the environment as little more than an accessory to econometric calculation. Does Goodall, in fact, intend to say that the integration between environment and economy is based on the total subsumption of ecological relations to market dynamics? I think not. But it is as if he is trying to say something that cannot be said in the terms available to him—terms that are profoundly obligatory for a politician in early twenty-first century Maine. How could one speak of the economy without acknowledging the *environment*? How could one affirm the environment without invoking the *economy*? How could one not, when speaking of economy and environment, engage with struggles around the needs, preferences, and fractures within *society*? It is all so common as to be almost unremarkable, and yet we must begin to see the water in which we swim: this trio—in myriad forms, contexts, and relations—as a fundamental horizon of modern life and thought.

Constitutional Geometry

Economy, society, and environment compose what I will call a *constitutional geometry*. Whether overlapped, triangulated, sandwiched, or nested (Figure 3), three core dimensions of reality appear as simultaneously distinct and related. We might think here in terms of three variably relatable positions—hence an array of *geometries* characterized by various permutations of a position *A*, *B*, and *C*. Multiple cognate terms may occupy these slots (Figure 4), and the specific definitions of the terms in each position may vary: *A*, depending on the formulation, might equal "economy," "market," "profit," or "prosperity"; *B* might include "society," "community," "people," or "ethics"; and *C* might designate "environment," "ecology," or "planet." Even the definitions of the terms in each slot might vary, as in the difference between a neoclassical and Keynesian economy. In all of these variations, however, there remains a triple geometry marking a similar set of presumed relations. This geometry is *constitutional* because it founds and continually performs a particular "problem-space" (Scott 2004) within which various relations between beings, configurations of values and interests, and parameters of viable negotiation appear as given. Diverse actions and concerns are subsumed and formatted into a single analytic or ontological triangulation, which is then posed as the fundamental terrain in which political struggle and imagination must play out. One cannot easily advocate for nonhuman living beings and their habitats without becoming an "environmentalist," just as one cannot seek to address human ethical concerns without participating in "social activism" or "social work" or engage with questions of production, consumption, employment, savings, or investment without speaking *of* or *for* "the economy."

In at least three of these geometrical variations of the trio, we find each category separated from the others, in tension or conflict and in need of (re)connection. The Venn diagram, exemplified by the image in *Maine Measures of Growth* (Figure 2), is perhaps the most common variation in articulations of sustainable development. Here, the task is to overlap and reconnect formerly antagonistic spheres in a "marriage" between elements that are nonetheless still distinguishable (e.g., Barringer 2004). Discourses of the "triple bottom line," which sometimes articulate the trio in alternate terms such as "people, planet, and profit" or "economy, environment, and equity," often *triangulate* the three elements (Elkington 1998; Coastal Enterprises 2009). Such a geometry portrays a connection and interplay while also emphasizing binary differences and (potential) oppositions. Not coincidentally, perhaps, "economy" is usually positioned at the top of what one might

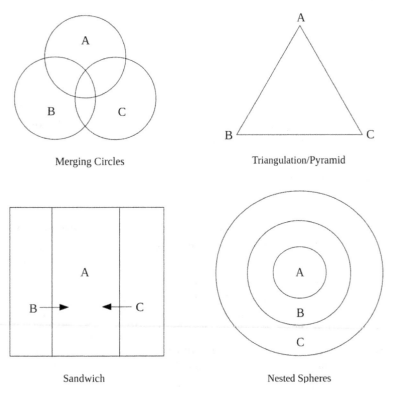

Figure 3. Variable geometries of the trio.

A	B	C
Economy	Society	Environment
Economy	Community	Environment
Economy	Equity	Environment
Profit	People	Planet
Prosperity	People	Place

Figure 4. Various vocabularies of the trio.

also view as a pyramid. Such hierarchy is also apparent in the "sand-wich" geometry of neoclassically influenced environmental econom-ics (e.g., Hackett 2006; Siebert 2008; Wiesmeth 2011). In this case, both environment and society are positioned as *outsides* that must be accounted for in economic (monetized and marketized) terms in order to appear as legitimate objects of intervention and management. Soci-ety is the source of "preferences," hidden behind a veil of subjectivity but "revealed" through the monetary behavior that animates markets. The environment remains the ultimate externality—the outside from which resources can be extracted and into which wastes can be dumped according to limits set primarily by the economic balance sheet.

In contrast to these three figures, a more radical version of the trio is presented in many formulations of ecological economics. Opposing the notion that economy, society, and environment constitute three separated spheres or positions that must be linked, ecological econom-ics *nests* the trio like Russian dolls. The economy is a "subsystem" (Daly and Farley 2010) located within a wider social domain that is, in turn, nested in a planetary ecosystem or environment. As Michael

Common and Sigrid Stagl (2005) describe, "The economy is located within the environment, and exchanges energy and matter with it. In making their living, humans extract various kinds of useful things . . . from the environment. Humans also put back into the environment the various kinds of wastes that necessarily arise in the making of their living" (1). Philip Lawn (2001) conceptualizes these relations in explicitly ontological terms, where a nested macroeconomy, a "socio-sphere," and an "ecosphere" are seen as characteristic elements of the "logos of nature." For Lawn,

> the three major spheres of influence represent different systems at varying degrees of complexity. Each can be considered a holon insofar as they manifest the independent and autonomous properties of wholes and the dependent properties of parts. . . . The macroeconomy acts as a component of the sociosphere which, in turn, acts as a component of the ecosphere. . . . In a sense, this makes the sociosphere something akin to the interface between the macroeconomy and the greater ecosphere. (2001, 144)

Economy, society, and environment have been spared in this geometrical articulation from any assumed *external* separations. Yet the fundamental problem-space itself remains unchanged. We remain in a world of three domains, each animated by distinct dynamics—even "laws"—and each in need of relational reconfiguration relative to the others. In fact, many versions of ecological economics tend to shift the focus from an *analytic* distinction to a more robust *ontological* one. Each system, now nested rather than simply linked, is viewed in terms of a realist epistemology that systematizes the domains and renders them "natural" in the sense of *given* in the world prior to discourse. A questioning of the geometry itself remains unthinkable.

In all of these configurations, we are confronted with articulations that Gilles Deleuze and Félix Guattari (1987) refer to as both "molar" and "majoritarian." As *molar* articulations, contemporary assemblages of economy, society, and environment are "unifiable, totalizable, [and] organizable" (33). They constitute singular "wholes" in which difference is subordinated to, or derivative of, a larger unity or identity. Even when ostensibly derived from empirical observation, these categories function as if they preexisted the populations of elements that inhabit them, and complex dimensions of the world are subsequently sorted and sliced according to a particular set of criteria—becoming "economic elements," "social dimensions," or "environmental factors." As *majoritarian* articulations, the trio's components are defined "by the power (*pouvoir*) of constants" (1987, 101). Majorities are understood here not in quantitative terms (as in a majority vote), but rather in terms of a takeover that subordinates variation to similarity. To be major is to enforce or conform to a dominant norm that renders differences into derivative variations. Economy, society, and environment constitute assemblages, which become their own measure or standard or, variously, become the measures of *each other* as the three categories vie for priority. Is it economically viable? Is this socially acceptable? Are the environmental standards adequately enforced? These are prime examples of majoritarian questions.

Why is this a problem? Part II will engage this question in depth, but for the moment I will suggest three core dangers that inhere in major molarities. First, and perhaps foremost, such categories are easily *ontologized*—rendered into objective descriptions and enactments of the structure of reality itself (Connolly 2002). Economy, society, and environment (among other molarities) frequently make their own power-laden construction invisible by seeming simply to name or identify that which already exists. The background context of debate and struggle, *the framing itself*, is effectively depoliticized as a possible site for contestation and transformation. Molar articulations, furthermore, can quickly shift from descriptive to explanatory functions. Once they have been identified to exist in the world, economy, society, and environment can be studied as objects, and constituted as relatively discrete and systematic domains in which particular patterns, processes, and even laws can be "discovered." They become sites of what Deleuze and Guattari call "royal science" (1987, 109), where the irreducible complexities of problems are captured by a theoretical reduction that seeks "to define equivalent relations by discovering, on the one hand, the independent variables that can be combined to form a structure and, on the other hand, the correlates that entail one another within each structure" (1987, 234). Once such dynamics have been posited, these domains become capable of confronting us from beyond with demands, constraints, and necessities. Rather than standing before a field of possibility, we find ourselves trapped in a web of predetermined limits.

Finally, in such a scenario it is all too easy for any one of the molar categories to claim the mantle of King. We are thus encouraged to think in terms of which domain rules all others (even if by prescribing limits) and which therefore should or must be prioritized. Conflicts between domains unfold predictably. Environmentalists understand that "the environment" is primary, conditioning and constraining all else. Social advocates see that questions of equity and well-being in human society are primary, or that "social capital precedes rather than follows upon general economic prosperity" (Barringer 2004, xxxii), providing the foundation upon which the health of all other relations depends. Economists know, beyond the shadow of a doubt, that we need a strong economy before we can afford the luxury of adequately caring for either the environment or the poor.[2] Everybody is right, everybody is wrong, and very few, it seems, are engaged in the politics of *problematizing the constitutional geometry itself*.

Triplets, Separated at Birth

There is a powerful tendency to project an economy, a society, and an environment across all domains of human life, past and present, thus treating them as universal categories inscribed into the nature of things. It is difficult to avoid this kind of thinking precisely because these foundational articulations shape our core understandings of reality. How could there be a human community without an "economy"? How can human groupings be understood if not in terms of various "societies"? How can we not have always lived in and depended upon "the environment"? There is, of course, no denying that all human and nonhuman groups engage in activities and relations through which they are sustained, materially and otherwise. We do, indeed, form various collectivities, and they certainly depend upon wider constitutive relations with other living beings and ecological processes. But these things take the *particular* forms of economy, society, and environment only under specific historical circumstances.

This historical emergence must not be taken as merely a matter of developing new language for spheres of life that already existed, that is, as a discovery by which human investigation exposes an objective reality that was hitherto obscured. The "birth" of economy, society, and environment involved their very *construction* as material domains of experience, subjectivity, measurement, and intervention. "The object," writes Michel Foucault, "does not await in limbo the order that will free it and enable it to become embodied in a visible and prolix objectivity; it does not pre-exist itself, held back by some obstacle at the first edges of light. It exists under the positive conditions of a complex group of relations" (2007b, 45). There are no economic, social, and environmental "dimensions" that await our discovery of them, and our identifications of such dimensions do not trace or amplify the contours of a nascent, objective distinction awaiting categorization. For an economy, a society, and an environment to exist, they must be produced—*initially*, via their historical emergence as new ways of formatting reality, and *continually*, through ongoing, iterative processes of composition.

As numerous scholars have shown, the elements of this trio are relatively recent inventions, co-constructed as products *of* and interventions *in* the unfolding of European capitalist-colonial industrialism and its various ongoing crises. The ability to distinguish between something "economic," something "social," and something "environmental"—to *format* our collective relations of sustenance and interdependence in these particular terms—is scarcely older than the first oil well (Pennsylvania, USA, 1859). A whole structure of thought and practice was laid out over the course of little more than a hundred years by which people came to find themselves living in a society, confronted by and dependent upon an economy, and surrounded by an increasingly domesticated and imperiled environment. These articulations are, one might say, *triplets separated at birth* and struggling with each other ever since.

Undoubtedly the terms "economy," "society," and "environment" all existed in English prior to the nineteenth century. "Economy," derived from the Greek *oikos* (household or home) and *nomos* (customary law or management), was used at least since the mid-fourteenth century to refer to either the frugal use of resources or to regimes for governing interdependent systems—the economy of the body, the economy of the farm, or the divine economy of God. By the eighteenth century, discourses of "political economy" focused on the management of national resources, but no domain of life was yet marked as distinctively "economic" (Tribe 1978; Poovey 1995). Even Adam Smith, the mythological founder of economics, used the term only in its earlier sense (Mitchell 2008). Society, from the Latin *socius*, has long been used to designate particular associations between various beings—human, nonhuman, and divine (Wolf 1988). In the early seventeenth century, the term was taken up by natural law theorists as "civil society" to contrast the mass of free-willed people from those who ruled over them; yet society was a still a particular *constituency* in this usage, and not yet an independent domain of life (Gierke 1957; Wolf 1988). "Environment," from the French verb *environner* (to surround), was used occasionally prior to the nineteenth century to refer to local configurations of encirclement (as in "the environment of glands" in the neck), but it was not yet a name for the totality of that which surrounds and sustains human societies.[3]

It was only amid the rapid and profound transformations of the industrial revolution that the contours of the trio began to emerge, and only in the middle decades of the twentieth century that the familiar terrain of economy, society, and environment described earlier in this chapter was fully consolidated. Our ability to distinguish something "economic" in the world can be traced to the ascendancy of dynamic, large-scale markets as a core organizing force of collective life. It is no coincidence that John Stuart Mill could, in 1848, make reference to "economic arguments" and "purely economic reasons" for the first time (Schabas 2005). This was the moment of the "great transformation" (Polanyi 2001) in which vast numbers of people, displaced from traditional access to the means of subsistence, found themselves subjected to the vagaries of an expanding market structure in which their very life-force was transformed into a commodity. The emergence of an economic assemblage was made possible by the enclosure of common land, the separation of activity into differentiated geographies of home and work, the growing collective dependence on market-mediated sustenance, and—among other elements—explanatory discourses of "economy." Amid such change, emerging practices of statistical measurement and liberal government increasingly rendered people into self-responsible members of a "population," and it became possible to speak in new ways of "society" and "the social" as aggregate domains of existence, to develop interventions around these domains, and to study them in terms of a new "sociology" (Rose and Miller 2008). Meanwhile, the composition of these new spheres produced a particular *outside*, a domain that would serve as a resource, a model, an external determination, or a realm of lost unity toward which to yearn. The Scottish writer Thomas Carlyle, a conservative critic of the industrial assault on rural culture, translated Goethe's term *umbegung* as "environment" in 1828, using it for the first time to refer to a holistic, defining context in which human action develops (Jessop 2012).[4] By the 1860s, the concept of "environment" was widespread in social and biological theory, referring to the contexts in which organisms, societies, and economies are situated and by which they are shaped or even determined (Luke 1995; Macnaghten and Urry 1998).

At the turn of the twentieth century, the key distinctions of the trio were mostly in place and functioning as commonsense modes of encountering reality in Europe and its current and former colonies. Yet two further consolidations awaited: while "society" may have served as a singular noun to mark out an objective and manageable sphere of life, *the* economy and *the* environment, in their full contemporary significance as singular, systematic domains, had not yet emerged as such.[5] Until the Depression era, "economy" still functioned primarily in adjective form, as "the economic *x*." Amid the generalized crisis of global markets in the 1930s, however, economists and administrators drew on econometric modeling, input-output analysis, and growing statistical capability to compose—as a practice of management—"*the* economy." According to Timothy Mitchell (1998), it was the development of Keynesian macroeconomics and the construction of the system of national accounts by Simon Kuznets (manifest most famously in the measure of Gross Domestic Product) that definitively articulated the now-familiar, overarching, law-governed, and growth-addicted economic sphere in which we find ourselves and to which we are subjected. This is the moment when policymakers and analysts in Maine and beyond could begin to tell us how "the economy" is doing, what "it" needs, and what we need to become in the face of its demands. A little over two decades later, the emerging awareness of profound ecological disruption diagnosed in Rachel Carson's justly famous *Silent Spring* (1962) gave rise to a parallel "thingification": the now commonsense notion that we inhabit—and must now defend and protect—a singular something called "*the* environment." Like the economy (and often in conflict with it), this articulation simultaneously encapsulated its subjects inside a definitive sphere to which all are at the mercy and constituted this sphere as a new object of planetary-scale management and intervention (Ingold 1993; Luke 1995).

Economy, society, and environment are categories born from struggles to understand and respond to the fitful throes of modern life. It should be no surprise, then, that we can map their rise onto the emergence of what many are now calling the "Anthropocene"—the geological moment in which (certain) humans come to substantively act as a planetary geological force (Crutzen 2002). Two juxtaposed illustrations serve to dramatize this connection. Figure 5a shows the steadily rising and ever-accelerating human-induced carbon emissions since 1750, tracing one way in which humanity has been increasingly constituted as "a collective being capable of geomorphic force" (Yusoff 2013, 779). Figure 5b is an "n-gram," drawing from Google's digitized corpus to visualize the relative frequency of usage of the terms "the economy," "the environment," and "the social" from 1750 to 2000.[6] There is a clear parallel, and this is no coincidence: economy, society, and environment were born at the very same moment that Europeans were beginning to transform fossil fuels into a massive industrial-technological complex and a vast accompanying expulsion of world-altering gas, and these assemblages were definitively consolidated in

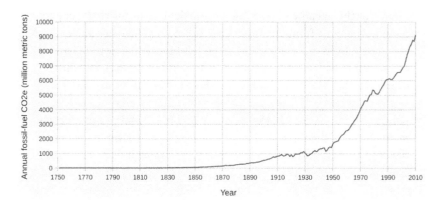

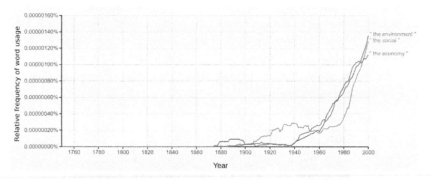

Figure 5. Two accelerating trends that co-characterize the development of industrial modernity: (a) Fossil-fuel CO2 emissions, 1750–2010. Data from Boden et al. 2017; (b) Google n-gram of the relative printed frequency of the terms of the trio, 1750–2000. Data from the Google Books corpus. Made with Google Books Ngram Viewer. http://books.google.com/ngrams.

the opening years of the dramatic mid-twentieth century upswing of human planetary impact known as the Great Acceleration (Steffen et al. 2015). Planetary anthropogenic climate change and the hegemonic trio arose *together*, as symptoms of a wider, emergent assemblage. In sum, it should be clear that our crisis-ridden era has been produced *by* and *as* this triple separation.

Much more can and should be said about the historical co-emergence of economy, society, and environment. Though historians have addressed each of the three categories individually and in various pairs, the story of the production of the trio *as a trio*—including nuance I have not touched upon—remains to be further elaborated. But that is not my task here. It is merely to suggest that such a history *exists*, for the purpose of opening these articulations to critical engagement at the most fundamental levels. If humans have not always had economies, lived in societies, and inhabited environments; if such modes of life are products of a particular, situated, and contingent history; if, in fact, this history suggests that these articulations are *implicated in the very crises they purport to address*, then a whole new level of politics—ontological politics—opens up for critical and creative engagement. None of the three dominant categories can continue to stand as the objective ground upon which the others can be judged, structured, governed, or into which the others can be merged or "re-embedded." The distinction of an "economic" presupposes the existence of a "social" upon which it depends yet to which it cannot fully be reduced. The separation of livelihood activity into particularly "economic" and "social" forms, likewise, constitutes the conditions of possibility for a notion of "environment" as the nonhuman constitutive outside, from which the other two domains are separated and yet from which they continually draw. This is the core structure of the assemblage I am calling the "hegemonic trio."

Articulation, Assemblage, Hegemony

I use the terms "articulation," "assemblage," and "hegemony" extensively throughout this book and their specification at the outset is crucial. By "articulation," I follow Deleuze and Guattari (1987) in referring to a complex process of world-making in which meaning and materiality are inextricably linked. Humans neither encounter a ready-made world nor fabricate one solely in our minds; we come into existence as provisional, ever-changing expressions of a material-semiotic compo-sition that precedes, exceeds, and also *involves* us (1987, 238). "Articula-tion" is a particularly powerful term because of its multiple valences: it refers to an effective speech act (in phonetics); to the capacity for speech itself (in literature and law); to a dynamic point of linkage between moving parts (in biology and engineering); to a point of conceptual connection (in theory discourse); to the simultaneous distinction and sequencing of serial elements (in music); and to the effectuation or actu-alization of an abstraction (in philosophy).[7] I intend this word to in-voke all of these senses at once, in variable combinations that cannot be determined outside of specific instances. There is not simply a sub-ject who speaks, nor is there a language that speaks the subject (as in Lacanian theory), but rather there are myriad articulations—some-times linguistic, sometimes not—through which things such as subjects and words are more or less durably stabilized.[8]

Understood as articulations, the categories of economy, society, and environment are "performative": they directly participate in constitut-ing the reality that they appear only to designate or represent (Austin 1975; Butler 1993). This performativity should be viewed not just in terms of the social power of certain human utterances, but rather in reference to the complex processes through which multiple vital ele-ments, including words, concepts, objects, and agencies of various kinds, come together to compose more or less durable stabilizations or "assemblages." Economy, society, and environment are performed into being through what John Law (2009) describes as "the provisional assembly of productive, heterogeneous, and . . . quite limited forms of ordering located in no larger overall order" (146). To speak of their articulation is to refer to the provisional stabilization of particular assemblages through processes that include material enclosures and exclusions, the construction of stable references and measurements, the circulation of visual representations, theoretical narratives and concepts, practices of habitutation, enforcement, and obligation, and various modes of subjectification.[9] I follow, here, an important shift in some scholarship from a focus on categories as substantive or con-stantive *nouns* to engaging them as *verbs*. Koray Çaliskan and Michel Callon (2009; 2010), for example, have moved from examining "the economy" to an analysis of *economization*, "the processes through which behaviors, organizations, institutions and, more generally, objects are constituted as being 'economic'" (2010, 2). Similarly, one might shift from an emphasis on society to *socialization*, and from the environment to *environmentalization*.[10] In each case, the focus in on material-semiotic ontogenesis: the *making* of particular assemblages and modes of life.

The term "assemblage" is a translation of Deleuze and Guattari's concept of *agencement*, which, in French, refers to an arrangement, a connection, a fitting-together of things.[11] It is not simply a happenstance collection of objects in a common place, but rather a particular set of dynamic interrelationships that constitute a relatively stable and durable "something" understood without recourse to a notion of essence (De Landa 2006). If articulation is the process of *composing* provisional stabilizations, then the assemblage is, in part, that which is stabilized. "The economy," for example, is an assemblage produced by various practices of articulation described above, and these include the mobilization of very category "economy" itself. But articulation is only part of the picture. Always more (and less) than its stabilization or territorialization, an assemblage is also perpetually engaged in processes of *deterritorialization*, of coming-undone, or becoming-otherwise. An assemblage is that which is articulated, but it is also that which articulation *fails* to fully stabilize, that which is "swept away" by other articulations and other assemblages (Deleuze and Guattari 1987, 55). Think of a deer in the Maine woods: on one hand, a continual process of self-making, an anti-entropic movement producing functional order from a flow of matter and energy, a singular coming-together of muscle, bone, blood, breath, tree buds, forest paths, weather, and leaf litter; on the other hand, a process of constant transformation, a becoming-new, and a movement toward death, decay, and ingestion by others that is the very condition of possibility for its existence *as* a living assemblage. Similarly, and as I will elaborate in numerous ways in chapters to come, the assemblages of economy, society, and environment are not simply produced, once and for all, as things with which we must now live. From the moment(s) of their initial articulation, they can be sustained only on the condition that they are also sites of becoming-otherwise, constituted by points of instability and transformation that beckon toward other modes of being.

Some assemblages are more durable than others, and some are also more potent in their ability to articulate myriad beings and relations into webs of mutual influence and interdependence that come to seem eternal or inevitable. At a given historical moment, particular assemblages become *constitutional* in the molar and major sense described earlier—establishing dominant standards of judgment, reinforcing "central points" of power and control, articulating grids of identity, and constituting widely obligatory problem spaces in which all viable forms of reason must subsist (Deleuze and Guattari 1987, 292). I call such assemblages "hegemonic."[12] This language of hegemony has most recently and prominently been associated with the work of Ernesto Laclau and Chantal Mouffe (2001), and my use of it here is in many ways indebted to their influence. For them, hegemony is a political process of instituting forms of order and meaning through articulations that seek—yet never fully achieve—universality and closure for a given collective. Such closure happens around particular representations known as "nodal points" (the economy or the environment, for example) that contingently rise above others to link multiple differences together, exclude other possible forms of unification, and become the momentary "common sense" of political life. My particular notion of hegemony, however, departs in two key ways from that of Laclau and Mouffe. First, while practices of representation may undoubtedly play crucial articulatory roles in hegemonic assemblages, hegemony may be *more* than just the effective, antagonistic articulation of nodal points. From an assemblage perspective, hegemony is established in ways that exceed language and representation. It is as much about affects, resonances, and material relations that are not fully taken up in discourse, and (as should become clear in subsequent chapters) it does not always require *identification* as its condition of success. Second, hegemony does not necessarily involve antagonism and the production of an "us and them"; it can, in fact, name the composition of the very space within which all such conflicts appear to play out. This is precisely the case with the assemblage of economy, society, and environment.

A key characteristic of a constitutional hegemonic assemblage is its ability to render its own provisionality so invisible as to become the very backdrop for other hegemonic and counterhegemonic struggles to unfold. The effects of such an operation can be seen clearly in a comment by Chad, the director of a Maine economic development nonprofit, referring to the triple circles of the *Maine Measures of Growth* report (Figure 2): "This Venn diagram is the most over-used, incorrectly used Venn diagram in the world. It drives me nuts. But I'll tell you why we use it. It grabs people, *and they get it*" (interview). What they "get" is simply an external reality in which these distinctions *matter* in both senses of the word. "Insofar as power operates successfully by constituting an object domain, a field of intelligibility, as a taken-for-granted ontology," writes Judith Butler, "its material effects are taken as material data or primary givens. These material positivities appear *outside* discourse and power, as its incontestable referents, its transcendental signifieds" (1993, 34). Despite the profound contingency, historicity, and performative constitution of assemblages, what emerges in the world is a set of self-evident, substantialized problem domains: *an* economy, *a* society, and *an* environment, about which we must ask crucial questions, to which (or from within which) we must respond, and which we may even attempt to alter through various forms of management or transformative intervention. The existence or stability of the domains, themselves, however, remains unquestioned.

"That Which Is Falling . . ."

I have taken the task of problematization thus far to entail two dimensions: first, the explicit articulation of a particular problem-space within which the conditions of possibility for certain kinds of thought and action become possible; and second, the rendering-contingent of this problem-space, showing it to be the provisional, historically specific result of concrete struggles and transformations that could have been (and might yet be) otherwise. But there is a third sense of problematization that is indicated by the notion of "assemblage" described above. Like Hegel's owl of Minerva taking flight only as the dusk of the present historical formation falls, problematization often seems to emerge just at the moment when a problem-space is shifting from constituting a foundational common sense to becoming itself a *problem*. In the final decades of the twentieth century, as economy, society, and environment were definitively established as apparent foundations for negotiating collective futures, they began to unravel both conceptually and practically. Or perhaps, more accurately, their always-present instabilities and impossibilities became ever more apparent. As part of what many have perceived as a generalized crisis of the core categories of modernity (Latour 1993), economy, society, and environment have been simultaneously subjected both to increasing critical scrutiny and to profound instability as modes of organizing institutions and collective negotiations.

As I described in the introduction, numerous scholars in recent decades have challenged conventional renderings of each of these assemblages, chipping away at their self-evidence and casting doubt on their descriptive and explanatory power. But such conceptual challenges are only a small part of a much wider crisis of sense that is unfolding at the level of materiality as much as at the level of ideas (both, of course, ultimately inseparable). Ongoing shifts toward new forms of affective labor and "immaterial production" across multiple scales (Hardt and Negri 2009), along with growing mass exclusion from participation in conventional economic activities, increasingly render a distinction between society and economy impossible to sustain. The colonization and transformation of planetary ecosystems under regimes of economic development (Fischer-Kowalski and Haberl 1998), and especially the forcing of global climate destabilization by the growth demands of "the economy," render the line between economy and environment untenable. Growing awareness of the crucial role of ecological relations for the sustenance of human sociality and acknowledgment of the complex sentiences of nonhuman living beings (Lestel 2014; Despret 2016), combined with an understanding of the "human" itself as a multispecies assemblage (Gilbert 2013), forces the distinction between society and environment toward effective collapse. It is as if the g-force of the Great Acceleration has pushed its own constitutive categories to their breaking points.

And yet they are not actually broken. The challenge that I am confronting, and one reason why the story I am trying to tell is so difficult to narrate in linear form, is that two things are true at the same time: the constitutional geometry of the hegemonic assemblage is both alive and well and already dead. I will describe, in chapter 5, some ways in which Maine's economic, social, and environmental professionals not only violate the boundaries of the trio with their work, but also actively resist these distinctions when confronted with them. At the same time, they have few other constitutional articulations with which to think or act. It is tempting, given such a strange situation, to refer to economy, society, and environment as "zombie categories," that is, in Ulrich Beck's terms, "'living dead' categories which govern our thinking but are not really able to capture the contemporary milieu" (2001, 262). Yet *capture* is precisely what these articulations *do*. Despite a growing sense that these categories are problematic, we still seem to need them—or, rather, they continue to produce and sustain their own necessities or demands. Or do they?

My goal in this chapter has been to outline the pervasive nature of the hegemonic trio in Maine and beyond in order to begin opening a space for radically challenging these articulations, tracing their ethico-political effects, amplifying their failures and lines of flight, and imagining the world otherwise. Ultimately, the point is to follow Friedrich Nietzsche's Zarathustra: "That which is falling should also be pushed" (1969, 266). But first, we must be clear about what we are pushing on.

Part II. Tracing Hegemonies

"CRITIQUE IS NOT A MATTER of saying that things are not right as they are," writes Michel Foucault as he sets up his description of the work of problematization (1988, 154). Why would he say this? Are we not motivated to critique, even in Foucault's sense, precisely because the present order demands transformation? Doesn't problematization presuppose and fuel a desire that is, in Michael Hardt's (2010) terms, "*against* the life we are given and [toward] a new life?" Perhaps Foucault was afraid of affirming a practice of critique as a self-righteous, dogmatic judgment of the world that conjures specters of totalitarianism. Perhaps he was subtly challenging the very notion of a singular "as they are" that can be known and represented as a system or structure to be forcibly overthrown and then replaced. Perhaps he simply meant to say that "critique is not *just* a matter. . . ." Regardless, we are confronted here with key questions that lie at the center of contemporary debates about strategies for collective transformation. What does it mean to critique? What is at stake in the work of challenging, revealing, judging, or condemning particular assemblages and relations of power? Can this work accomplish the transformative task it claims to serve? Is critique an ethical imperative, more urgent than ever, or has it, as Bruno Latour (2004b) suggests, "run out of steam"?

Debate around these issues often appears in binary form, as a struggle between two constellations of perspectives on ontology, affect, and strategy.[1] On one hand, there are those who view critique as a crucial practice of debunking hegemonic narratives and revealing some form of truth about a world torn by suffering and oppression. A necessary responsibility of radical scholarship is to analyze the workings of dominant power, guard vigilantly against co-optation, and open up pathways for resistance and change.[2] To avoid such work would only be a mark of one's *privilege* to do so, since the analysis of hegemonic power is not optional for those whose bodies and communities are targeted by exploitation and violence. This view is often linked with a sense that the oppositional *affect* of such critique—feeding (and feeding on) a sense of injury and outrage—is a crucial ingredient to the construction of organized and effective collectivities motivated to make revolutionary change.[3]

On the other hand, many voices have challenged this "orthodox" critical revolutionary project, accusing it of complicity with the very relations it purports to challenge. Latour (2004b) famously argues that when critique seeks to debunk false perceptions and reveal underlying structures of power, it serves only to obscure the actual, complex compositions of the world, reinforce dualisms between objective "facts" and subjective "fetishes," and affirm the foolish arrogance of the critic. "The Zeus of critique rules absolutely, to be sure, but over a desert" (2004b, 239). J. K. Gibson-Graham (2006a) argues this point from a different angle: discourse about the world, she asserts, is never simply a *description*; it is an act of *production*, participating in generating the very realities it claims to only identify. When critics call out particular practices or relations as manifestations of capitalism, patriarchy, or other totalizing systems of domination, they risk affirming and strengthening that which they seek to oppose. This is, in part, because the supposedly vast power, systematicity, dynamism, and pervasive reach of such hegemonic formations are as much a construct of critical theory itself as they are actual realities to be found in the multiple becomings of a complex world. "While it affords the pleasures of recognition, of capture, of intellectually subduing that one last thing," proposes Gibson-Graham, such critique "offers no relief or exit to a place beyond" (2006a, 4).

The dangerous performativity of systematizing critique is linked, in this view, to a particular subjective formation and affective investment, "one in which the emotional and affective dispositions of paranoia, melancholia, and moralism intermingle and self-reinforce" (Gibson-Graham 2006a, 4). The critic stands as all-knowing seer and judge, able to take in the complex sweep of reality, reduce it to a set of discrete causal forces, and then proclaim "what is to be done." Paranoia is a name for this subjectivity: a desire to "show intricately and at great length how everything adds up, how it all means the same thing"

(2006a, 4). Everything is enrolled into the narrative of hegemonic power, and the critic comes to inhabit a world dominated by forms of rule that are effectively undefeatable. Defining themselves primarily in relation to that which they oppose yet cannot defeat, "excluded from power yet invested in the powerful" (2006a, 5), they slip into resentment. What remains is a Nietzschean "slave morality," a valorization of weakness in the name of moralizing purity and virtue. To escape such a fate, our theoretical and practical strategies must instead highlight difference and multiplicity, cultivate hope and experimental openness, and focus on possibility and creation.

This "critique of critique" is compelling on multiple levels, and it provides a powerful lens through which to view some of the most dangerous patterns in contemporary and historical leftist politics. Yet the binary tendency of the debate—even if unintended by many of its participants—is deeply problematic. Must we really choose between critical attentiveness to totalizing modes of oppressive power and openness to creative possibility? Does all judgment entail arrogance and totalitarianism? Do all forms of radical critique necessarily entangle us in knots of paranoid resentment and melancholy? Is all paranoia problematic? What if there *are* durable assemblages of power that merit analysis in terms of their totalizing, co-opting tendencies? The polarization of this debate should be viewed as a warning emerging from all positions taken collectively: "Beware all who tread here! It's a trap!" Critique *is* dangerous, and *so is our refusal of it*. We must experiment with approaches that enable us to navigate between the rock of resentful critique and the hard place of naive creation, while learning lessons from the perils and promises of each. This is what each of the three remaining parts of the book, taken together, aim to enact, and I begin here in Part II with the work of *tracing*.

I draw this term from Gilles Deleuze and Félix Guattari, who use it to refer to the analytical reproduction of a "ready-made" hegemonic actuality (1987, 13). To trace is to follow the dominant lines of power that compose an assemblage, generating a kind of "copy," a (re)presentation of its contours and relations that can be circulated, engaged, and ultimately challenged and transformed. As a critical analytical practice, it is simultaneously an embrace of what might be called, riffing on Gayatri Spivak (1996), "strategic paranoia," and an explicit acknowledgment of the dangers of such a move.[4] One who traces *knows* that the articulation generated is performative, is implicated in and complicit with that which is represented, and yet pursues the work nonetheless. Why? In part because there is no noncomplicit place in which one can stand, with clean hands, to do the work of "performing other worlds." Speaking personally, as someone who inhabits a body marked as male and white, living in relative material affluence in a minority world settler-colony, I understand that my complicity in reinscribing the dominance of capitalism, patriarchy, racism, colonialism, and other assemblages of exploitation and violence is not simply the product of the ways I choose to theorize. I *am* complicit, not only by what I *say or write*, but by the full array of material-semiotic relations in which my livelihood is implicated. To trace is to refuse a notion of a singular, objective "system" that is beneath all expressions and can be revealed as the ultimate power within which we are gripped, but it is also to acknowledge *that we are gripped* and that we must account for this capture.

To trace, therefore, is necessary but perilous, as one always risks too much proximity, getting "sucked in." And it is certainly not, by itself, sufficient. In the context of Deleuze and Guattari's broader pragmatics, tracing is a situated, strategic moment in a wider, multidimensional transformative process. "It is a question of method," they write: "*the tracing should always be put back on the map*" (1987, 13). The figure of the "map" is crucially distinct from the tracing, not a reproduction of "the same," but an invitation to experiment with new connections. Unlike the tracing, the map is "entirely oriented toward an experimentation in contact with the real. . . . [I]t is detachable, reversible, susceptible to constant modification" (1987, 12). Tracing, by itself, is anti-experimental and closes upon a singular reality; tracing when "put back on the map" (the aim of Parts III and IV) is a particular way of taking note of patterns that have been performatively constituted and into which we are—and might continue to be—enrolled. It does not purport to reveal a conspiracy of total and inevitable co-optation but rather seeks to generate a vigilant *prophylactic* against such a dynamic.

The tracing I enact in the following three chapters is not intended to produce a singular and totalizing account of how things "really are" in Maine, and therefore to constitute an undefeatable monster whom we can resentfully love to hate. Yet neither do I intend to enact what Gibson-Graham calls a "straw man" strategy (2006c, 10)—a purified, larger-than-life representation constituted solely for the purposes of more clearly articulating its alternative. I cannot merely say that things unfold "as if" economy, society, and environment constitute a

powerful, pervasive, and interconnected assemblage in which our institutions and imaginations are gripped. Rather, I intend to invoke
this image of a triple hegemonic formation as a simultaneously *real*
and *nontotal* articulation in Maine. We are *actually* in the grip of a
totalizing, hegemonic mega-assemblage, the material-semiotic power
of which is substantial and cannot be vanquished with the wave of a
performative-discursive wand; and at the very same time, this totalization is utterly incomplete, as Mainers are always already in the process
of rupturing, exceeding, and escaping this assemblage and enacting
others. Reality is multiplicity, and strategic paranoia is a way to identify dangers of capture and co-optation and to cultivate a *critical care*
that fortifies the many lines of flight that are already escaping.

2 FORCES AND DOMAINS

Dynamics of Mastery and Submission

Hegemony's Forms

The hegemonic trio of economy, society, and environment in Maine manifests, simultaneously, as a set of *forces* and *domains*. As forces, each of the three elements appears to stand above individual human agency, shaping and determining it from the outside; like the weather, they confront us as objective forces to which we are subjected and in the presence of which we become particular kinds of subordinate subjects.[1] As domains, these articulations appear as discrete, bounded zones or systems—collections of objects to be managed or mechanisms to be manipulated. Human collectivities (or at least particular professional groups of humans) are positioned in this case as masters and managers of an objective world rather than as its subordinates. Forces and domains are, in fact, the two forms that "objectivity" takes in a world divided into subjects and objects: on one hand, the objectivity of that which confronts human subjects as a force beyond the whims of interpretation and politics; on the other hand, a domain of passive things over which active subjects can exert control. The subject is, in fact, *defined* by the relation between these two modes of the object that simultaneously set the limits and possibilities for its agency.

J. K. Gibson-Graham (2006c) has noted this dual configuration, with its "twin dispositions of utter submission and confident mastery" (2006c, 93) relative to dominant articulations of "the economy." She describes how economic politics often oscillates between an image of the economy as "the supreme being whose dictates must unquestioningly be obeyed," and a view of it as "an entity that is subject to our full understanding and consequent manipulation" (2006c, 94). It is clear from my

encounters with the trio in Maine that this seemingly paradoxical movement is characteristic of *each* of the three categories, and is therefore
linked to a much larger ontopolitical configuration. As in Bruno Latour's
(1993) description of the "modern constitution," in which one can appeal
to apparently contradictory statements in order to justify a given action
or situation ("It's all a social construct!"; "It's an objective law!"),
hegemonic politics in Maine is a continual oscillation. At one moment,
the economy is a sovereign force whose rule must be obeyed ("or
else . . ."); at another moment, it is a machine with levers to be pushed
and pulled. If the economy poses a problem, blame the force of society;
otherwise, be sure to manage society appropriately so that this economy can function smoothly. The environment sets objective limits to
human action that must be obeyed, while it is also the ultimate source
of all resources and must be managed appropriately as such. This chapter traces some of the ways in which these complex oscillations play out.

Economy as Force

To get serious in Maine, to say something of substance, weight, and
authority, one must speak about the economy. This is the site of
"Maine's bottom line" (Lawton 2008), where matters of survival, material well-being, dignity, and the very future itself all appear to be
at stake. We are told by the authors of *Charting Maine's Future: Making Headway* that "Maine people are concerned, above all else, with
jobs and the economy" (GrowSmart Maine 2012, 1). Some of the state's
most prominent environmental advocacy groups remind us that "today
in Maine the economy is on everyone's mind," and frame environmental protection as a form of economic investment (Kelley 2010). The
economy is "hard," necessary, serious, and foundational; all else is "soft,"
secondary, and dependent (Nelson 2009a). Dana Conners and Laurie
Lachance, prominent economic development professionals in the state,
make the order of priorities clear when they argue that early child-
hood education in Maine "is not just a social and moral imperative; it
is an *economic* imperative" (qtd. in Cervone 2012, emphasis added).

From where does such an "imperative" come? The economy is
articulated, first and foremost, as a *force* that lies beyond the realm
of individual or even collective human agency. According to Frank, a
department director in a large Maine charity organization, the economy is "an incredibly powerful thing . . . you know, it's . . . relatively

unbridled, right? So it doesn't necessarily act for the *good* of anything. It's just this powerful force, right?" (interview). This force is beyond our control: "Economic forces are gonna happen," says Owen, the director of a statewide economic development organization, "and it's gonna go where it's gonna go, and we can try to control it, but at the end of the day . . . at some level it's gonna happen" (interview). For some people, this force is envisioned as a vast, anonymous agency or *being*: "It just seems like it's a machine that just keeps on moving," says Paul, a social worker (interview). "I get depressed," admits Elizabeth, a policy advocate for a major Maine environmental organization, "because I feel like there's an economic system that we're never going to *tame*, so to speak" (interview). For others, the economy is like the weather: a power that sweeps over us from above or beyond. Former Maine governor John Baldacci has spoken of "an economic and financial ice storm—unavoidable and unrelenting" (qtd. in Mills 2004). Dorothy, the director of a regional public health initiative, describes it like this: "When you talk economy, it's kind of like this big ball . . . the vision I have is, you know, is . . . lighting going through it or whatever [voice escalating, half-laughing, almost shouting], you know?!" (interview).

The force of economy is often associated with a set of "laws" that appear as integral to the structure of reality itself. "You *can't* contradict the laws of supply and demand. I mean, they operate. They *do* operate," says Ben, an academic focused on sustainable regional development (interview). His work normally emphasizes the role of institutions in structuring the political landscape, yet when it comes to supply-and-demand dynamics, such analysis apparently does not apply. In a surprisingly identical articulation, a conservative economic think-tank leader (normally antagonistic to Ben's approach) proclaims confidently that "politicians think they can repeal the law of supply and demand. It's never been violated. Economists have studied it for hundreds of years. It's a *law*" (interview). Law, in this sense, is the force of objective nature itself, "absolutely exempt from the agitations of the crowd and before which subjects must kneel in humility" (Latour 2004a, 78). It is thoroughly haunted by the image of the sovereign, the king, the deity, who stands as a final and irrefutable source of appeal and judgment.

A crucial vehicle through which the sovereign law of the economy is articulated or expressed is *measurement*. A measure is not only, as Massimo De Angelis describes, a "discursive device that acts as a point of reference, a benchmark, a typical norm, a standard" (2007, 176), it is also a *performative* device by which both an object and its index are brought into being as such. It is not that measurement fabricates reality out of thin air, but rather that it *fixes* a particular set of processes into a stable system of reference that enables new kinds of presence in the world as well as new forms of intervention (Latour 1987). Numbers, in particular, as Nikolas Rose describes, "redraw the boundaries between politics and objectivity by purporting to act as automatic technical mechanisms for making judgments, prioritizing problems, and allocating scarce resources" (1999, 198).

Things gain a particular kind of independence and apparent stability once they have been counted. That which is partially *produced* by measurement seems, then, to be objectively represented *by* it. In Maine, as elsewhere, the economy's numbers function as an *index of force* that renders myriad local relations into a coherent "economic" dynamic. Through the production and circulation of what Latour (1990) calls "inscription devices"—graphs, charts, tables, reports, quotes, PowerPoint presentations, and such—messy measurements are cleaned up, rendered stable, and inscribed into forms that can be transported through numerous sites of action. Measures are thus made into "objects which have the properties of being *mobile* but also *immutable*, *presentable*, *readable*, and *combinable* with one another" (1990, 6). Examples include the one-stop statistical grid of the *Maine Economy at a Glance* website (Bureau of Labor Statistics 2014); the *MaineBiz* magazine's (2013) visual summary by the same name; the colorful charts of *Measures of Growth in Focus* (MEGC 2013); and the biannual prognostications of Maine's Consensus Economic Forecasting Commission (Clair et al. 2013). Joseph O'Connell, referencing Latour, calls this process of performative measurement "the creation of universality by the circulation of particulars" (1993). Indeed, far from measuring *all* livelihood activity, "economic" measurement is usually restricted to the particulars of *monetary* flow and any relations of production or consumption that can be directly related to its magnitude.

Once inscribed and ontologized, there is no negotiating with the numbers and with the economy-as-force they participate in articulating. Right-wing governor Paul LePage (2013) and the progressive organization Opportunity Maine (Ginn and Brown 2009) both agree that the economy "demands" particular policies and fiscal actions. It "provides" us with the means of life (Brookings Institution 2006, 8). It "requires" specific actions and adaptations (Governor's Council on

Maine's Quality of Place 2007, 10). As Calvin, the director of an economic policy think-tank, says, "Most people can't stay [in Maine],
because the economy doesn't allow them to" (interview). There is a
powerful disciplinary force at work here, laying out a particular set
of possibilities and punishing anyone who transgresses their bounds:
"Businesses and jobs," proclaims the Maine Alliance, "must adopt the
ways of the new economy decisively or face extinction" (1994, 6). The
demands of this cutthroat economic reality call for "bold action," "courage and discipline," and "tough decisions" (O'Hara 2013; LePage 2014a).
"You know, in an economy, you have to make choices," says Owen, the
economic development organization director, "You absolutely have to
make choices. There are going to be winners and losers. That's how
economies work. There's no saving everybody" (interview).

The conviction that Maine must follow an inviolable dictate from
the economy manifests in a pervasive emphasis among economic
development professionals on market competition. All strategies for
improving human lives or environments in Maine must ultimately pass
a crucial test: Does this make our state or its private enterprises more
competitive? Ostensibly cutting-edge approaches focused on "bottom-
up" asset-based development, enhancing local capacity, and cultivating
"quality of place"—approaches that might, in another frame, suggest
a focus on endogenous development, regional sufficiency, and creative
action to meet local needs—are all circumscribed by the necessity of
competitive advantage. The only *assets* that count in the framework
of Mobilize Maine, a statewide asset-based economic development initiative funded by the U.S. Economic Development Administration, are
those that lend Maine an exclusive "competitive edge" over other
regions (NADO Research Foundation 2011). The only innovation that
counts in Maine Department of Community and Economic Development's "Innovation Index" is that which can enhance commercial productivity or catalyze the development of new marketable products
(Camoin Associates 2012). Maine's "quality of place" is developed or
preserved primarily in the name of attracting, as one economic development advocate put it, "young, talented, educated people . . . the hope
for the future, for Maine" (Calvin, interview).

Why competition? I asked Arnold, the director of a regional economic development authority: "Is this an optional game that we think
we're obliged to play?" His reply was clear: "Well, I think we're obliged
to play not because the game's being played, but because you need to

survive" (interview). We should be reminded here again of the material nature of articulation, for while the statistician Kathleen can propose to me that "a lot of what we talk about with the economy, well, it is all just sort of concepts and it works because everybody's bought in to this concept" (interview), this "buy-in" is enforced by forms of material-semiotic institution that render these concepts not only durable but *obligatory*.[2] When the owner of an alternative energy business described to me that the economy "boils down to one's ability to *survive*, to produce a good or service or work product that results in some type of compensation so that you can eat, provide yourself with food, shelter, and clothing" (Dennis, interview), his linking of "survival" with "compensation" can be read as an acknowledgment of a very real dependency on a hegemonic economy that has been coercively established in Maine.

A long and ongoing history of enclosure, cultural transformation, and desire-production in the state and in its larger socio-geographical context within European colonialism has produced a situation in which Maine people *actually do* require money to secure core portions of their livelihoods, wage jobs to secure this money, competitive businesses to provide these jobs, and economic developers to help attract and retain these businesses.[3] Few if any are wholly insulated from the addictive dynamics of market competition that so often punishes those who do not adequately compete, or from ongoing processes of "primitive accumulation" that unfold in the forms of debt, privatization, the elimination of public benefits, regressive taxation, and other such practices (De Angelis 2001; Harvey 2003; Perelman 2007). As Sean, a prominent Maine conservation advocate, states bluntly: "We need to *survive*, and we survive in this society through capitalism. So money *does*, economy *does* rule" (interview).

A stark picture emerges: Far from having the freedom to determine their own future, Maine people must recognize that economic forces provide the dynamic, non-negotiable parameters within which any creative engagement with development must take place. Economic developers, social advocates, and environmental activists all seem obligated to inhabit the problem-space that the economy-as-force articulates. All are subjected to a continually moving, ever-unpredictable flow of financial activity and market power that builds life possibilities and then sweeps them away. Living under the authority of a deterritorializing, lawlike force of aggregated competitive, monetized, market activity, Maine people can participate in economic life only as adaptive subjects—reacting, adjusting, or failing to do so.

Economy as Domain

This overwhelming disciplinary force is, of course, not the only form in which the economy is articulated. Simultaneously, as if in a desperate attempt to rein in or manage this force—to enact some form of agency in its presence—the economy also appears as a governable *domain*. This is what François Perroux (1950) refers to as "geonomic space," and what Timothy Mitchell describes as "the totality of monetarized exchanges within a defined space" (2002, 4). My interviewees simply call it "Maine's economy." As Kathleen describes regarding her daily work as a government statistician:

> People call me up and say, "What's going on with Maine's economy?" and I have to ask them to clarify: Are you talking about Maine's GDP? Are you talking about Maine's employment? Are you talking about the unemployment rate? Are you talking about the number of businesses we have? . . . Because usually they want numbers from me, and so they're asking for a very specific "this is what I'm thinking about in terms of the economy," so I have to find that for them. (interview)

The economy here is not a deterritorializing force or flow, but a specific, bounded space. "For a geographic community to survive over the long term," says Jane, the director of a philanthropic organization, "it needs to have an *economy*" (interview). Indeed, it is a particular economic *territorialization* that enables a set of common identifications ("our" economy, "their" economy, the "Maine economy," or the "national economy") and thus stabilizes this economy as a site for management and policy intervention.

The Gross Domestic Product (GDP), in particular, and its state-level equivalent (Gross State Product) function to constitute a bounded political space as having "an economy." As a core dimension of the system of national accounts, produced and maintained by the U.S. Bureau of Economic Analysis, the GDP does not simply "take the pulse of the economy" (Landefeld, Seskin, and Fraumeni 2008), but rather works to constitute the very "body" through which such a pulse appears to flow.[4] A specific array of monetary transactions are tied to a bordered space and aggregated into a singular indicator, the content of which becomes the crowning measure of economic health, success, and well-being (Harvie et al. 2009). "You know, probably most people when they think about the economy, they're really meaning Gross Domestic Product," says Kathleen (interview). Even if economists such as Eric, an academic regional analyst, know that the GDP and other measures are "just another measure; . . . they're not the economy" (interview), these inscription devices appear nonetheless as objective representations of a reality that is independent of them.

In such a context, Maine is merely a small part within a larger whole to which it is subjected. The broader field of "geonomic" economization unfolds as the articulation of a structure of nested containers, each of which exerts asymmetrical force upon its subordinated contents—the global economy upon the national, the national upon the regional, and the regional upon the local (Gibson-Graham 2002). "Maine is not an island unto itself," write Allen Pease and Wilfred Richard. "Its economic and social well-being are determined largely by national policies" (1983, 65). The economy-as-domain thus becomes a system of cascading determinations in which politicians, policy advocates, and other players seek to intervene at each level to maximize benefit (or at least the *appearance* of benefit) for their pertinent population (Rubin 1988). The articulation of a "Maine economy," where this domain appears coextensive with the political boundaries of the state, thus renders it possible for Maine's economic development advocates to at least *speak* of the need to "create a focused strategy[,] . . . make the tough decisions and carry it out," and to aspire to "re-create the engines of growth in Maine's economy" (O'Hara 2010, 1).

If the articulation of economy-as-force constitutes a dynamic of subordination and subjection, then the economy-as-*domain* can be seen as a moment of tenuous, provisional aspiration toward control and mastery. In a widely mobilized image, the economy becomes an engineering site, a machine, a series of "levers" or "gears" that can be manipulated to achieve various desired effects (Gibson-Graham, Cameron, and Healy 2013). Carol, who works for a government social service department, used such an image to describe the mechanisms by which conventional economic development interventions might generate positive outcomes for "social" practices: "Those people who are economic developers, what they know is that *if they get that piece moving, then these other parts will also move*. . . . If they focus on what's traditional, and measurable, and cash-based, these other parts all also move too" (interview, emphasis added). The discourse of leverage, of strategic intervention in the economic mechanism, is what enables the very *field* of "economic development" and fuels the image of a political infrastructure that can, with the right policies, "get the economy moving." Dorothy, a community health worker, expresses the political hope often associated with such a discourse: "I said, the last presidential election, 'I want a president that can make gas less than two bucks a gallon, that will give us 3 percent on our savings account, and either everyone has health insurance or no one has it.' If there was a president like that running who could promise those three things, I would vote for them and I think our economy would turn around" (interview). Politicians build their electoral prospects on the promise this image of mastery suggests: that they—unlike their competitors—can harness and transform the economic field, as former U.S. senator Mike Michaud (2014) says, to "build a stronger economy and create jobs."

The economy-as-domain is inseparable from the *state* as a territorial unit of governance. Coextensive with state boundaries, constituted in significant part by state-sponsored technologies of inscription, and presented as an object for state management, "the Maine economy" is as much a property of the State of Maine as it is of Maine's population. Timothy Mitchell outlines the mutually constitutive relation in these historical terms: "The idea of 'the economy' provided a mode of seeing and a way of organizing the world that could diagnose a country's fundamental condition, frame the terms of its public debate, picture its collective growth or decline, and propose remedies for its improvement, all in terms of what seemed a legible series of measurements, goals, and comparisons" (2002, 272). In this sense, the economy can be seen as a stabilization of deterritorializing flows for the purpose of rendering them *governable* and thus constructing an apparently reliable "hold" on economic life that can be mobilized for a variety of political purposes (Rose and Miller 2008). Foucault describes such a scenario in terms of the emergence of "liberal government," no longer a state built on despotic rule but rather one built on the "management and organization of the conditions in which one can be free" (2010a, 63–64). These conditions are, most fundamentally, the forces of the *market*.

The state is, therefore, not *actually* the master of the economy-as-domain, despite opportunistic rhetoric to the contrary (*x* politician will "turn this economy around"). Contemporary economic government is, in fact, another form of subordination to forces beyond human agency.

Even Keynesianism, a key theory in the origin of the economy-as-domain articulation, is far from the "command and control" model that its critics might ascribe to it. It functions, rather, at the level of *how much* and *what kinds* of interventions a government should make in light of the dynamics of the economy itself (De Angelis 2007, 89). Keynes himself argued that there has simply "been a fundamental misunderstanding of how . . . the economy in which we live actually works" (1936, 13). In Keynesianism as in neoliberalism, says Foucault, "the basic principle of the state's role, and so of the form of governmentality henceforth prescribed for it, [is] to respect these natural processes, or at any rate to take them into account, get them to work, or to work with them" (2007a, 352).

On one hand, the economy-as-domain provides the state with a particular *mode of rule*, a context or vehicle through which to exert various forms of coercion, obligation, and enticement upon a population in the name of its own well-being. Neoliberalism constitutes only a more disguised form of such rule, in which coercion is outsourced to the market rather than located in a mediation between state intervention and market dynamics. On the other hand, this governmentality on the part of the state can be seen as an ultimate *concession* to the rule of the economy-as-force. "Government," writes Foucault relative to a lesson gleaned by the seventeenth-century Physiocrats, "must know these [economic] mechanisms in their innermost and complex nature. Once it knows these mechanisms, it must, of course, undertake to respect them" (2010a, 61). Engagement with various economic "levers" provides mastery only *relative* to a broader concession to economic forces. Indeed, the very image of pulling levers belies a structure of power: lever-pullers are rarely the inventors of the machine, and while mobilizing their positions of mechanical influence for various pragmatic purposes, they remain functionaries of the sovereignty of economic force.

Society as Force and Domain

The articulation of economy as either force or domain is inseparable from the composition of a "society." This is clear in genealogical terms, as I described in chapter 1. It is also true in practical contemporary terms, as a statistically constituted form of the social stands as the nearly coextensive "body" of the economy (Poovey 1995). It is variably articulated as a distinct domain of life and as a lawlike force of collective determination though a whole host of "social" measures and indexes: population changes, age and identity compositions, educational attainment, crime rates, health indexes, employment rates, income levels, aggregate market preferences, election results, and more. In all of these cases, society is articulated as some variation of an aggregate "us," the sum total of Maine people taken as a coherent population. It is therefore, on one hand, a realm of subjects bundled into a singular object (or as various "populations," a collection of objects) to be measured and managed. On the other hand, this very aggregation constitutes a kind of objective force that determines the contours of the collective life it emerges from. In neither instance, though, is society easily distinguished from economy. The social body is at once fed by the economy as its external source (force) of sustenance, and it is also itself the sustaining force that animates all economic articulations. In both senses, there is no society that can clearly stand apart from the economy that it generates, sustains, serves, or is definitively dependent upon.

As an aggregated collective force, society is the fundamental driver of economic dynamics and its ultimate source of determination. It is the origin point of what economists like to refer to as "exogenous preferences"—manifestations of desire, expressed in monetary transactions, that come from outside the economy itself yet are its source of animation. "An economy is nothing more than the voluntary exchange of goods and services between people," proposes Marvin, the director of an economic policy think tank (interview), and this exchange is driven by desire rendered "social" though its aggregation via market-signaling mechanisms. Even if one challenges the individualism of this formulation, the dynamic remains, since public policy decisions and the actions of collective institutions can also be viewed as expressions of social force. To the extent that something problematic or beneficial is unfolding in the economy (or, for that matter, anywhere else), this can be explained or justified by recourse to society: "Are we investing as a society enough in our education, in our health, in our creativity, and in our community?" asks Chad, the economic development director (interview). "Mainers as a society value nature," says Carl, an ecologist working for the state government (interview). For Kathleen, the government statistician, whether we should measure things in monetary terms "depends on whether we as a society want to be able to do . . . dollar-value comparison[s]" (interview). In all cases, "we" confront ourselves as a kind of alienated, aggregate force of our own preferences, choices, and instituted agreements.

Yet even as society stands as a force capable of challenging or even constituting the economy, it is simultaneously and paradoxically composed as a site of dependence and subordination. Economy and society are articulated, to borrow a term from anthropology, in an "asymmetrical reciprocity" (Orenstein 1980) in which the economy most often appears as the master term. For while the economy needs society as its matrix and its justification for existence ("The economy is about people," says Kathleen), society's dependence on the economy appears as a more determinative and politically potent articulation. Recall Sean, the conservationist: "We *survive* in this society through capitalism. . . . Economy *does* rule" (interview). Isaac, an economic development consultant, proposes that "the whole infrastructure of society is evaporating" in some northern Maine communities, "because there aren't enough jobs" (interview). And as the sustainable development researcher, Ben, observes: "We've got a society that to some extent operates through the laws of supply and demand" (interview). It is apparent here that when society constitutes a force, the substance of its force *is* quite often the economy.

Society as *domain*, articulated via social statistics of (certain) livelihood characteristics and outcomes, is like a hungry body in need of economic food. Sean's articulation of economic rule ("We have to *survive*") is a commonsense formulation. Of *course* society needs an economy! Isn't an economy precisely the means by which society provides for its material needs? Isn't the "hungry body in need of food" not just a metaphor, but the *actual form* of the society-economy relation? Perhaps; but then "economy" could refer to only a particular set of *actions* taken collectively—a *process* of instituting livelihood (Polanyi 1992)—and not to either a distinct force or a separated domain. What is seemingly so normal within the hegemonic assemblage, yet actually quite bizarre, is the ease with which one can speak of an economy that rules over the sources of its own animation and a society that is ruled by its own creation now confronting it as a fickle external force.[5] In a dizzying tangle, society-as-force appears to *generate* economy-as-force, which in turn becomes this social force's most powerful expression (social preferences translated to market allocation). Economy-as-force then provides (or not) the dependent and needy social-as-domain with its sustenance. To measure the health and well-being of the social-as-domain, one can then use economic indices.

Within such a configuration, economy-as-domain necessarily comes to stand in for society itself, since the health of economic force is dependent on the management of the populations and resources that compose (and are subjected to) it. Society in *both* possible forms (force and domain) is therefore rendered into an instrumental *accessory* to economy. Chad, the economic developer, inverts "people" and "economy" in a way (perhaps inadvertent, but nonetheless telling) that makes this dynamic quite clear:

> A critical piece within any economy is the people within that economy. So whatever they're doing, they are important . . . they need to be functioning at the highest level they can, you know, their full potential. . . . We use a measure that's pretty easy to get and commonly used, which is *productivity* . . . you know, how much are you doing? And that is tied hard to a person's education and their training and experience and knowledge, their potential in life, which in turn is tied directly to their health. So you want people to be healthy, to live healthy lives, because they actually are more *productive*. (interview)

The economy, which Chad would agree is "about people," is figured here as that to which people are ultimately in *service*. People, or populations, come to constitute sites of economic productivity, cogs in the wheel of growth, serving the demands of that which was ostensibly intended to serve them. This is a manifestation of Marx's (1964) notion of "alienation" par excellence.

Environment as Force and Domain

The analysis thus far has only involved *humans*, and a consideration of "the environment" might seem likely to shift this focus. But despite a sense in which environmental issues are often associated with endangered species and images of undisturbed wilderness, there remains a particular human subject at the center of hegemonic articulations of the environment (Evernden 1988; Luke 1995). Indeed, the human is often the *only* subject to be found, or at least foregrounded, when environmental concerns are at stake.[6] While both economy and society, when manifested as forces, rely on a notion of (aggregated, abstracted) human subjects generating dynamics that exceed and then act back upon them, the environment involves only *objects* in the double sense described earlier. On one hand, the environment can be presented as synonymous with "nature" as a source and force of objective law. Environmental advocates and economic developers alike can appeal to this notion in an attempt to close down political debate and present their advocacy as a matter of *fact* rather than of *value* (Latour 2004a). On the other hand, the environment-as-domain sits, in its various forms, outside human society as a collection of resources to be *used and managed*—whether in a spirit of accumulative exploitation or restorative recreation.

Environment-as-force is, in one of its manifestations, quite familiar: the drought that causes the blueberry crop to fail, the ice storm that takes out electric service for three days, or the epidemic of deer ticks spreading Lyme disease to thousands of rural inhabitants and visitors. The environment in such instances is articulated as that which is *out there*, beyond human control and agency; it confronts us with myriad welcome and unwelcome surprises. By enrolling these more-than-human processes into its articulation, the hegemonic assemblage of "the environment" constitutes a particularly powerful force. As the very name for nature itself, undistorted by human cultural projections or political agendas, the environment becomes the ultimate source of objective (understood here as incontrovertible) knowledge. To align oneself with this force, to make claims in its name, is to gain tremendous power to "naturalize" things that might otherwise be understood as complex, contingent articulations. Environmental determinism is only the most common and obvious of such moves, and one can find some notion of "the indisputable laws of nature" (Latour 2004a, 174) lurking behind articulations on all sides of the political spectrum.

David, for example, a prominent Maine environmental activist, presents a classic "environmentalist" discourse in this vein: "There are limits on a finite planet," he says. "There's just too many people, *that's* the problem. . . . We're like a cancer growth" (interview). He describes an experiment done with undergraduate ecology students in which bacteria were isolated in a nutrient-rich petri dish: "These bacteria would just grow like crazy, and eventually they'd stop growing and the whole colony would die. It wasn't that they had completely consumed the medium which they were living off, but they died because of the toxicity of their waste. I use that as an analogy, the planet being a petri plate and we're the bacteria" (interview). The environment here, as objective nature and its agents, functions to naturalize a particular political discourse of limits on population growth.[7] Even the most strident pro-development, procapitalist, wilderness skeptic can become an ardent "environmentalist" in this ironic sense. Recall, for example, the pronouncements about the unbreakable "law" of supply and demand by David and Marvin. Responding to a challenge regarding the necessity of competition, another private economic development consultant offered a common trope of nature: "Yeah, but you gotta compare yourself to something. We're an animal. We have to be better than others. . . . Everything is competition. It's just the nature of being an animal" (Harold, interview). Not only the economy, but the *environment itself* demands that we compete—or die.

This environment-as-force, which is often articulated in forms that avoid explicitly invoking "environment" as a key word, can paradoxically come to serve as a strategy for subordinating its non-identical and more explicitly articulated twin, environment-as-domain. One can thus appeal to a natural law (e.g., supply and demand) to pose an economic sovereignty over and above the domain of an environment figured as a domain of passive, potentially commodifiable resources or amenities. The notion of the "environmental Kuznets curve" exemplifies an articulation in which the environment appears as *dependent* on economic development (Grossman and Krueger 1995; WCED 1987b). Eric, the development economist, summarizes this concept:

> You've got to take care of the base first, and the economy speaks to that. . . . Environment gets far more attention from wealthy places than poor places, and it gets far more attention in good times than bad times. It's related to the stresses on the hierarchy of needs. So, ironically, we have the economy growing and moving ahead in order for people to deal with the environmental changes. . . . The economy gets more attention in times of stress, and it *needs* attention because it's the only way in which society as a whole is able to focus on some of the other things. It's a trade-off. (interview)

It is the *economy* (naturalized via environment-as-force) and not the environment (as domain) that constitutes "the base" in this articulation, and only market-centered development can save us from the very destruction that it has generated in the first place.[8] Such a view refuses to ask about the very composition of "the environment" that low-income people are supposedly refusing or unable to care about in the face of "economic" imperatives. Could it be that this articulation of the environment as an instrumentalized domain of objects and amenities is always already produced as an adjunct to the economy? Might its

very form be part and parcel of what generates the eclipse of the ecological and sustains the seeming necessity of economic development as
a first priority?

If, as Owen, the economic development director, says, "everyone
in Maine is an environmentalist," this is because a domain called
"the environment" has been widely articulated as little other than "an
immense mine from which to endlessly extract the basic raw materials
necessary to feed the processes of commodity production" (De Angelis
2007, 67), a space for dumping and discharging the wastes of production, and a set of services to be rendered "sustainable" in their avail-
ability to human enjoyment and endless economic growth (Healey and
Shaw 1994). This articulation unfolds—as with economy and society—
via multiple practices of measurement and mapping. Through geological and ecological surveys, ongoing inventories of forest tree composition, fishery health, wind energy potential, invasive plants and
insects, fire danger, fragile ecosystems and endangered species, flood
risk areas, soil nutrient levels, water and air quality, ozone levels, food
dangers, and more, a "Maine environment" is ontologized as a domain
of *things* to be used, managed, or avoided. The Maine Department of
Environmental Protection and the Maine Department of Agriculture,
Conservation, and Forestry, the latter self-described as "the State of
Maine's support center for our many land-based, natural resource interests" (Maine DACF 2014), are key institutions in this production. Not
simply representational practices, these inscriptions constitute an entire
set of material-semiotic relations in which ecological relations take on
particular forms as sites of optimization, risk management, and "trade-
offs" (Asdal 2008). This is the production, as Timothy Luke describes, of
the environment as "something to be managed by expert managerialists
armed with coherent clusters of technical acumen and administrative
practice" (1996, 3). Moreover, this is a domain that can be *economized*
and thus brought into the zone of economic governmentality—to be
managed efficiently by market forces (Lemke 2002).

If the environment is a bundle of natural resources to be conserved
for a production paradigm oriented toward the manufacturing of tangible commodities, the growth of a "service economy" in Maine, along
with the rise of discourses about the competitive demands of the "new
economy" (Reneault 2014; Caron 2015), has translated this instrumental articulation into the language of "amenities" (e.g., Colgan 2006).
Accompanied by a rhetoric that purports to end the conflict between

economy and environment, Maine's natural resources and landscapes take on the role of providing an attractive backdrop for economic investment and population growth. "Prosperity," says economic think-tank director Calvin, is "a function of protecting the character of the place" (interview). As the authors of *Charting Maine's Future* describe, "Maine possesses a globally known 'brand' built in images of livable communities, stunning scenery, and great recreational opportunities" (Brookings Institution 2006, 6). Ecological concerns appear in this report only as an awareness that "often-haphazard residential development is more and more *blurring those crisp scenes* as it impinges on forests, fields, and waterfronts all around the state" (2006, 8). In scholar-activist Raymond Rogers's words, it appears here that "environmental concerns are important so that economic development can continue" (1998, 75).

Such an articulation is not restricted to economic development professionals. In fact, some of the strongest expressions of the amenity view can be found among environmental advocates, where protection efforts sometimes appear to be more about consumer advocacy for potential Maine settlers than about ecological concern. Carl, a state government ecologist who is clearly committed to work beyond this discourse, seems obligated to describe it this way: "I see the protection of the environment as such a strong selling point for the economy of Maine, and I always have. That's why I live here. That's why I think a lot of people retire here, or summer here. Because they like the environment in Maine. Land conservation and conservation of our resources—air, water, all those things—are tied to the economy of Maine probably more so than if you lived in Philadelphia or Southern California" (interview). One of the Maine Environmental Priorities Coalition's key publications (Kelley 2010) is called *Investing in Maine's Environment: A Trail Map to Prosperity*, the name of which indicates the extent to which the hegemonic environment is bound up with the economy. One does not protect, defend, or restore the environment; one *invests* in it. The trail map takes us neither to health, fulfillment, connection, ecological integrity, nor even to the top of a wild mountain, but to *prosperity*. The instrumental framing of the report is crystal clear: "Maine's extraordinary environment forms the *backdrop* for who we are and what we value as individuals and as a state. Our jobs, our health, our leisure activities, our community values, and our identity as Maine people all have their roots in our beautiful environment. *When we work together to protect it, Maine people and Maine businesses can thrive"* (2010, 2, emphasis added). To protect "the environment" in Maine, we must protect investment opportunities. "We have to think about the natural resources in a new way," proposes Sean, the conservationist, "and think about how to capitalize on conservation" (interview). Why? Because as Stephen, a well-known Maine environmentalist, says, "We're in competition with every other big beautiful place in the world" (interview). All that cannot be constituted in terms of market competition is rendered invisible, impossible to care for as part of a public contestation. Such an approach may be strategic, as environmental politics has often faced challenges in expressing a more "radical" stance in public (Dobson 1990, 20). But the instrumentalizing effect nonetheless remains.

Whether in the form of "sustainable" resource extraction, tourism, or the continual fabrication of "quality places" constructed in the image of an outside investor's eco-fantasy, more than human lives, relations, and spaces are subjected to an ongoing process of socioeconomic rule and colonization. Unlike a parallel dynamic within the domain of society, in which human subjects enact economic force even if it returns to rule them, all of this unfolds without an accompanying environmental subjectification. Nonhumans are articulated as *objects* of both society and economy, but never as *subjects* in relation to these domains. One might imagine a political slogan in this context: *"No subjection with out subjectification!"*[9] Only humans get to be subjects in this assemblage, and even then only in a limited sense.

The articulation of "the environment" as a domain of either resources or amenities assures a focus on particular humans attempting to secure the status quo of their ways of life in particular places. The verb "to environ," as Luke notes, means "to encircle, encompass, envelop, or enclose. It is the physical activity of surrounding, circumscribing, or ringing around something" (1995, 64). This implies, then, that *something* is always encircled, something is always at the center of this enclosure. "An environment," writes Tim Ingold, "exists only *in relation* to the being whose environment it is. . . . [T]he environment is reality *for* the organism in question" (2009, 143). In the case of "the environment" as conventionally composed, it is clear that *particular human beings* and their livelihoods are at the center. The environment appears as such, and certainly as valuable, only to the extent that it supports the activities, visions, and narratives of these specific humans.

Which humans? Those who are properly assimilated and subjected to a hegemonic articulation of the triple categorization: individualized, competitive, "responsible" colonizers; historically speaking, Western, white, wealthy men (Argyrou 2005).

The classic critique of "environmental" politics as a domain for privileged subjects seeking respite while remaining indifferent to core issues of exclusion and oppression is not, then, simply a commentary on the problematic choices of certain activists or organizations (though it is this, too).[10] It is also an expression of the ways in which "the environment" *itself* names a key element in the topography of modern, capitalist-industrialist, settler-colonial anthropocentrism. In other words, it is the case not simply that "the environment" has been the concern of those who are rewarded by the hegemonic articulation, but also that the very construction of this environment within the larger assemblage of the trio is always already bound up in these relations of power. Of *course* one might end up asking: "Are you and environmentalist, or do you work for a living?" (White 1996); the environment has been produced as that which is *not* the site of work, industry, economy— modern livelihood in its hegemonic form. If, within the hegemonic assemblage, the economy manifests as the alienation of labor, and society appears as the alienation of human agency, then the environment is the alienated form of the matrix of life itself. What if many of us have been seeking to "save" that which must, in fact, be radically questioned and perhaps even undone?

3 ENCLOSURES AND OUTSIDES

Making and Unmaking Boundaries

The Co-capture of Domains

Exiting the hegemonic assemblage of economy, society, and environment is no simple task. As bounded, measured domains (or "spheres") of life, each element captures and encloses some things while also constituting an "outside" into which other things are relegated. A dynamic of enclosure, exclusion, and subsequent disciplinary reintegration, particularly when all three domains are taken as an interrelated "whole," constitutes a powerful apparatus of capture. While the previous chapter focused on ways in which hegemonic versions of economy, society, and environment are articulated as dynamic oscillations within a space of forces and domains, this chapter takes a closer look at how each of the domains relates to one another. How are their boundaries constituted? What is included and excluded? How do the excluded elements of one domain come to constitute the contents of another? If the force/domain view expresses the hegemonic trio as a set of co-produced, conflictual divisions, this chapter's tracing enables a clearer view of the constitutive *inseparability* of economy, society, and environment in their hegemonic forms. Not only does each articulation lend force to, or steal force from, the others, but each is also constructed in and through the very process of boundary-making that its existence as a domain entails.

Enclosures

As I suggested in chapter 2, the articulation of the hegemonic trio can be understood as a historical and ongoing process of *enclosure*. I use this term in two distinct but related senses, referring not only to processes of privatization and deprivation that "increase people's dependence on capitalist markets for the reproduction of their livelihoods" (De Angelis 2007, 133), but also to a much broader sense in which assemblages are constituted through processes that draw boundaries, ossify relations, enforce dependencies, and produce exclusions that these assemblages are, in turn, dependent upon. To produce "the economy," for example, a line must be drawn at both material and conceptual levels: this is what *counts*, this is what can and should be *valued*, and this is what *must* now be done in order to survive, since the economy itself is a hegemonic capture of the means of life. Economic enclosures have variously involved the forced separation of people from access to direct means of subsistence, the degradation of the means of this subsistence, and a subsequent construction of particular "economic" spaces and practices through which livelihoods must be produced (the "workplace," the "job," the "enterprise," the "market"). These are often accompanied and reinforced by the "conceptual enclosures" (Hyde 2010, 215) associated with the discipline of economics that render these spaces intelligible, stable, and legitimate. As Koray Çaliskan and Michel Callon proclaim: "No economization without either economics or the institutional assemblages that act as socio-cognitive prostheses to ensure the coordination of agents" (2010, 22).[1]

Though the concept of enclosure has been predominately applied to the domain of economy, it is crucial to see this process as constitutive of society and environment as well. The composition of a "society" is enacted first and foremost through the articulation of boundaries that delimit its legitimate membership. Who counts as part of a given social domain? The politics of undocumented immigration in Maine is a case in point. In June 2014, Maine governor Paul LePage issued an executive order threatening to cut funding to state municipalities that provide general assistance for undocumented immigrants. In his radio announcement, he stated that "illegal aliens who choose to live in Maine are not our most vulnerable citizens. We need to take care of Mainers first. I think most Mainers would agree" (LePage 2014b). With the term "illegal aliens," he was referring to a group of people who have come to Maine as refugees from brutal violence in their home countries (e.g., Besteman 2016), and as low-paid migrant workers who produce $137 million of the state's annual GDP raking wild blueberries, planting trees, processing eggs, weaving Christmas wreaths, and harvesting apples, cauliflower, and broccoli (Perryman Group 2008). LePage's designation of "illegal" points toward the boundary-making function of citizenship institutions, while his addition of "alien" addresses the very boundary of humanity itself. Maine "society" or "community" is stabilized and defined by this move, particularly when attached to material sanctions. On one side of the enclosure are "real Mainers" who *count*; on the other are those whose needs, vulnerabilities, and contributions can be discounted and dismissed. If any doubts remain about this example as one of enclosure, witness LePage's statement to a group of senior citizens a few months after his order: "If we can't build a fence high enough," he proposed, "we ought to go to China and see how they built a wall" (qtd. in Gluckman 2014).

What of "the environment"? Is this not the ultimate non-enclosure, the very manifestation of the "outside"? In some sense, yes, as I will describe later. But in its hegemonic form the environment is not the opposite of enclosure but rather a *product* of it. As I have already argued, when articulators of the hegemonic assemblage speak of "the environment," they do not refer to a radical space of wildness that threatens the very stability of all that it escapes. Rather, the environment is the measured, bounded, and managed domain of the *source* and the *sink*—the recreation area, the mine, and the dump. One has only to consider, for example, the ways in which environmental concerns often take the form of creating and stewarding the delineated spaces known as "parks," "refuges," and "sanctuaries." Various versions of a proposal for a Maine Woods National Park in the forested center of the state have been, in this regard, major sites of conflict as local people fear—and experience—exclusion from the ability to continue long-time land-use practices and to determine the long-term fate of their immediate habitat (Docherty 2000; Auerbach 2018). As both William Cronon (1996) and Bruce Braun (2002) have argued in different ways, such "environmental" spaces are not the last bastions of a noncultural nature but are actively produced by a particular set of settler-colonial processes that articulate a division between the environment and (certain versions of) humanity while speaking of "preservation."[2]

Indeed, one is hard pressed to find humans in Maine's "environment" in the literature and rhetoric of many of Maine's environmental advocates except as potential despoilers to be guarded against or as beneficiaries of the "second paycheck," that is, "of a quality of life above and beyond what is spent: access to beautiful natural areas, stable and safe communities, outdoor recreation opportunities, and proximity to wildlife" (Maine Audubon Society 1996, 7). Humans "enjoy" an instrumentalized, romanticized, aestheticized—indeed *anesthetized*—environment that is produced as a literal "outside." The Maine Natural Areas Program, for example, articulates Maine's environment in terms of a curated collection of "natural communities and ecosystems" (Gawler and Cutko 2010), none of which include humans despite most of Maine's landscape being constituted by human cohabitation with other species. *Natural Landscapes of Maine* does not list "parking lot edge mixed invasives" (including grasses, poison ivy, Japanese knotweed, ragweed, some aluminum cans, and a few cigarette butts) among their "assemblages of interacting plants and animals and their common environment" (Gawler and Cutko 2010, 8). As one interviewee, an ecologist, described in reference to a similar project, "if we were curators of a museum, we would want to have an example of each type of artifact that we could put in our museum and say, 'Look this is an example of *x*, *y*, and *z*'" (Carl, interview). Who and what are made visible in such a museum? Who is erased? Who decides?

The enclosures associated with all three categories are barely separable, for it is the demarcation of "society" that enables "the economy" to have both a subject and an object, and this social boundary-drawing that also significantly shapes people's access to the enclosed means of subsistence. Meanwhile, the enclosure of the environment differentiates landscapes into some that are more disposable than others and some that are more purified of apparent human influence than others. A whole host of dynamics play out in and between these spaces by which certain humans straddling the margins of "the economy" may be pitted against those who are able to afford the seeming luxury of "the environment" while never questioning the relations between their wealth, social exclusion, and the degradation of places that will never appear on the cover of a glossy conservation brochure.

Externalities and Domesticated Outsides

It is the nature of enclosure to constitute, and to be in turn constituted by, an outside. Michel Callon (1998), following Erving Goffman (1986), has referred to this process in terms of "framing and overflowing." Building on the economic concept of externalities, he argues that entities such as "the economy" are produced by a material-semiotic boundary-making that simultaneously constitutes an inside and an outside. The framing of action is essential for any negotiation, calculation, or decision, and it depends on both its *exclusion of* and *relation to* that which it has externalized. "Framing would be inexplicable," writes Callon, "if there was not a network of connections with the outside world" (1998, 249). On one hand, "all framing thus represents a violent effort to extricate the agents concerned from this network of interactions and push them onto a clearly demarcated 'stage' which has been specially prepared and fitted out" (1998, 253). On the other hand, such staging is impossible to fully isolate: "A wholly hermetic frame is a contradiction in terms because flows are always bidirectional, overflows simply being the inevitable corollary of the requisite links with the surrounding environment" (1998, 255).

In the case of each hegemonic articulation, then, one can examine the overflows produced by the framing and trace their constitutive relations with that which they have been excluded from. What is essential for the framing of economy, society, and environment, yet overflows their boundaries? What forces and relations make each category's apparent stability possible while themselves never appearing as part of the categories themselves? Callon notes that not all such relations are necessarily exploitative or "outrageous" (1998, 246), since it is the very nature of order that it must exclude some elements of chaos. But the ease with which he dismisses the ethical perils of the framing/ overflow relationship is problematic, as it risks rendering invisible the substantive forms of constitutive violence often associated with enclosure.[3] Callon thus sterilizes his theorization, rendering it into something that would seem to be merely a neutral description of articulation processes rather than an apparatus for a critical, ethical tracing of the operations and effects of hegemonic power. It is for this latter purpose that I am interested in mobilizing the framing/overflow perspective.

What, then, are some constitutive overflows of "the economy" that must be traced in Maine? First, the economy is able to stand as an independent and objective domain, delinked from questions of ethics and politics, precisely because its articulation has pushed ethico-political dynamics out into the domain of the "social." This is clearest in the neoclassical economic theory that informs much of Maine's economic development policy landscape, where the very force of "the economy" is constituted by the subjective preferences of consumers understood as "exogenous." If the "law of supply and demand," celebrated by Ben and Marvin (interviews), sometimes generates problematic effects, this is not a problem with the *economy* but one of *social preferences*. As Marvin, the economic policy think-tank director, states starkly: "Why do some people like Van Gogh? I don't particularly care for his paintings. But people, some people, are willing to spend hundreds of millions of dollars for it. It's not for me to say what you should value in life. Some people prefer saving insect species, others prefer to look at a Van Gogh" (interview). Kathleen, the government statistician, similarly is able to deflect critiques of economic dominance over social and environmental concerns by blaming social preferences: "We, as Americans, tend to value work and money over just about everything else," she said (interview), effectively rendering the coercive nature of this particular valuation invisible.

Third, while externalizing normativity to the social, the assemblage of the economy in Maine nonetheless draws significant normative strength from its ability to stand as the singular source of subsistence, survival, and necessity. One cannot argue with economic imperatives because these are immediately seen as coextensive with the imperatives of earthly sustenance itself: "We need to *survive*, and we survive in this society through capitalism" (Sean, interview). At the very same time, however, a vast proportion of the relations that Maine people actually rely on for survival are utterly excluded from hegemonic articulations of "the economy."[4] Over the course of my fieldwork, interviewees variously mentioned practices of hunting, fishing, trapping, foraging, home gardening, barter, gifting, sharing, parenting, elder care, housework, homesteading, informal care for land and waters, voluntary reduction of consumption needs, nonprofit business models, worker- and consumer-owned cooperatives, and the work of "ecosystem services" as some of the many ways that Maine people are sustained.[5]

In very few cases did any of these activities or practices constitute legitimate "economic" activity upon which development efforts might be focused. For at least a few interviewees, in fact, dependence on such practices was seen as problematic, something to eradicate through *genuine* economic development. In a successful economy and society, says economic development network director Owen, "all of those [non-market] things that people are using to survive hopefully go away, or [stick around] because they're fixed, meaning 'I'm no longer hunting for food, I'm hunting because I like hunting.' . . . [We are] trying to get to the place where the other stuff doesn't *matter* as much" (interview). Paid work in competitive capitalist firms is thus established as the ultimate goal, and the material-semiotic violence of its own enforced necessities is rendered invisible by a tacit discourse of progressive modernization (Escobar 2012). Adam Smith's mythological narrative of the movement from the primitive hunter to the pin factory employee is alive and well in Maine.[6] Meanwhile, the actual array of relations that Maine people require to survive are either relegated to the "social" and the "environmental" or rendered effectively invisible with no clear place in any of the categories of the hegemonic assemblage.[7]

What, then, of society's overflows? What elements are crucial for the framing of society yet excluded from its domain? First and foremost is the economy itself. It is the dynamic of asymmetrical reciprocity (chapter 2), which constitutes the social in its hegemonic form as the "body" of the economy, yet this economy is nonetheless excluded from the boundaries of the society it pertains to. If there is something worth retaining in Karl Polanyi's (2001) much-debated notion of the "disembedding" of economy from society over the course of the nineteenth century, it is this: while the dynamics of framing and overflowing ensure that such delinking can never fully unfold (some have accused Polanyi of suggesting the contrary), there has indeed been a process of *articulation* by which an economy-society assemblage has been produced. This assemblage is characterized by both a "disembedded" disjunction between the two domains and their simultaneous, total co-implication. In other words, there was no "society" that preexisted a disembedding, no prior embedding that was violated, but there is rather a *single assemblage that comes into being as simultaneously separated and inextricably interdependent*. I break here with economic sociologies that would present the economy as inherently "social" and thus collapse the categories without interrogating their mutual constitution as historical assemblages (e.g., Parsons and Smelser 1956; Granovetter 1985).

Apart from the externalization of the economic, society is also constituted by the ongoing exclusion of all the relations, places, and human and nonhuman beings that render it possible yet never appear as viable, visible, or legitimate members of its domain. The example of undocumented immigrants in Maine is such a case, and this extends to other groups and relations as well. Maine's "society" depends on myriad relations that it simultaneously excludes, from the outsourcing of lumber production to the southern United States and South America to sustain wood consumption habits while conserving regional forests (Berlik, Kittredge, and Foster 2002) to the widespread discursive exclusion of people "from away" (that is, from other states and nations) as fully legitimate participants in public deliberations (M. W. Anderson 1997; Shuman 2007). Perhaps most fundamentally, the social in Maine and elsewhere is constituted by the exclusion of the entire web of more-than-human relations that are the focus of ecology. Society is, indeed, the space of non-nature, the primordial *human* enclosure of civilization against the howling wilderness (Evernden 1992; Soper 1995; Wright 2010). Yet it is this very "wilderness" on which all that is social utterly depends.

What, then, must be excluded from "the environment" in order for it to appear as a coherent domain? There is a pattern here: the environment is constituted by its exclusion of and simultaneous dependence on the social and the economic. The humans who write guidebooks such as *Natural Landscapes of Maine* cannot themselves appear as constituents of "the environment" they describe. Other humans who depend upon these "natural landscapes" for daily subsistence—collecting fiddlehead ferns (a common spring food in rural Maine), fishing, hunting, gathering medicinal herbs and materials for basket-making and wreath-weaving (Baumflek, Emery, and Ginger 2010)—can never appear in such guidebooks, either, for they are "social" interlopers in a space that is not theirs. On a wider scale, the complex market dynamics that shape and reshape the forested ecological patchworks of northern Maine along with weather systems, insect populations, and soil microbes cannot count as "environmental" impacts, but must appear as external forces against which the environment must contend. Meanwhile, the often-unacknowledged backdrop to such articulations is the forcible removal and continued exclusion and erasure of indigenous people from these places that were once, and for some still are, a *home* rather than an "environment" (Braun 2002).

All of these examples of overflowing that I have described are clearly of very different natures. What they have in common, however, is that they are not entirely excluded from the hegemonic articulation *as whole* but rather take the form what I will call "domesticated outsides." These are outsides that overflow, yet maintain clear relations with that from which they remain excluded. They "[put] the outside world in brackets . . . but [do] not actually abolish all links with it" (Callon 1998, 249), and their recognition or even assimilation does not necessarily threaten the stability of the larger assemblage itself. In fact, their recognition and domestication in some form may be crucial to the ongoing maintenance of hegemony. An economic developer acknowledges, for example, the existence of nonmarket modes of sustenance but renders them secondary (Owen, interview). A social worker recognizes the constitutive importance of sociality with nonhuman companion animals, but this remains a mere instrumental accessory to human-centered work (Dorothy, interview). An environmental scientist tells a story about meeting human subsistence gatherers on a trip into a "remote wilderness area," but this is granted only the status of a quaint experience (Carl, interview).

Such overflows must be distinguished from what Judith Butler, following Henry Staten's (1986) reading of Jacques Derrida, refers to a "constitutive outside" (1993, 188). This latter form of "outside" is that which cannot even *appear* within a given symbolic-material order. It is "the excluded and illegible domain that haunts the former domain as the spectre of its own impossibility, the very limit to intelligibility" (Butler 1993, xi). The domesticated outside, on the contrary, is an externalization that can be named, mapped, and given a relation to that which has been enclosed. Domesticated outsides are representable within the hegemonic order, even as this representation does violence to their other (nonhegemonic) becomings. I intend this term "domesticated" to invoke a sense of the relative containment and taming of an otherwise potentially dangerous material-semiotic "wildness" or excess (Bataille 1985), and I also seek to make discursive connections with feminist critiques of the ways in which domestic labor constitutes a particular, exploited outside/inside relative to many modern, patriarchal assemblages (Federici 2012). My naming of this domesticated outside, and its association with various examples above, should not be taken as suggesting that a clear line can actually be drawn between the "domesticated" and the "wild," and my critical tracing here is not intended to ultimately reinforce such distinctions. The line, in practice, is utterly blurred, and that which appears assimilable at one moment can threaten the coherence of an assemblage from its very heart at the next. It may be more useful, in this regard, to think of the domesticated outside as an ongoing *process* of domestication that never wholly succeeds.

Abject Outsides and Assimilation

There are certain relations that lurk on the very edges of the domesticated outside, located in the liminal zone between radical, unrepresentable excess and that which can be at least partly captured and assimilated. These relations are what Callon attempts to avoid in his refusal to be outraged, "disgusted," or "disturbed" by the dynamics of externalities (1998, 246), for they are often quite disturbing in multiple senses. These are elements of yet another kind of outside—one that is quite complex and strange. It is an outside that is at once outside *and* inside, simultaneously located at the very limits of domesticable overflows and also within the very heart of enclosure itself as its *underside*. This is where we find economic subjects who have failed to perform or have been rendered "redundant" or "surplus"; social subjects who have reached the limits of acceptable sociality and must become the objects of "social work"; environmental dynamics that deface beautiful images of "wilderness"; and environmental subjects who render monstrous the very distinction between subjects and objects that the environment is supposed to affirm. I will call this the "abject outside," invoking Julia Kristeva's theorization of "the jettisoned object," that which "lies outside, beyond the set, and does not seem to agree to the . . . rules of the game" (1982, 2). The abject is neither fully object nor fully subject, positioned at the limits of acceptable boundaries and often appearing as the disgusting and disturbing *mess* that troubles and threatens the stability of the order from which it excluded.[8] As a site of violence that underwrites appearances of peace, the abject is painful to encounter and acknowledge. As the site of unruly transgression that shows a given assemblage to be rotten at its very core, the abject is dangerous. If an assemblage is to remain territorialized and hegemonic, the abject outside must (yet cannot fully be) be either eliminated or assimilated.

The abject economic takes the form of people who are excluded from access to enclosed spaces, pushed to their very margins while still remaining in their grip, and who embody the failures of the economic itself while nonetheless appearing in the hegemonic articulation as *personal* failures. This is the zone of existence beyond the "industrial reserve army" where people are no longer able to appear as potential employees. Marx and Engels (1970) call this the "lumpenproletariat," William Corlett refers to it as "the damned" (1998, 159), and

Serge Latouche (1993) speaks of "development's castaways." Economic developers in Maine often use the abject economic as a justification for various policy interventions, as when Owen asks, "Have you drove through Princeton and Dartmouth [Maine]? I have. It's freakin' abject poverty there. Those people need *jobs*" (interview). And yet those pushed into the abject economic do not always conform to the desires and demands of economic development. Some refuse to be "energetic and responsible workers" (Lawton 2008, 37) and forge other paths. As regional planner Oscar describes:

> You have people on the low end of the economic scale who like it just the way it is. . . . They've come up with a system in some fashion that involves wages, subsidies, and welfare and those sorts of things in order to maintain a lifestyle that they're comfortable with. And many of them will juxtapose that economic situation with the fact that they can go out in the backyard and there's nobody there, and they can see the hills. (interview)

This is Oscar's own story, of course, and people's lived realities are often much more complex and problematic. The point is that the economic produces subjects that it cannot then fully assimilate and whose existence and trajectory challenge its core articulations. There are good reasons why Maine economist Charles Lawton writes of "the social unrest inherent in our capitalist world" (2008, 41).

The reality of the abject economic often invokes a sense of repulsion, horror, or fear from those located more firmly within the hegemonic articulation. It is this marginality and vulnerability that the economic is intended to overcome, and the possibility (or reality) of life on the "outside" is terrifying.[9] Hence the economic developer Owen's desire for people to move beyond dependence on hunting for their sustenance: "Yeah I like the taste of deer meat, so I kill a deer once a year, but I'm not [going to], like, have anxiety over if I don't get the deer I don't know how I'm going to eat this winter" (interview). Who with access to the relative stabilities of "the economy" would *not* be averse to dependency on a successful hunt? What horror, so many might think, to *rely* on local ecological relations, on our own skill as hunters, and on the health of the deer herd! And yet it is Owen who also proclaims that "economic forces are gonna happen, and it's gonna go where it's gonna go, and we can try to control it, but at the end of the day . . . it's gonna happen" (interview). To contrast the fear of dependency on a local ecology with the enthusiastic embrace of dependency on an anonymous economy is to see the strength of the hegemonic articulation and to touch something quite dangerous that the presence of the abject offers: the possibility of *other forms of life*.

This abject economic is also a key site of the abject *social*, since those who are excluded from the economy are also placed at the margins of a society that stands as that economy's body. This is where "social work," in its complicit hegemonic form, enters as an assimilatory practice. "Social work is . . . having impact for people that are in the lower tier of economics," says Fred, the director of a Maine community development organization. "How do we get capital, resources, skills, various things to those folks?" (interview). Even as a crucial redistributive politics is clearly present here, Fred's description of social work links unsettlingly with a more problematic dimension: the "social" articulated in its abject form as the domain of all of those who have *failed* to become adequate economic subjects. As sociologists Marie Pellegrin-Rescia and Yair Levi describe: "There is an ongoing integration (to which center?) of populations that, classified by the category of imaginary completeness, are described in the negative as 'inactive,' 'non-affiliated,' 'miserable,' subject of 'shame' to themselves and objects of 'pity,' for they lack the 'control' over their situation and themselves" (2005, 5). The abject social appears as a *gap* that needs to be filled, a problem that must be solved with economic development: "What we try to do is to identify what's missing, where the gaps are, and then try to fill those gaps with existing resources" (Dorothy, community health worker, interview); "We work to fill gaps in the marketplace" (Brent, community development finance specialist, interview); "The nonprofit sector comes in to fill the gap" (Fred, community development worker, interview).

We find, then, at sites of the abject social, an ongoing articulation of a host of "social problems," failures of assimilation, normalization, or discipline (Foucault 2007a). As Robert Castel writes, "Marginality itself, instead of remaining unexplored or rebellious territory, can become an organized zone within the social, towards which those persons will be directed who are incapable of following more competitive pathways" (1991, 295). Multiple spaces of diverse livelihood practice— some quite problematic and some not—are thus transformed into the uniform measure of "poverty" as a lack of *monetary income* (A. Acheson 2007). People must be brought into the fold of proper economic life, rendered into "confident, productive members of society" (Helen, interview). For many social workers, economic developers, and other agents of liberal government, such an articulation demands an emphasis on the movement of people into more and better forms of "employment," presumably in predominately private (capitalist) firms: "A lot of the things we're talking about," says Frank, director of a social charity organization, like "living a healthier life, accumulation of assets[,] . . . those types of things come with employment. That's really what it is. It's a function of employment" (interview).

Social work, in this sense, can function as an accessory to the process of hegemonic articulation, as institutional interventions seek continually to (re)make individuals and populations into "an engaged workforce that's ready to do the jobs of the century"(Brenda, researcher for a social policy organization, interview). A whole host of disciplinary measures are deployed here, from incentive structures linked to food stamp benefits to mandatory home visits by social workers, all seeking to bring the abject back into the fold of society and economy, or—especially in the form of police and prisons—to neutralize their threat as aberrant and potentially unruly subjects. This is not to say that all such practices are inherently and wholly problematic; indeed, many people depend on social workers and social benefits for key dimensions of life, and many of the people who do this work are deeply motivated, generous, heroic, and sometimes life-saving. The point here is that the hegemonic articulation renders the line between solidarity and collective care, on one hand, and assimilatory discipline, on the other, quite blurry, and the latter is all too often justified by appeal to the former.

There is much more to the abject social than economic failure, of course, since this is the outside edge to which so many people, bodies, practices, ways of life, and forms of desire are forcibly pushed in the process of stabilizing a particular normative assemblage of society. It is not within the scope of my work here to analyze these complex contours, and significant work has been done by others to trace the ways in which, for example, black and brown bodies, transgendered bodies, and queer bodies and desires of myriad shapes have been rendered abject as a mode of white supremacist, masculinist, and heteronormative articulation (e.g., Andrea Smith 2005; Lowrey 2008; Weheliye 2014). It is no coincidence that Paul LePage's so-called aliens are primarily immigrants from Latin America and Africa, and that as the demographically "whitest" state in the United States (Koenig 2013), Maine has long been a site of violence and hostility toward people of color (see, e.g., Thistle 2012; Woodard 2012). Economic abjection and social abjection intersect quite brutally in this state where African Americans experience the highest relative rate of poverty in the nation (Ross and Sullivan 2014).

There is also a clear sense in which transgressive relations between humans and nonhuman animals also constitute key sites of social abjection. In my interviews, the social abjection of human-nonhuman relations was most often expressed via a sense of the *ridiculousness* of linking nonhumans with human categories and with forms of respect and desire associated with the social. I risked rendering my whole project suspect and was met with awkward silence when I suggested to two different interviewees (Irene and Nora) that we might consider speaking of "deer economies" or "dog economies." When I asked Sandra, the director of a regional economic growth council, what would happen "if I were to get up and say, 'We need to take nonhumans seriously in our thinking about this,'" she responded, chuckling: "You'd be laughed right out of the ATV store, dear [puts on strong Maine accent], if you came up with that. They'd laugh you right out of the snowmobile shop!" (interview). The abjection signaled by humor here is inseparable from the actual violence visited upon so many nonhuman living beings whose presence never appears as a legitimate site for ethical consideration. To be excluded from the social, even with its own ambivalences, is to face non-existence as a subject—to become merely a *thing*, and to be treated as such.

There is an *abject environment* as well, and it is constituted as all the relations and beings that cannot be fully assimilated into the hegemonic articulation of "the environment" yet nonetheless render it intelligible at its limits. Consider, for example, particular inconveniences that mess up pretty pictures. Some of these were introduced by one interviewee with regard to romantic environmental framings during the struggle against a proposed dam project on the Penobscot River in the mid-1980s. Matthew, an economic development consultant, described the battle over the fate of Big Ambejackmockamus Falls (or "Big A"):

> That was saving a so-called wilderness waterway, which was not a wilderness waterway, but can be depicted as one. You know, you can position your camera in such a way that the logging road isn't visible, that the power lines along it aren't visible. You get away from the dams and away from the crowds of fishermen, and you do it at a time when the dust from the logging

roads is not rolling over it, and you can depict it as a wilderness waterway. (interview)

The problem here was not that people were struggling to prevent dam construction or to constitute a different ethical relation to the river but that this struggle took place on a terrain that could not render the relational and ethico-political complexity of contemporary ecologies visible. An abject outside haunted the environmental articulation in such a way that to permit its entry would be to risk having to confront the very limits of the hegemonic configuration.

The environment-as-domain is commonly constituted as a realm of amenities through the exclusion of all ecological entities and relations that refuse to fit into the metrics of management or the images of romantic advocacy. One will rarely find, in the literature or in public discourses of Maine's environmental advocacy organizations, an articulation of the environment as dangerous, disgusting, or generally unattractive.[10] To sustain the image of the "good health, good jobs, and quality of life that Maine's environment provides to all of us" (Kelley 2010, 2) requires the exclusion of—or at least an uneasy relationship with—all that is not "good," "healthy," or "beautiful." As Maine forest activist Mitch Lansky writes, "It is easier to rally behind something big and furry than something small and slimy" (2003, 25). Or as Carl, the ecologist, describes:

> Yeah, we want to live in a town that has preserved farmland around it so we can feel like we're living in a rural area as we're driving in. . . . It's not quite the same as saying "We've preserved this nasty thicket of a cedar swamp because it has all of the intact species and natural processes that are inherent in it." You know, nobody wants to look at the nasty, tangled cedar swamp. They think it's just a big bug factory, but that's what nature *is*! (interview)

As a site of "monstrous and illegitimate" hybrids (Haraway 1991, 154) lurking at the edges and undersides of its enclosure, the environment continually threatens to exceed its hegemonic articulation and undermine its own stability and purity with a wildness that cannot be assimilated.

Maine's environmental advocates are clear, to be sure, about many of the threats posed to the environment by pollution and other forms of degradation. Yet it is around such issues that the dangers presented by an actual grappling with the abject outside become clear: antipollution action risks becoming a challenge to the very structures of capitalist production and accumulation, and must therefore be tempered and held within the confines of the hegemonic assemblage. "Most importantly," says the website of the organization Maine Rivers, for example, "we need to be conscious of our own role in contributing to river pollution in many everyday activities: using toxic household or lawn/garden chemicals which end up in rivers" (Maine Rivers 2014). Wholly unaddressed in such an individualizing articulation are questions of financial and cultural access to such "environmental" actions (Sandilands 1993); the legitimacy of the entire assemblage through which individuals end up possessing such toxins in the first place; the ongoing operation of 329 known corporate Clean Water Act violators in Maine (Duhigg 2012); and—last but not least—questions about the ways this "green" consumer emphasis might deflect from more harrowing questions about the patterns of power and accumulation that generate and sustain planetary destabilization (Alfredsson 2004; Akenji 2014). One might argue, as Naomi Klein (2014) does relative to climate change, that the overt acknowledgment of toxic pollution in its fullest sense would demand a radical undoing of the core institutions of the hegemonic assemblage itself. Pollution is, then, double faced: partly a "safe" object of environmental concern, and partly an abject site of concern that must be tamed or assimilated. The abject environment cannot be permitted to threaten the structure of the inside from which it is constitutively excluded; externalities must only be *internalized* into a structure of colonial, capitalist anthropocentrism that remains unchallenged.

4 A DIAGRAM OF POWER

Nature-Culture, Capital-State,
and Development

Critique beyond "Structures"

The politics of the hegemonic assemblage bounces and shifts within a strange, multiply triangulated space that divides humans from non-humans, some humans from other humans, agency from its objects, monetized livelihood activities from all others, and at the same time is able to both naturalize these arrangements and pose them as subjective projections without ever challenging the problem-space itself. On one level, economy and economic development often appear to be pitted against other key concerns including rising inequality and poverty, traditional forms of community and connection, climate change intervention, wilderness preservation, and the development of sustainable local and regional food systems. Yet on another level, so many of these struggles serve to affirm the sovereign status of the economy relative to other elements of the triple assemblage: social workers seeking to assimilate people and communities into formal employment and market integration, or environmental organizations rendering ecological relations into amenities, job catalysts, and new sites for investment. This is the tiny, stifling world that the problem-space of the hegemonic assemblage enables.

A common critical approach to this situation would be to describe economy, society, and environment as products of larger "structures" of ideological or material organization. To pose two extremes between which many variations can be found, the hegemonic trio can be viewed as either the outgrowth of problematic *ideas* (the concepts, for example, of human separation from the natural world, or of markets as independent, lawlike forces), or as the results of *material relations* of production and exchange (namely, modern industrial capitalism). I could say, like a good deep ecologist or new age culture critic, that this is all the result of cultural stories that have alienated us from our true relational integration with the natural world and with each other. Or, I could proclaim, like a good critical Marxist, that it all obviously comes down to capitalism, "the system" within which we live and that configures the dominant ideas and institutions that we live by. In either case, I would not be entirely off the mark; there *is* something going on here that is more than just the appearance of a set of three problematic categories. Yet getting at this "something" without eliding the power of material modes of organization or performatively strengthening hegemonic modes of life is a challenging task. How to engage critically with the hegemonic trio, tracing patterns of power at a fundamental level, without recourse to a notion of some kind of predetermining structure or system of causation? And how to avoid a notion of "system" or "structure" without ending up in a kind of idealism, affirming only the power of the stories we tell about the world? Engaging these questions is the tricky task of this chapter, and I will step back from close engagement with conversations in Maine to consider some broader patterns. I begin, though, by reading one of my interviews thorough the lens of what Gilles Deleuze and Félix Guattari refer to as a "diagram" (1987, 100).

The Prism

I asked Carol, the director of a Maine state government social services office, about her broad view on the relations among economy, society, and environment. "It's a *prism*," she said, "and it depends on where you're shining the light, what you're going to talk about. It doesn't make the prism any less whole" (interview). Carol seemed intent on showing that these three categories are little more than analytical tools, invoked in particular contexts to expose differently useful facets of an essential unity. It is a common understanding, apparently shared by many others I interviewed: economy, society, and environment are not so much real things in the world as they are *conveniences* to help us make sense out of a complex reality that is ultimately indivisible. While pragmatic, such a view does not easily square with the common sense also articulated by many of the same people; namely, that you can't argue with the economy, that society is in need of help, or that the environment sets biophysical limits to human action.

I want, then, to carry Carol's figure of the prism in a different direction. How does it actually function in her statement? At first glance, it might appear that an essential unity of light (the "real world") is diffracted into three differentiated bands (economy, society, and environment) depending on particular analytical needs. In fact, it is not the *light* that remains reliably "whole," but the *prism itself*. Carol suggests here, perhaps inadvertently, a powerful image of articulation: a non-totalizable multiplicity ("white" light) is composed into a particular set of differences through a refractive apparatus that itself does not contain or embody these distinctions. Although it might appear to an observer that white light is "really" made up of a set of distinct colors that the prism only reveals, it is the *assemblage* of light, prism, and observer that generates this distinction. The prism, we might say, is an *ontologizing device*, a machine that refracts assemblages of economy, society, and environment into their particular concrete forms and then disappears as the very source of refraction. The prism, in this figurative sense, is an operation of material-semiotic power, the construction-in-action of hegemonic articulation.[1]

This image can be understood more precisely through Deleuze and Guattari's philosophy of becoming, which is intimately linked to their notions of articulation and assemblage. In Deleuze's (1994) terms, the assemblage of economy, society, and environment is continually composed as an "actualization" of a "virtual," which its articulation does not exhaust. The virtual/actual distinction is a conceptual strategy for thinking about reality as an ongoing process of composition while still being able to explain apparent stabilities. If the *actual* is that which we encounter as everyday "reality," as a collection of molar entities and identities, the *virtual* names the molecular dimension of reality that is unformed, always *becoming*, a zone of "intensities that cannot be accounted for in terms of actual identities" (Williams 2003, 8). The virtual is pure process out of which the things of the world continually materialize. Contrary to common uses of the term that might imply something fake or false (as in "virtual reality") it is quite *real* (Deleuze 1994, 208). But it is not something that can, in itself, be seen or experienced; as a reservoir of un-encounterable potential, it must always be *actualized* in specific and limited forms. Economy, society, and environment are instances of such forms.

The virtual is not totally amorphous and undifferentiated (indeed, it *is* pure difference), nor can its "contents" be separated from the

actual that it enables (Deleuze and Parnet 2007, 149). At the interface
between the virtual and the actual, at the surface of intensity that is
continually becoming the world-as-we-know-it (and is also, as I will
describe later, unmaking this very world), we encounter what Deleuze,
building on Michel Foucault, calls "diagrams" (1988, 35).[2] These are
"map[s] of relations between forces" (1988, 36), particular *patterns* by
which actualizations are produced in some ways and not others. Every
collective historical formation has a set of specific diagrams that function simultaneously to describe and produce the contours of that formation's shared reality. These diagrams or "abstract machines" (1988,
34) can be said to have *names*, in the sense that certain images, figures,
or entities express diagrammatic patterns in particularly high resolution (Deleuze and Guattari 1987, 511). "Descartes," for example, might
be one name for the abstract machine that "draws" the subject-object
distinction across the interface between the virtual and actual, rendering it expressive in the world. Foucault's initial usage of the term
"diagram" was in reference to Jeremy Bentham's Panopticon, the late
eighteenth-century architectural model of disciplinary surveillance
that he uses as the figure of a collective assemblage of power: "The
Panopticon . . . must be understood as a generalizable model of functioning; a way of defining power relations in terms of the everyday life
of men" (Foucault 1977, 205). A diagram is not necessarily something
that is drawn on paper, but it *is* something that is "drawn" in the world
as the ongoing realization or "effectuation" of a pattern of power that
produces (and is produced by) assemblages in particular forms. If economy, society, and environment are actualized "concrete assemblages"
then it is clear that there is a diagram or abstract machine (or a bundle
of these) that they express or actualize.

But what *is* this diagram? The hegemonic trio effectuates, among
other things, a distinct pattern of power that can be presented visually
in the form of three axes: two crisscrossed binaries of *Nature-Culture*
and *Capital-State* with a third directional axis of *Development* coming up through the middle (Figure 6).[3] These axes and their relations
name particular lines of compositional force that influence the space
of possibility in which articulations of the economic, the social, and the
environmental are continually consolidated, and which these articulations, in turn, work to enact. This is to say that the various ethico-
political dynamics described in the previous chapters—permutations
of the constitutional geometry—can be more effectively understood

when viewed in relation to a complex interplay between ongoing productions of Nature-Culture divisions, Capital-State oscillations, and an
ever-onward normative push toward a Development that never quite
arrives. I will turn to these dynamics momentarily, but first it is crucial
to be clear about the nature of this analysis and its claims.

These diagrammatic elements are *more* than just ideas circulating in
the heads and books of particular humans (though they are these, too),
and they are at the same time *less* than "systems" or "structures" within
which various dynamics unfold. To say that the hegemonic trio effectuates a diagram of Nature-Culture, Capital-State, and Development
is not to say that it is caused by them, determined by them, or that it is
manifested "within" the system of power that they compose. This notion
of the diagram should not be mistaken for a theorization of "structure"
as a system of (pre)determinations within which agency unfolds. "This
has nothing to do," says Deleuze, "either with a transcendent idea or

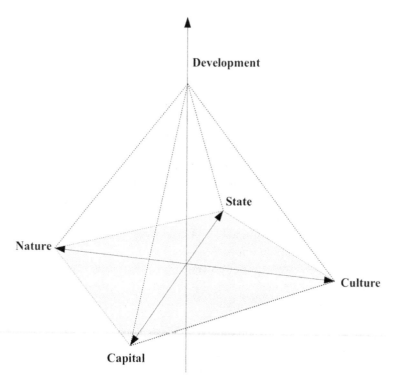

Figure 6. A diagram of contemporary power: mapping of the dynamic
problem-space effectuated by the hegemonic trio.

with an ideological superstructure, or even with an economic infrastructure, which is already qualified by its substance and defined by
its form and use" (1988, 36). Diagrams are not pre-established things,
which then subsequently cause or determine what unfolds; they do
not preexist their articulation. Actualizations (economy, society, environment) effectuate diagrams, not vice versa, and this term "effectuate" is crucial: it is not to *cause*, but to render capable, to make *actual*.
That which is effectuated has no existence outside of those actual articulations through which this effectuation occurs. This is a challenging
perspective to think, since it scrambles conventional notions of linear
causality. There is no diagram that simply *sits there*, producing effects;
rather, the diagram itself emerges as the very production of these effects.
One cannot, for example, go and find "the Nature-Culture dualism"
as such outside of particular ways in which it is effectuated in actual
articulations such as a lived, material experience of division between
a society and an environment. Hence Deleuze's notion of the diagram
as "immanent cause," a cause that is "realized, integrated, and distinguished by its effect" (1988, 37).

Diagrams may best be described in terms of the notion of "problem-
space" that I invoked in chapter 1. If economy, society, and environment help to define the actual contours of a collective problem-space
within which certain things appear as visible or invisible, possible
or impossible, then it is a *diagram* that is the rarely spoken "name" of
the problem-space itself. The hegemonic trio is one particular way to
"solve" the challenges this space presents. Diagrammatic forces are
not often themselves explicit dimensions of public conflicts and negotiations, but rather remain as part of the background that makes such
conflicts possible in their actual forms. This is why opposing forces
such as those involved in the Plum Creek struggle can be said to share
something despite their opposition—they are all participating in effectuating the same diagram of power. A problem-space is composed in
which the abstract machine itself is rendered invisible while its actualizations appear as inevitable.

Nature-Culture

The first movement that constitutes the trio's diagram is the Nature-
Culture dualism—what Alfred North Whitehead (1920) refers to as
"the bifurcation of nature," the division of reality into a domain of

(nonhuman) objects and a domain of subjective (human) interpretation. This division is associated with a whole host of parallel dualisms that together mark out the shapes of modern hegemonic power: man/woman, human/animal, mind/body, rational/irrational, civilized/ savage, and subject/object, among others (Plumwood 1993). For some critics, dualism appears as a set of problematic ideas (perhaps a danger of the name "Descartes," referenced above, as if that singular philosopher invented rather than effectuated core elements of Western dualism), but in a diagrammatic understanding the distinction between Nature and Culture is continually actualized in *practices* and *relations*. These include ideas, but also material modes of life and affective (dis)connections. Nature is not just an idea of a separation of humanity and human subjectivity from all else; it is the actual production of demarcated spaces (the Nature Conservancy, for example, functions to compose that which it then "conserves") and hyperseparated experiences (how easy it is to encounter birds as pretty objects when one didn't grow up learning the news of the day from their songs!). The diagram of Nature-Culture names a mode of power by which worlds are produced as "always already" separated into these domains, and which patterns other forms of articulation in ways that continually shape their relational contours and affirm the reality of the distinctions. This is why a distinction between a society and an environment, for example, makes such intuitive sense to so many people, and why the invocation of these terms cannot easily escape these deeper diagrammatic bifurcations.

A common view of dualism would suggest that power is on the side of one term while subordination is necessarily on the side of the other (e.g., Plumwood 1993, 42). This is correct in the sense that association with certain terms can serve to justify or deepen relations of hierarchy and violence, as when the association of certain humans with "animals"—thus with "nature" and with the realm of "objects"— becomes a strategy for white supremacy or male domination. But it is crucial to recognize on another level that power is what circulates in (or perhaps *as*) the *whole diagram itself* and enables the production of all of its elements and their variable tensions and oscillations. Culture is, on one hand, a site of agency and freedom, where "human beings, and only human beings, are the ones who construct and freely determine their own destiny" (Latour 1993, 30). Yet it can also be the site of ephemeral fantasies, projections, "soft" articulations that cannot stand up against

the durable facts that an appeal to "nature" enables. Nature can therefore subsist as "that which has always already been there" (1993, 30),
immune to contestation; and it can also be articulated as a domain of
passive objects, a "kingdom of means" separated from a (human-only)
"kingdom of ends" (Plumwood 1993, 145). Domination and exploitation can be justified and enforced via any and all of these angles.
Hence the "forked tongues" of European colonizers: "By separating
the relations of political power [Culture] from the relations of scientific
reasoning [Nature] while continuing to shore up power with reason
[Nature] and reason with power [Culture], the moderns have always
had two irons in the fire" (Latour 1993, 38).

This is precisely how the economy, variably articulated as a manifestation either of Nature or of Culture, can be justified and legitimized as being fundamentally "about people" (Kathleen, interview)
while also appearing as an incontestable force. It is how society can
appear as an objective domain to be measured and managed, and as
a slippery realm in which complex values shape action and generate
surprise (thus requiring markets as a form of nonstate coordination
based on decentralized signaling of "exogenous" preferences). And it is
how the environment can appear, variously, as a mine, a dump, and a
source of appeal to "natural laws" and natural analogies of competition.

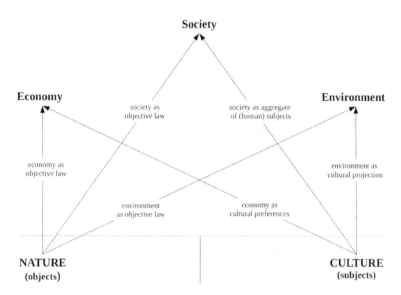

Figure 7. Dynamics of hegemonic actualization: Nature-Culture.

Because all three of these assemblages are composed as expressions of the Nature-Culture diagram, their hegemonic contours follow and amplify the ethico-political dynamics of the bifurcation in multiple ways. Indeed, one can barely invoke any one of the three elements of the trio without also effectuating some kind of distinction between a Nature and a Culture, and without playing out some form of power dynamic implicated in this diagram. A whole space of ethical and political possibility is, therefore, laid out (Figure 7) in which contradictory versions of the Nature-Culture binary are simultaneously reinforced and transgressed while relations of separation, domination, and exploitation among humans and between (certain) humans and nonhumans remain invisible or incontestable.

Capital-State

Cutting across the Nature-Culture binary on an intersecting axis is a second pair of diagrammatic elements: Capital-State. Their ongoing effectuation is widely visible in the form of partisan debates and struggles over the relationship between "free markets" and "government." The positions are well-worn: those who see generalized markets as the key to efficient resource allocation and say that "government should stay within its bounds" (Marvin, interview), and those who view markets as limited and flawed and position government as a key agent for (re)distribution and the enactment of social solidarity. "The government's role is to do that which the individual cannot" (Carol, interview). But this policy seesaw—More markets! More government! More Markets!—is merely the distracting tip of a diagrammatic iceberg, which is ever-present yet rarely itself rendered into a site of politics. It may already be clear from the previous two chapters: economy, society, and environment are articulated in relation to a complex dynamic of synergy, oscillation, and tension between the territorializing power of the State (producing and managing various "domains") and the deterritorializing force of Capital that so often rises to sovereign position even in the face of other forces of "Nature."

The State is arguably the most visible element of the Capital-State axis, particularly to the extent that Capital can hide its processes of coercive accumulation behind the veil of "the market." As a clearly demarcated center of authority with a name (Maine, USA), an ostensible location, an associated territory, a seemingly unified structure of decision-making, and a potent set of enforcement mechanisms, the State often appears as the sole site of "politics," the singular mechanism through which human collectivities are able to enact or influence the shape of economy, society, and environment on a large scale and with durable results. It is commonplace to hear people in Maine say things like, "Oh, I'm not political," or "I don't follow politics," and thereby affirm that "politics" happens only in big white buildings in the state's capital, in posh offices inhabited by people in suits, or (occasionally and superficially) in voting booths at the local elementary school. The State appears here at once as the container within which life unfolds and as a narrowly defined and exclusionary authority over these sustaining domains. Yet such articulations are only particular modes or *moments* of the effectuation of the State as a diagrammatic process.

By "State" in this context, I do not mean a definite array of governing institutions, a sovereign national entity, a particular apparatus of policing and legitimized violence (M. Weber 1994), or a mere tool of capitalist accumulation (Sweezy 1942), though all of these might be its partial expressions. I mean, rather, a *process of power* that is both the "other" of Capital and its most crucial condition of existence. The State names a force of authorization, unification, order, control, inscription, conscription, repression, law, and judgment—an "abstract principle of power and authority" (Newman 2011, 4). It operates, according to Deleuze and Guattari, via processes of "overcoding" (1983, 199) that link elements within a system of unified meaning or representation, "facilitating [their] insertion into a whole new level of synthesis: a conjunction with numerous other categorized individuals or persons, in a complex assemblage of thunderbolt judgment" (Massumi 1996, 51). The State *is* the production of identifiable populations that can be tracked, measured, cared for (or not), and governed, the maintenance of the boundaries within which they are contained and from which they are variably excluded, the composition of terrain—economy, society, environment—over which coercive power can be exercised, and the ongoing legitimation of sovereign force to hold it all together at its fraying edges. The effectuation of the State, in varied forms, is the construction of "a whole to which it will render its law immanent" (Deleuze and Guattari 1983, 221), simultaneously producing government, governed spaces, and governable subjects (Rose 1999).

If, on one side, the elements of the hegemonic trio can be seen as enactments of the territorializing power of the State, then on the other side of the axis this trio effectuates the power-pattern of Capital. Unlike key manifestations of the State, the diagram of Capital as such remains submerged, taking form as "market forces," "competition," "the need for jobs," and "the economy" itself. But the power of Capital is why these articulations all seem so commonly bound up with the unspoken assumptions that dependency on money and volatile markets for basic human flourishing is inevitable (or even desirable!), that profit-driven competition is the most effective and efficient mode of human productive organization, that jobs are primarily produced by capitalist firms, that the economy stands on the bedrock of accumulation-driven private enterprise, and that production and consumption must grow endlessly in order for people and communities to thrive. But what is Capital? How does it work as a diagrammatic element?

In Marxian terms, Capital is a relation and process of addictive money-value accumulation, premised on a particular form of market freedom while coercively sustained by (often invisible or denied) forms of enclosure and exploitation. In its functioning, Capital enacts two simultaneous movements: on one hand, it renders all things commensurable through the transformation of radically heterogeneous life values into universalizable exchange value. All things are (potentially) marked by the sign of money. On the other hand, this assignment of equivalence—a kind of territorial marking—is an incredibly potent form of deterritorialization, as things and relations are wrenched from their concrete habitats and rendered quantitatively abstract. Capital, in these two movements, is that process by which a forest ecosystem, an oil pipeline, a health insurance package, a pound of marijuana, a crate of plastic water bottles, a public school, and a nuclear-equipped battleship are all not only rendered into things exchangeable in variable ratios, but also translated into generic indices of "economic health" that can be mobilized by politicians, policy professionals, and activists of all stripes to advocate or challenge whatever element they are attached to. Do you want something to happen or to be avoided? Turn it into a money value, or at least call it "capital," and your argument may be heard.

The nonprofit research organization Independent Sector (2016) values volunteer time in Maine at $21.61 per hour. Why should this matter? Because the work of caring for our elders must be defended in terms that speak to the "bottom line" and at the same time reduce this work to a value that is (theoretically) exchangeable for anything else. How else could *Homo economicus* make a good decision about allocating scarce resources? "You've got to come up with some sort of apples-to-apples comparison to be able to make a valid decision" (Kathleen, interview). Thus in Maine we can find valuations of the Plum Creek resort development proposal and a liquefied natural gas facility sitting alongside a study concluding that the state's total "ecosystem services"—ostensibly the most fundamental processes that sustain life—are worth $14.7 billion (Troy 2012). This is approximately 27 percent of the state's annual GDP, *less* than the 2012 GDP contribution of Maine's combined finance, real estate, and professional services sectors.[4] The absurdity (or insanity) produced by Capital should be clear here: utterly incommensurable and often immeasurable life values are rendered into quantitative equivalents for an impossible yet obligatory comparison. The stage is set to conceptualize economy, society, and environment as a series of "trade-offs."

But while these trade-offs appear as careful, rational considerations of costs and benefits, the deck is always already stacked against anything that cannot clearly generate and amplify monetary value. Capital's universal commensuration presupposes, depends upon, and enables two further operations: the construction of dependency and the demand for growth. Given the (often invisible) history of enclosure noted in chapter 3, the negotiation of life via money value is not optional for most people. "Money does rule," or at least it constitutes one key mode of rule among others. But dependency on money, in itself, is not Capital. It is the *setting-in-motion* of this dependency, along with the process of universal commensuration, in order to generate the ongoing accumulation of privatized wealth that constitutes the heart of Capital as a process. The diagram of Capital is effectuated in the complex articulation of a universal equivalent, money dependency, consumer freedom, market organization, private property divisions between workers and owners, objectification of living labor (including nonhuman labor), and the collectively sanctioned or coerced legitimation of unequal money accumulation, among other elements. A core outcome of this process is that "growth," defined very particularly as an increase in monetary transactions (and the things, such as jobs, that generate and sustain this), is rendered not only desirable but necessary. Of *course* environmental advocates would be required to argue their cause in terms of a "trail map to prosperity" and become, effectively, amateur economic developers: to do otherwise would be to advocate for death and decline. Economy, society, and environment become obligatory effectuators of the growth machine.

Capital as a process must be distinguished here from any concept of "capitalism" as a unified and total *system*. J. K. Gibson-Graham has generated a powerful critique of the ways in which such accounts often end up consolidating and strengthening that which they claim to challenge. "Capitalocentrism," as she calls it, is a discourse that "situates a wide range of economic practices and identities as the same as, opposite to, a complement of, or contained within capitalism" (2008, 11). Gibson-Graham calls for the performative rejection of a focus on this seemingly undefeatable monster, seeking to amplify other (noncapitalist) forms of knowledge and practice. But what *happens* to the relations formerly known as capitalism? How do we conceptualize and engage them? I propose to follow Massimo De Angelis in asserting that there is no singular capitalist *system*, as a sphere that encloses our world and names our "economy," but there *is* a process of capitalization and capitalist colonization. "We are not talking about a *state*, a fixed condition in which *the whole* of . . . life practices are actually colonized" (De Angelis 2007, 43); rather, we are talking about an ongoing, always-incomplete, and always-threatened process of *colonization*, a "social force that *aspires* to colonize the whole of life practices" (2007, 43) yet "*continually faces the threat of its extinction*" (2007, 40).[5] If the notion of "capitalocentrism" risks suggesting that the force of capital lies only in our discourses about it, then perhaps we might shift to a critical thinking in terms of capitalo*centering*: Capital, in material practice and not just in performative discourse, *does actually seek to become the center*, even as this aspiration never fully succeeds. The problem with being capitalocentric is not the naming of Capital as a dire problem, but active participation in discursively amplifying a process that is already in motion—namely, the process of capitalizing the world, of transforming as much of life as possible into new opportunities for the exploitative, private accumulation of monetary wealth.

Deleuze and Guattari refer to this process as the "capitalist axiomatic," arguing that Capital functions not by "coding"—that is, by rendering things into homogeneous regimes of identity, meaning, or structure—but by an abstract quantification that refuses such unity while also rendering everything exchangeable. "Capitalism," says Deleuze, "is founded on a generalized decoding of every flow: flows of wealth, flows of labor, flows of language, flows of art, etc. It did not create any code, it created a kind of accounting, an axiomatics of decoded flows, as the basis of its economy" (2004, 270). An axiom is a rule of operation that "deals directly with purely functional elements and relations whose nature is not specified, and which are immediately realized in highly varied domains simultaneously" (Deleuze and Guattari 1987, 454). This is what enables Capital to cut across myriad geographical, cultural, demographic, and political contexts, adapting to seemingly endless difference while never ceasing to render it into a market relation oriented toward accumulation. "How much flexibility there is in the axiomatic of capitalism," they exclaim, "always ready to widen its own limits so as to add a new axiom to a previously saturated system! You say you want an axiom for wage earners, for the working class and the unions? Well then, let's see what we can do— and thereafter profit will flow alongside wages, side by side. . . . An axiom will be found even for the language of dolphins" (Deleuze and Guattari 1983, 238). This formulation quite clearly describes the flexible, adaptable, and powerfully co-opting capacity of Capital as a process of colonization and accumulation.

Yet in the face of the apparent power and reach of what they call "capitalism," or even at times "the capitalist system" (1983, 233), Deleuze and Guattari sometimes seem to lose their bearings and betray their most compelling ideas and intuitions.[6] The great theorists of ontological becoming who challenge molar organization, royal science, and majoritarian articulation end up, at key moments, composing a vision of Capital as a kind of universal, ahistorical, determining structure of sameness. "There is only one world market, the capitalist one," they proclaim, and this "world capitalist axiomatic [can] tolerate a real polymorphy, or even a heteromorphy, of models" (1987, 455). It is a classic instance of capitalocentrism, by which Capital is ascribed a power that effectively subsumes difference into the "sign of the same" (Butler 1992), and heterogeneous assemblages become "models" within an effectively inescapable process of capture. To be sure, Deleuze and Guattari are quite clear at moments that capitalism must be understood as a historically contingent and even accidental assemblage: "The only universal history is the history of contingency" (1983, 224). But they seem to lose this view when they also propose that "it is correct to retrospectively understand all history in the light of capitalism" because "in a sense, capitalism has haunted all forms of society, but it haunts them as their terrifying nightmare, it is the dread they feel of a flow that would elude their codes" (1983, 140). Their move here is to map Capital, as a deterritorializing process, onto a more general and generic movement (or threat) of decoding and thus render it "universal" to all social formations. Can they have it both ways? Can Capital be understood as a particular historical, non-universal assemblage composed by an accidental convergence of forces *and* as an ever-present possibility waiting to be born? Only by risking a dangerous naturalization of capitalism and betraying the most potent elements of a philosophy and politics of becoming.

Capital, then, may function as a series of malleable axioms in the sense that variable strategies must be continually deployed in order to produce new needs, construct new markets, make the best of emerging crises, and ultimately maintain the process of accumulative growth. But these axioms do not add up to a "capitalist system" that singularly defines a "world market" or that "distributes [heterogeneous social] formations, determines their relations, while organizing an international division of labor" (Deleuze and Guattari 1987, 454). Markets always exceed capitalism (Roelvink 2016), heterogeneous "social" formations are composed and decomposed by myriad forces, and international divisions of labor cannot be reduced to a determination (even if powerfully influenced) by Capital. What *can* be said is that Capital is an addictive process of capture in the service of accumulation. It is actualized continually in multiple ways, many of which are potent but none of which are all-powerful or even in themselves generative.[7] We do not live "in" a capitalist system, we are not determined by capitalist "structures," and we are not subjected to a singular rule of "the worldwide capitalist axiomatic." We *are*, however, continually confronted with the process of Capital's colonization, and we are variably swept up in the addictions of accumulation as well as in the kinds of critical enthusiasm for capitalist power that can end up contributing to the process of capture.[8]

How do Capital and State relate? Unlike Nature-Culture, they are not locked in a strict dualism in which each term maps onto a host of other analogous articulations and in which one term clearly stands as the master element. They are neither wholly opposed nor dancing in collaborative synergy, though elements of both dynamics are variably present at different historical junctures. Capital might be said, by some, to name a force of creative liberation from the essentially conservative capture of the State.[9] Karl Marx and Friedrich Engels (2012) were not the only critics of capitalism to see the radical possibilities opened by the deterritorializing flows of Capital in the face of ossified hierarchies; the frenzied freedom of "creative destruction" (Schumpeter 2003) is a compelling image and temptation. But this view of Capital risks conflating the anarchic force of creativity and innovation with its domestication in the name of accumulation ("Innovate to produce and sell!"). Even more important, it elides the myriad ways in which the effectuation of Capital is only ever a partial deterritorialization accompanied by ongoing recapture.[10] The State, on the other hand, might be said to constitute a force of stability in the face of Capital's deterritorializations, yet this would be to confuse the *actualized* dynamic that is often called "market versus state" with the *virtual* diagram that is Capital-State.[11] Eternal stability is only the impossible desire from which the State launches and sustains an endless procession of transformations, including but not limited to territorial conquest and colonial pillage. To speak in simplified terms: if Capital is a form of durable capture that appears as continual destabilization, then the State is a force of continual destruction that appears as stability.

The two processes work hand in hand, even if at times in the form of combat. At one moment, the State appears as sovereign, all the

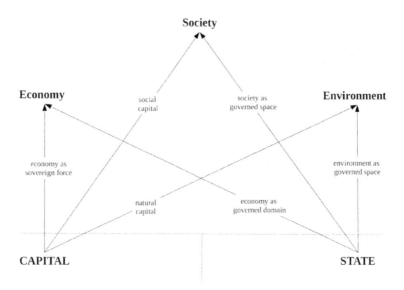

Figure 8. Dynamics of hegemonic actualization: Capital-State.

while handing over sovereignty to Capital. At another moment, Capital's assertion of sovereignty enables the State to appear as the only solution to the danger it poses. Or, to put the dynamic in terms of an effectuation similar to that described with regard to the Nature-Culture binary above, each term of the hegemonic trio can be said to variously effectuate the Capital-State dynamic (Figure 8). On one side, the economy stands as the force of Capital itself, shaping and demanding obedience as if from beyond. Society and economy are rendered accessories, becoming little more than "social capital" or "natural capital" in various manifestations. On the other side, and at the same time, each category is measured, mapped, and "overcoded" as a domain of government(ality) that appears to master Capital while at the same time giving itself over to its rule. Whether valorizing key dimensions of life via a "capitalization" or regulating and controlling via government (in Foucault's sense), one remains within the diagram of power.

Development

While Nature-Culture and Capital-State can be conceptualized in terms of two crossed axes, a third axis of Development can be seen to travel up through the middle, pushing the whole diagram forward on a trajectory of endless "progress" toward a future which never quite arrives. This is a crucial animating force for the entire diagram, for it renders what might otherwise be a series of violent and monotonous purifications and clashes into apparent "growing pains" on the way to something better. Development as a diagrammatic element composes a singular, linear and progressive movement of "improvement" (Gidwani 2008, 70), in which humanity is articulated as moving (or needing to move) in a particular direction toward ever-increasing well-being, knowledge, and material wealth—all defined by the cultural specificities of the European industrial revolution (Esteva 1992; Shanin 1997). On an everyday scale in Maine, Development is effectuated in its hegemonic form as a discourse of poverty and lack combined with a demand for growth of jobs, population, and material wealth. Development is the identification of a problem, the normative demand for its solution, and the strategy by which it is to be (ostensibly) solved.

It is a tremendously flexible diagrammatic element. As Vinay Gidwani points out, Development's core focus on improvement can be taken up in multiple ways: "It is a peculiar machine, unusually adaptive, that has worked in conjunction with a range of other powerful machines or diagrams: pastoral, sovereign, liberal, disciplinary, communist, governmental, communitarian, and capitalist" (2008, 70). And yet Development as a pattern of power is not often expressed in the full range of its potential (as *all* possible pathways for "improvement") but is quite restricted even in its adaptations. When "development" is spoken of in Maine, it refers to two distinct yet interconnected phenomena: the process of growing the economy (in its various guises), and the production of new *stuff*. The only people who *really* develop things are "job creators," commodity inventors, and real estate developers. It would be laughable in most circles to claim that someone seeking to defend an endangered species, protect an old-growth forest, organize against workplace exploitation, fight for welfare benefits, or create a cooperative subsistence farm is engaging in "development." If development means progress toward endless betterment, then why would it *not* fundamentally entail the construction of collective forms of life in which ecological well-being is no longer antagonistic with dominant forms of human production and consumption? Why would it *not* involve active struggle against all forms of exploitation and oppression? Because Development does not stand alone as an operative diagram; in its hegemonic form, Development draws its force from its relation to the other two axes.

In one dimension, as Bruno Latour argues, Development's "arrow of time" is explicitly linked to the Nature-Culture binary as a trajectory of purification by which modernity progressively "differentiates the radiant future from the dark past" (2004a, 188), separating Nature and Culture, fact and value, subject and object and liberating them from the savage, superstitious hybrids of past eras and "primitive" peoples. It is here that we can see the ways in which Development maps particular temporalities with spatialities, constituting some places as "developed," thus further along on the line of progress, and others (particularly in the majority world) as "undeveloped" or "underdeveloped," even "backward" (Sachs 1992; Latouche 1993; Escobar 2012) One could read Owen's preference for being subjected to the economy rather than to local ecologies (described in chapter 3) as one instance of this developmental purification in action: "better" always means leaving dependence on Nature behind in the name of human freedom and mastery. At the same time, Nature can be mobilized to justify and "naturalize" this very process: "Because, at the end of the day," observes Matthew, an economic development consultant, "we're animals, and we're all seeking to improve ourselves as animals, right?" (interview).

Development is fueled, perhaps even more crucially, by the Capital-State dynamic. On one hand, the arrow of progress embodies the drive (habit) of Capital toward endless accumulation and serves to justify this addictive treadmill in the name of a forward motion toward something better. Development gives Capital a teleology, an "uplifting sense of both material and moral destiny" (Norgaard 1994, 43), and thus injects it with a certain kind of *hope*, where alone it might have cultivated nothing but cycles of manic depression. At the same time, it is the State that is to grid, manage, and facilitate Development (Wallerstein 1984), reducing barriers to its movement and assuring that "everyone" has access to the "opportunities" it provides (if they do not take these up, of course, it would be their own fault). The State also provides a collective locus for Development, enabling its articulation as a project beyond the interests of individuals: a national project, a people's project, a project in which "we"—an "imagined community" (B. Anderson 2006)—are *in it together*.

In Maine, economist Charles Lawton effectively articulates the hegemonic demand of Development when he describes a divide in between those who want to keep things the same and those who seek to embrace change. There are "two Maines":

> One characterized by traditional industries and institutions struggling against the forces of globalization and another, smaller and less easily defined, Maine struggling equally hard to embrace these forces. . . . One Maine is weary, discouraged, narrow-minded, angry, and above all stubborn—determined to bring the world back to the way life was and ought to remain. The other Maine is energetic, hopeful, curious, happy, and above all stubborn—determined to make this special place home to both their houses and their dreams. (Lawton 2008, 21)

Maine people, Lawton suggests, are poised between succumbing to a barbaric refusal of economic progress and enthusiastically embracing adaptive subordination to the forces of Development. It is the same demand posed by *Charting Maine's Future*, described in chapter 1. The arrow of progress is moving; get on board or get left behind! But what to do with the Mainers who refuse this choice?

Geometries of Power (and Beyond)

The five elements of the hegemonic diagram come together in "commonsense" articulations of economy, society, and environment. When a politician, a business owner, or a forest defender speaks about any one of the trio's categories, compositions of Nature-Culture, Capital-State, and Development are unfolding at the very same time. Economy, society, and environment are not mere illusions through which gullible subjects inadvertently reinforce the power of Capitalism and other hidden monsters. Nor are they innocent categories that simply describe the world "as it is." They are *generative* of particular forms of life. Diagrammatic thinking is a diagnostic tool for naming these forms of life so as to notice their patterns, to trace their particular forms of composition and capture, and to therefore increase our capacities to resist and create.

This chapter, and the two preceding it, have only scratched the surface of what might be done with such a tracing. If the interacting dynamics of economy, society, and environment are complex, then the interactions of this trio with the five elements of the diagram can only be dizzying.[12] Imagine taking the two crown-like figures above (each with six lines of relation linking the diagrammatic elements with the trio), folding their triangles together into a pyramid, and inserting the arrow of development, itself articulated as a movement between seven elements. Economy, society, and environment are articulated at the point, the tip, where it all converges: this is the actual shape of the prism. In Doreen Massey's terms, it is "a power-geometry of intersecting trajectories" (2005, 64). One could spend many volumes unpacking these tangled relations. My intentions in the previous pages have been twofold: to indicate a possible direction and strategy for analysis that embraces critique without succumbing to performative complicity, and to generate just enough of a concrete tracing of the hegemonic trio in Maine that its patterns of power might be more effectively identified, challenged, and warded off as we follow lines of flight to new places. For though I have now worked to constitute economy, society, and environment as durable and powerful stabilities, this is not the place where I intend for any of us to end up.

Part III. Decomposing the Trio

> The function of any diagnosis concerning the nature of the
> present . . . does not consist in a simple characterization of what
> we are but, instead—by following lines of fragility in the present—
> in managing to grasp why and how that-which-is might no longer
> be that-which-is.
>
> —Michel Foucault, *Politics, Philosophy, Culture*

IN ORDER TO STABILIZE THE HEGEMONIC NARRATIVE of Part II for strategic effect, I have excluded a whole array of hesitations, uncertainties, resistances, and messy articulations that emerged and circulated throughout my research in Maine. Although these multiple flows of difference and disruption do not all constitute active opposition or alternatives to the hegemonic articulation—and indeed, some of them are quite assimilable to it—their presence indicates the fundamental impossibility at the heart of any hegemony. In Ernesto Laclau and Chantal Mouffe's terms, this is "the impossibility of a final suture" (2001, 125), of a definitive tying-up of any social formation. Gilles Deleuze and Félix Guattari view this through the lens of *multiplicity*: because no reality is singular, because all being is becoming, and because difference is the operative principle of existence, there can be no ultimate unification or completion. "Multiplicities," they write, "are defined by the outside: by the abstract line, the line of flight or deterritorialization according to which they change in nature and connect with other multiplicities" (1987, 9). A hegemonic assemblage may be quite powerful, and a great deal of its power may in fact consist in recapturing, domesticating, obscuring, or denying the lines of flight that are carrying it away at its edges. But such an assemblage will never succeed in becoming the "structure" or "system" it appears to be. Hegemony is always becoming-otherwise. This means that "counterhegemony" is not just an external operation that one poses against a hegemonic assemblage; it is also *internal* to the (un)working of hegemony itself.

If the task of tracing is to strategically (and perilously) focus on the contours of dominant power in order to open the possibility for effective opposition and escape, then the next step must be to unravel this very tracing while not losing the strength of its warning. "One elaborates a punctual system or a didactic representation," say Deleuze and Guattari, "but with the aim of making it snap, of sending a tremor through it. A punctual system is most interesting when there is a musician, painter, writer, philosopher to oppose it, who even fabricates it in order to oppose it, like a springboard to jump from" (1987, 295). "Decomposition" is the name I give to this work of undoing or unraveling. Drawing resonance from Bruno Latour's (2010) notion of "composition" as well as from Donna Haraway's (2016) "compostist" provocations and my own farming practice, I intend the term to invoke the coming-undone of bodies, the *becoming-compost* of all things, while also indicating a purposeful act.[1] If hegemonic assemblages are always unraveling, then a crucial task is to amplify these lines of flight, to open the cracks further, to make the assemblage "snap." To be sure, decomposition occurs on its own, without help; but the conscious work of decompositional analysis can serve to introduce potent new bacterial and fungal cultures to the mix—accelerating and channeling the process in particularly fertile directions.

The question of directionality is important here, though tricky. "Lines of flight" are not, taken cumulatively, headed on any particular trajectory. Other resonances of "decomposition" (think zombies, dead bodies, sewage) make this clear. Just because a given assemblage is coming undone does not necessarily indicate anything about what it might be in the process of becoming, or what it might yet become if enrolled into other assemblages. Decomposition cannot, therefore, be a simple matter of disinterested empiricism, since there are many ways to decompose and many directions to carry a line of flight. We must choose what to amplify and what to leave behind, even as our choices will always at least partially betray the intentions that directed them.[2] This issue marks a major distinction within various scholarly approaches to performativity and ontological politics. On one hand, much work inspired by actor-network theory tends to approach the multiplicity of world-making articulations as something to be documented in a fairly standard mode of academic distance. Donald MacKenzie, Fabian Muniesa, and Lucia Sui's *Do Economists Make Markets?* (2007) is a case in point: gathering numerous rigorous and informative instances of economic performativity (and its failure), this collection refrains from constituting a politics of performativity toward a radically different composition of "economy." J. K. Gibson-Graham's approach, on the other hand, is explicit about the project of "performative practices for other worlds" (2008), seeking to amplify some forms of world-making and not others. Like her, I strive to enact an ethically driven practice of decomposition: composting in order to grow something *new*.

5 CRACKS IN THE ASSEMBLAGE

Uncertainties, Resistances, and Swerves

Openings

I expected to find a whole array of instabilities and un-becomings at the heart of even the most hegemonic of spaces and institutions in Maine, and this was indeed the case. What I was less prepared for was the possibility that the entire formulation of my project would be overtly challenged by many of the people I interviewed, *on the grounds that it assumed and reproduced the validity of the hegemonic trio.* I had imagined a far-too-simple scenario, one in which professionals, captured by hegemonic versions of economy, society, and environment, would reproduce the stability of these domains in the face of a world that resisted and exceeded any ultimate capture. Maine's economic, social, and environmental professionals, I thought, would mostly tend to believe in these categories and thus work to reinforce them, while it would be the unconscious or inadvertent excesses of their work, along with other human and nonhuman actors beyond their institutions, that would disrupt this closure. I was at least partly wrong.

Even amid a pervasive reproduction of these categorical distinctions in professional reports and public discourses, many of my interviewees expressed significant degrees of discomfort and skepticism toward them when speaking in private. Indeed, as I reflect on my interview strategies in terms of their performative effects, I find an unsettling dynamic. If the distinctions among economy, society, and environment were reinforced in my conversations, it was often not my interviewees who were guilty; it was *I*. Focusing questions on the three categories served to re-perform their presence and affirm their importance. I demanded that my interviewees describe their world in terms of an economy, a society, and an environment, all the while intending to disrupt such a description. In some cases, resistance to this demand took the form of evasion, with interviewees eliding my attempts to format the conversation in terms of the trio, instead describing the details of their daily work: specific meetings, projects, negotiations, and interventions. In other instances interviewees answered my questions but with visible discomfort—hesitation not reducible to a reaction to an unexpected query. Many people spoke of "shades of gray" rather than categorical divisions. One statewide development agency director went so far as to question the validity of my project framing. Focusing on these distinct categories, he said, "is wrong. It'll get you to some place, but it won't get you to talking about the things . . . the whole package that makes us good" (Chad, interview). A director of a statewide rural development coalition rejected the trio outright as "false divisions" (Harriet, interview).

At the same time, it is not exactly the case that my interviewees proposed an abandonment of the three categories in favor of some other articulation. For every moment of evasion or resistance, there were numerous other moments in which economy, society, and environment reappeared as ontological givens or at least stable points of reference. What is going on? Are people, myself included, simply confused? Full of unreflective contradictions? Bruno Latour's understanding of modernity might be helpful here. For him, "the word 'modern' designates two sets of entirely different practices that must remain distinct if they are to remain effective" (1993, 10). The work of "purification" refers to the ongoing stabilization and maintenance of crucial modern divisions, while "translation" designates the continual mixing of beings, the "proliferation of hybrids" (1993, 51), which can be clearly seen in phenomena such as climate change, genetic modification, and human enhancement technologies. Purification continually attempts to clean up that which translation makes a mess of. To be "modern" is to maintain an absolute divide between these concurrent ontological processes, enacting translation in ever more complex and often problematic ways while simultaneously denying it through practices of purification.[1]

Are Maine's policy professionals quintessentially "modern" as they both affirm and resist the distinctions of the hegemonic trio? There is merit to this view, and it enables us to place some of the tensions and contradictions of my conversations into a wider context. But things on the ground seem more complicated and interesting. In many of my interviews, it was not exactly the case that people were adamantly purifying what they were also scrambling; rather, I heard the variably self-conscious expression of what might be called a *nonmodern yearning*. Unlike the strong articulations of modernity that Latour highlights, the hegemonic trio in Maine seems to find few adamant defenders in the face of questioning. It is as if my presentation of the trio often served to reflect back to my interviewees a self-image that they wanted to refuse, an articulation seen as problematic from an outside that our encounter helped to generate. It is as if substantive belief in the "modern constitution," or in the constitutional geometry of economy, society, and environment, can no longer be sustained in the face of this world's complexities. It is as if, despite the grip of hegemony, "everyone knows" that these categories no longer (or perhaps never did) adequately name the processes and dynamics in which we find ourselves.[2] This is not just a matter of confusion or contradiction; this is a constitutional crisis in the making.

Politics in the Cracks

But what are the *politics* that one can find emerging from the doubts and ambiguities of a professional class of policymakers, researchers, and advocates? If my interviewees partially resist conventional categories, or embrace ontologies of complex hybridity alongside hegemonic representations of purified categories, this is not necessarily because they are actively seeking or even secretly desiring radical transformation. Acknowledging or embracing blurred boundaries, hybridity, or the collapse of traditional distinctions does not make one a revolutionary.[3] There is no necessary correlative relationship between rupture and liberation, between cracks in the hegemonic formation and the actualization of more just, democratic, and dignified assemblages. As Gilles Deleuze and Félix Guattari make clear, referencing their notion of a "smooth" or "nomadic" space that deterritorializes forms of striation and structure, "never believe that a smooth space will suffice to save us" (1987, 500). At the same time, it is the continual becoming-undone of hegemonic formations that offer the *possibility* for all transformation; they are its necessary but insufficient conditions.

One could, therefore, raise justifiable questions about the political limits of fieldwork focused on Maine's professional economic, social, and environmental advocates. My tracings in the previous three chapters would indeed suggest that many of them are significantly (perhaps hopelessly) captured by, complicit with, and invested in the ongoing composition of hegemonic assemblages. Aren't they, in Gustavo Esteva and Madhu Suri Prakash's terms, "the economic men and women who work for modern institutions wedded to spreading the global economy" (1998, 193), or at least wedded to reproducing the conditions under which such a hegemonic spread remains essentially unthreatened? There is little doubt that this is at least partially the case. Moreover, aren't the most radical and creative forms of resistance and creation found precisely *outside* these institutions of power? Should we not look for ruptures and lines of flight primarily "in the margins," emerging from the "social majorities" (1998, 194) who are already constructing new realities and forms of life? Such efforts are proliferating in Maine, and I hold strongly to the view that more liberatory modes of life must be built from the interconnected, creative work of these grassroots activists and initiatives, "enacting de-centralized, non-hierarchical logic[s] of self-organization" (Escobar 2009, 351). No amount of engagement with (relatively) elite professionals can substitute for the crucial work of organizing "from the bottom-up" (Esteva 2010).

And yet we must also be careful to avoid a binary formulation. It is not the case—in Maine, at least—that there are simply, on one side, professional "economic men and women" reproducing hegemony and, on the other, liberated grassroots subjects building alternatives. It is exactly such an account that I aim for this decompositional analysis to disrupt. If a liberatory "post-modernity" already exists, as Esteva and Prakash suggest, "where people refuse to be seduced and controlled by economic laws" (1998, 194), then this must be seen as cutting *transversally* through multiple spaces, institutions, and even subjects. No voice presented in previous chapters as a representative of hegemony is the only voice in which my interviewees can (or might) speak. Even those who remain consciously wedded to a hegemonic articulation of economy, society, and environment are also subject to doubts, hesitations, and confrontations with a complexity that disrupts the possibility of total suture. Others are much more open, seeking alternative articulations and working to cultivate small spaces of transformative possibility within otherwise (seemingly) hegemonic institutions.

"Inside" and "outside" are rendered more complex here, folded into one another as fluid *moments* rather than as fixed topological positions. "Center and periphery thus emerge," writes Arturo Escobar, drawing on Stephen Gudeman and Alberto Rivera (1990), "not as fixed points in space, external to each other, but as a continuously moving zone in which practices of doing conversations and economies get intermingled, always shifting their relative position. Marginality becomes an effect of this dynamic" (2012, 96). One cannot know prior to direct and careful engagement where the cracks, ruptures, or transformative possibilities might lie. Who would have expected, for example, that it would be the director of a sub-regional *economic growth council* who would tell me that the GDP is "baloney," and that "all the economic development stuff you read is . . . pretty ethnocentric" (Sandra, interview)? Or that it would be a private business owner who, of all my interviewees, would most clearly express a critique of capitalism combined with a commitment to sufficiency over profit: "The little tiny scintilla of hope," said Dennis, "is that by rejecting the premise [of maximizing profit], we might be able to disrupt the conventional capitalists' recipe or game plan" (interview).

While it is not my intention to suggest that professionals working in Maine's mainstream institutions might or should constitute a leading force for revolutionary transformation or to propose substituting semi-elite "inside" strategies for robust grassroots organizing, I remain interested in exploring potential openings where fruitful connections might be made. Donna Haraway's "cyborg" approach to politics is a guide here: "I am made to recall," she writes amid a description of her subjection to the violent either/or politics of ecological purists at a conference, "those researchers even at Monsanto who may well take antiracist environmental feminism seriously and to imagine how alliances might be built with them" (2008, 10). Can we identify and encourage potential lines of flight that traverse even the most hegemonic of spaces and subjects? Might we find unexpected connections, alliances, and potential co-becomings between those on the "inside" of hegemonic institutions and those on their "outside"? This is to explore, in other words, the possibility not only of an "in and against" strategy (Escobar 2012, 181), juggling institutional engagement with oppositional action, but also an "in/out and *for*" strategy through which we might find and develop linkages, resources, and new footholds for imagining and enacting other forms of collective life. This is one dimension of what some have called a "transversal politics" (Guattari 1996; Yuval-Davis 1999).

As I turn to the work of decomposing, my interviewees begin to turn against themselves, challenging the hegemonic articulations in which they have already shown themselves to participate. It is not that any one person enacts a radical change and wholly betrays the trio but rather that many otherwise disconnected micro-fissures offer the *possibility* of opening larger and larger cracks. These cracks begin with hesitations and uncertainties expressed in spaces where confidence and mastery might be expected, spill over into more overt acknowledgments of the limits of hegemonic forms of knowledge and the performativity of discourse, and finally open toward the possibility of swerves or even defections—however small—from the ongoing assembly of the trio and its world. The larger picture of instability that emerges here is quite consciously fabricated from bits and pieces, from glimmers—an image provisionally and incompletely stitched together with scraps that only appear (for now, at least) in the pages of this book. And this is the point: to use this space of writing to dramatize what might emerge from processes of assembly that can only be prefigured here in suggestive forms.

Hesitations and Uncertainties

Eric is an academic economist focused on regional development. Much of his work involves constructing economic models that forecast the effects of planning interventions and development proposals. Numerous policymakers, private companies, and economic development advocates rely on his reports to make their cases about the benefits of particular projects. From a performative perspective focused on the effects of what Eric produces, he can be seen as a key figure in sustaining Maine's local implementation of the hegemonic assemblage. Yet in private conversation, a different subject emerges: far from sounding like the Voice of the Economy, he focuses on the limits of measurement and modeling, the dangers of confusing representations with that which they seek to represent, and on his aspiration to offer deliberative resources to decision-makers. I will return to some of this in the next section. For the moment, I highlight a provocative uncertainty that emerged in our conversation. Eric describes his analytical work on the categories of economy, society, and environment as a matter of clarifying "trade-offs":

I think it's important that everybody have the best information available about each side. Each of those circles [referencing the Venn diagram from the *Maine Measures of Growth* report, Figure 2, chapter 1] has to be dimensionalized. And the dimensions have to be understood, because at the end of the day, you're going to do trade-offs, and you have to figure out how much you're trading. Otherwise you tend to get into absolutes, in which case . . . *augh* . . . if you have no idea what it is you're trading off, your tendency will be to trade nothing for fear of trading everything. . . . My job is to make sure that [people] get the best information available about the part of it that I'm most qualified to deal with. (interview)

This is a familiar approach among those advocating "sustainable development," one that accepts the general contours of the hegemonic trio and then seeks the conditions under which its elements can be "balanced." Economists become crucial arbiters in this process, since one dominant stream of their discipline has positioned itself as the very "science of trade-offs" (Lewis and Widerquist 2013).[4]

But what is really being traded off? What choices appear as trade-offs only because they have been formatted as such, and what other options for negotiating livelihoods are closed off by this formatting? What if these are false choices? Is the development of Moosehead Lake, for example, really a trade-off between local jobs and something called "the environment," or is this frame itself a set-up that elides other—perhaps more unsettling—questions about power and possibility? I asked Eric: "How do I know a trade-off when I see one, and how do I distinguish between what seems like a trade-off and what might be a failure of imagination?" His answer was as anticlimactic as it was powerful: "Yeah, that's a really good question, and it's one that I struggle with. . . . *I don't know* [chuckles], I *really* don't know. I've put that in the 'I'll cross that bridge when I come to it' box" (interview). This is no minor uncertainty: one of the most prominent and widely respected agents of the hegemonic articulation of economy in Maine—one often charged with providing the core data for negotiating "trade-offs"—can neither ask nor answer serious questions about the foundational terms of his work.

Yet while Eric's reports lay out Maine's preformatted choices and trade-offs in the forms of figures and charts, costs and benefits, pros and cons, he also knows on some level that this a dangerous pathway and leans toward something different: "I want to use modeling to provoke question-asking rather than answer-giving," he tells me. "People are a lot more comfortable with answers than they are questions" (interview). There is a crucial *gap* (a crack?) here between, on one hand, Eric's desire to open spaces of negotiation and collective creativity and, on the other, the professional and financial gains to be made by giving his contract employers what they want: hard facts and trade-offs that render the hegemonic articulation seemingly inevitable.

Such a gap was also apparent in my conversation with Kathleen, a statistician employed by the State of Maine. Her job, like that of Eric, is to provide people and institutions with data about Maine's economy and society; in her case less about costs and benefits and more about the vital signs of the aggregate domains: GDP, population growth, employment, business starts, and such. Kathleen is a key mediator in the chain of articulation through which the Bureau of Economic Analysis and other agencies participate in composing an entity that can be known and measured as "the Maine economy." Moreover, she is asked to comment in various public situations about the state of things: How is the economy doing? What do we need to improve? What is in store for our economic future? With the appearance of confidence and quasi-omnipotence, Kathleen joins with other such professionals to articulate the ongoing stability and inevitability of the hegemonic trio. In confidential conversation, however, a different story emerges: the apparent objectivity of numbers upon which economy as both force and domain rest their power is, in fact, a thin veneer. Economic prediction, Kathleen tells me, is not science but is "actually more of an art-form because it's based pretty much completely on different assumptions that you're making. . . . It's very subjective" (interview). She describes her work in a surprisingly self-conscious manner as a problematic, though necessary, process of distilling numbers from impossibly complicated assumptions: "We make assumptions and then we come out with a number at the end . . . because that's what people want" (interview).

Who are these "people"? We might think of this word as a stand-in for all who are interested in, invested in, addicted to, and coercively trapped by the necessity of hegemonic metrics. The diagram of power itself, one might even say, "wants" these numbers, *needs* these numbers, and certain trained professionals are paid to provide them. "I mean you've got to be able to come up with some sort of apples-to-apples comparison to be able to make a valid decision," says Kathleen, speaking in the voice of hegemony. And yet five minutes later she finds herself lost in the open sea of assumptions that render her work (im)possible:

> In a lot of cases, the challenge is that we don't have this apples-to-apples comparison. . . . I get questions frequently about the economic impact of different industries, and people don't realize that there are so many assumptions that you have to make going into that. Depending on what those assumptions are and how your model is set up, you could come up with two completely different answers for the same thing just by changing one small assumption. And so, on the surface you might think it should be really easy to find out if changing the minimum wage will make people better or worse off. But in actuality, it's really hard to measure. You can make arguments on both sides, depending on what assumptions you're making and how you're tracking that, and how you're defining well-being. . . . None of it, in reality, takes place in a vacuum. (interview)

On one hand, Kathleen resonates with the demand for hard facts and commensuration: without this, no decisions can be made, no planning effected, no population measured, no rational intervention made. Like Chad, the economic developer, Kathleen (though perhaps more so her employer) needs "established fact[s]—data . . . that you can't dispute" (Chad, interview). Yet, on the other hand, these facts are clearly open for questioning and impossible to sever from ethics, politics, and history.

In the face of this complexity, Kathleen expresses an unfulfilled sense of responsibility. Economic professionals often fall short of communicating their assumptions, and the media does not help:

> They're not reporting the assumptions. They're not in many cases even reporting what the definition is, they're just saying, you know, "forty-two." Everybody goes, "forty-two," not really understanding what that is. . . . Someone somewhere along the line is going to have to step up and say, hold on a minute, we've got to talk a little bit about this! You know, when we announce a number, are we going to give the background, or are we going to say, "Yep, let's just let the economists do whatever they want, and we'll take their word for it, and we'll take those numbers and run with them"? (interview)

Kathleen expresses here the same yearning as that of Eric, and one that she, too, often violates in public practice: to render the complexity and contingency of metric construction *explicit*, to constitute "facts" as sites of public negotiation, questioning, and exploration. This yearning may be dampened or even squashed by the ongoing demands of the hegemonic machinery, by the fact that depoliticized, naturalized, objectified measures are "what our culture wants" (interview). It may subsist more in its violation than in its effectivity, remaining little more than an unfulfilled yet occasionally expressed rebellious desire. Yet it nonetheless remains a crucial opening, a small but quite real crack present at the (broken?) heart of hegemony.

Acknowledging Construction and Contingency

If one set of cracks can be found in the tensions between the demands made by a hegemonic diagram of power and other yearnings and experiences circulating within non-unified subjects, another can be found in the ways that some professionals are able to acknowledge the constructed, provisional, and contingent nature of the categories they are also gripped by. In multiple interviews, I was confronted with this surprising theme: despite an often simultaneous acceptance of the three categories as ontological givens, interviewees also spoke of them as pragmatic, collective fabrications. As with the hesitations and uncertainties described above, there is nothing inherently liberating in the recognition that certain things are *produced* and not simply given. Yet such a move is a crucial precondition for transformative action and agency, offering at least the possibility that things could have been— and might yet be—otherwise. Moreover, the explicit recognition of this construction and contingency may open spaces in which politics can shift from questions of trade-offs and inevitable tensions between forces and domains to public struggles and negotiations over political epistemologies and ontologies themselves. Can the amplification of discourses of construction enable us to engage the ethico-political effects of certain performative practices of world-making and open creative spaces to imagine such practices differently?

The starting point for such an opening is *recognition*, and this is expressed in numerous forms. Harold, a private economic development consultant, tells me, "We created the economy. It's a made-up thing, a made-up way to measure stuff going back and forth, right?" (interview). Kathleen, the government statistician described earlier, says similarly, "A lot of what we talk about with the economy, well, it's all just sort of concepts and it works because everybody's bought into this concept" (interview). When I ask the program director of a major Maine environmental nonprofit how "the environment" gets defined in her work, she responds: "Um, well . . . by our board . . . [laughs] . . . and staff working with our board!" (Irene, interview). The environment for Dana, the director of another prominent environmental advocacy organization, is "a catch-all term for a variety of things," and these things are determined as much by the politics of the moment as by any particular conception of "nature" (interview). The social domain, for Fred, the director of a statewide community development organization, is constructed by a particular set of "lenses" though which one looks, including a specific "social impact tool" used by his agency to measure (and thus constitute) their work in explicitly "social" terms (interview). The list of such examples could go on.

The economist Eric, my star witness for contradictory articulation, pushes this recognition even further, offering a clear sense that these constructed terms and measures function to *produce* what they claim to describe: "It's in the measurement that we tend to give form to the concept of the economy. . . . And so the question of 'what is the economy' ultimately comes down to what it is you're exactly measuring and what it is you're doing [with that] measuring" (interview). In this understanding—not unlike that of Michel Callon (1998)—the economy is constituted through a framing, overtly produced by human beings, necessarily selective in its metrics, and inevitably partial in terms of that which it brings into view or obscures. "Measurement increases precision," says Eric, "but creates its own distortion" (interview). Kathleen, too, recognized that various representations of the economy are influential: "*Talking* about the economy, particularly in the media, has more of an impact on the economy than just about anything else" (interview). Bradley, the director of a sub-regional environmental protection effort and also an ecologist, speaks more generally about the three categories as constructs that work to produce certain realities and reproduce particular power relations. He could be reading from a critical constructionist manifesto: "What we're talking about is contesting for *meaning*, and contesting for the access to *power* that meaning generates" (interview).

If some interviewees recognize performativity, others name a profound provisionality and contingency at the heart of the hegemonic articulation. Chad, the economic development director cited frequently thus far as enacting significant oscillations between hegemony and its rupture, begins by affirming the necessity of "established facts" and offers the relationship between economic productivity (value-added per worker in Maine) and social well-being as a prime example. But the more I ask him to describe the nature of this linkage, the further we get from such objectivity. Soon, the whole trio of economy, society (in the form of "community"), and environment becomes an arbitrary convenience masking an impossible-to-capture complexity:

> People's interpretations sometimes are problematic, in that they're looking for definitive black-and-white statements of what economy is, community, and environment. And they're looking for very specific relations, and causal relationships, and we just don't live in that world. . . . Once people let go of that, this is a lot easier to digest and understand. But I think we have to start with some kind of lines and structure to just begin. (Chad, interview)

We move from a lawlike causal relationship, premised on an objective economic dynamic, to "lines and structure" meant only as prompts for collective exploration. An indisputable foundation, a matter of fact, becomes, in Chad's very words, a "good story" or a "jumping-off point" (interview). Looking for a sovereign economy whose mechanisms determine our spaces of possible action and whose workings can be predicted via causal analysis? Give up the search, because "we just don't live in that world."

Swerves

One could read the various hesitations and self-reflections described thus far as minor and inconsequential instances in which professionals express reasonable yet non-actionable doubts about the nature, trajectory, or use of their work. Perhaps both Eric and Kathleen will remain relatively comfortable with these tensions, performing effectively on the side of hegemony even if offered a chance to defect (though perhaps not; one never knows . . .). Other interviewees, however, demonstrate much more potent destabilizations that gesture toward possible "swerves" (Gibson-Graham 2006a, 14) or defections. Brenda, a researcher working for a nonprofit social advocacy organization, is a bold example. I cited her in chapter 3 as providing an example of socialization tied to a normalized (hegemonic) economic subject. Early in our conversation, she described her goal as providing "opportunity" for young people: "They're the future of society. They are the future leaders. . . . If they grow up more whole and more resourced, with better opportunities in terms of education, you'd hope to see an outcome of an engaged workforce that's ready to do the jobs of the century" (interview). While her work is framed around "young people," it focuses in practice on *particular* young people: "low income is a common thread" (interview), because it is these youth who are seen as needing intervention, needing various kinds of programs to enable proper participation in the workforce and larger society. One could easily see Brenda as performing a key dimension of hegemonic articulation in which poor people are positioned as needy subjects, social agencies as institutional saviors, while upper-middle-class people remain the tacit normative measure of success and well-being.

As the conversation went on, however, and as I asked questions that sought to interrupt or open this narrative to other directions, a wholly different voice emerged, one that essentially reversed the public stance that Brenda often takes:

> EM: What kind of person is social work trying to create? We have specific ideas about what makes a good person, an effective person, right?
> BRENDA: Right, and who *decides* that? . . . We have this middle-class mindset for the world, you know, that everyone . . . If you look at most of the kids in child welfare they're mostly from families that are poor. That doesn't mean that abuse isn't going on in a middle-class home, it's just that to start out, that family isn't *like* the middle-class view of the social worker. Because the social worker has achieved a goal of . . . *status.* (interview)

Her tone grew more urgent as our conversation progressed:

> EM: So is a certain kind of middle-class human the kind of norm that we're trying to make everybody into?
> BRENDA: I *know*! I wrestle with that personally, because I think, you're right, I get mad about that sometimes, like, what are we saying, that it's not OK to not have enough? To be just getting by? Is that not OK? And what do we *want*? Do we want everyone to be the same? (interview)

Brenda raised here the possibility of a complicity between well-intentioned social work and a pathologization and stigmatization of poverty. "We totally get sucked into it," she confessed, "because [of] this idea that we all have to be these high-achieving [people]" (interview). In a more affirmative sense, Brenda opened up a space in which the very definitions of poverty, well-being, and "enough" can be radically questioned. Are the sufficiency practices enacted by many Maine families truly a problem to merit intervention? Can one use income as a measure of need? How are we to challenge an articulation that demands accumulation and economic "success" as the primary standards of human achievement? What if there are other ways to approach this? As Brenda exclaimed finally, "How do we *stop* this madness?!" (interview).

It is as if a spell had been broken: the hegemonic assemblage (in this case primarily of economy and society) no longer appeared to Brenda as the inevitable horizon of thought and action, and a whole different set of emotions, thoughts, and political articulations bubbled up. New questions began to emerge that shifted the problematization from poverty to the "middle-class mindset" that had stood as an unquestioned norm. What if *this* is a site that demands critical attention and intervention? Brenda raised grave concerns about the damaging pressures of what she called "overparenting" and the expectations associated with a certain notion of "success":

> No one's talking about the way that the middle class, upper class are raising their children now, keeping them in this bubble-world. And I've read some statistics about how, especially in high-pressure colleges, the number of kids who seek out counseling once they get there is just skyrocketing. They've been hovered upon all their life by a parent telling them to overachieve, overachieve, do this, do that. And then you get a little bit of freedom and you don't know how to do it. But no one would name that *child abuse*. But if you *didn't* provide your kid with things then you have neglect, but we judge one worse than the other. (interview)

Brenda expressed a sense of her work opening up in our conversation: What if a focus only on poverty was leaving out other key realms of ethico-political intervention? What if income measures at least partly miss the point, and transformative action could unfold instead around questions of the kinds of people we seek to affirm and become? What if her organization could be working toward creating people who are not *competitive*, but rather, in her words, "*compassionate*" (interview)? I asked her, toward the end of our encounter, if she is able to find space in her work for stepping back to have such conversations and to challenge conventional assumptions. "No, I don't," she responded, and proceeded not only to explain the coercive conundrum of dependency on funding from entities who would discourage such questioning, but also to level a powerful critique of profit and exploitation:

> We don't talk about Wall Street. We don't scream about wealth and the accumulation of it, like the disparity, the economic disparity. We might talk about the wage issues and median household income, but we're not talking about. . . . Because the philanthropists we are talking about [chuckles] are giving us [money]. . . . So no one's really speaking out about it! I would love to see more of that occur! I told you [earlier] about the [person who founded a social service organization in New York City with the support of a Wall

Street investor]. Why didn't he turn to that hedge fund guy and say, "It's because you make that much money that my children's families live in poverty! Their low wages give you the profit that you are just basking in, and then you can throw some my way to help kind of *soften* the blow." (interview)

One can imagine small cracks forming in the reports that Brenda produces, words bending and shaking on the page, tiny tremors yearning to open up something that the hegemonic diagram of power cannot assimilate. Combining her analysis of the relation between Wall Street profits and families who struggle to eat with her questions about our definitions of poverty, well-being, and success offers a powerful glimpse of a counterhegemonic politics lurking behind, beneath, and alongside hegemony. How can such sites of ethico-political (in)articulation be named, amplified, and connected? This is a key strategic question that clamors for attention.

Brenda is not alone in her double (or, perhaps more accurately, multiple) existence. It is a condition shared by many in her position— perhaps by all of us in some sense—caught between the coercive necessity of a hegemony that we can neither think nor live without and the multiple dimensions of life that exceed it. What emerges here renders the singular, hegemonic composition of economy, society, and environment wholly questionable: there may be real activities and exchanges that measurement brings into focus (and also enable), real bodies aggregated (and thus shaped) by population statistics, and real nonhuman spaces, beings, and relations that participate (unevenly) in composing an "environment," but these are never fully captured by any dominant territorialization. An excess of activity, thought, speech, and desire always escapes the process of articulation through which these categories are performatively produced. They are thus always *potentially* de-ontologized, vulnerable to ethico-political questioning, transformation, resignification, and perhaps even abandonment. Such a possibility depends, of course, on the construction of concrete interventions that amplify and expand the cracks. The work of *multiplication* is a crucial next step.

6 MULTIPLYING ARTICULATIONS

How Many Definitions Can Maine's
Professionals Produce?

Multiple Worlds

Momentarily resisting the allure of the closure, certainty, and mastery associated with the hegemonic trio, Chad provocatively reminds us that "we just don't live in that world" (interview). What world do we, in fact, live in? *Multiple* worlds, and this multiplicity is made explicit by a proliferation of aberrant (i.e., not-quite-hegemonic or even counterhegemonic) articulations of economy, society, and environment encountered in my fieldwork. While the hegemonic themes described in the previous chapters were continually and often boldly present in my conversations, the terms of the trio also broke into a barely countable array of divergent fragments: each of the categories *expanded* in multiple ways, including elements ignored or excluded by the hegemonic articulation; *divided* into separate and sometimes conflicting dimensions; *blurred* into processes through which various agencies were continually and differentially produced and engaged; *transformed* into constellations of values and localized accounts generated from particular lived experiences. Such lines of flight, if taken seriously, amplified, and further materialized, might ultimately defy any reassimilation into the hegemonic articulation and open new pathways for becoming otherwise. In what follows, I describe these multiplications relative to each category.

Multiplying the Economy

What is the economy? At first glance, private business and monetized market exchange appear to constitute the entire domain (chapter 2).

Harold, the economic development consultant, however, begins to complicate things: The economy, he says, is "the interchange of ideas or products or services that lead to, presumably, a positive exchange for both parties" (interview). This does not necessarily—though it might also—include exchanges of *money*. Helen, a high-ranking professional in a government community development office, is even more specific in this regard. The economy, she says, "may also be the exchange of services *without* dollars. It may be people who are doing *x* number of hours of babysitting, you'll give me *x* amount of vegetables from your garden. There's a number of people bartering ... when there are few dollars within the town." (interview). Marvin, the conservative economic policy think-tank director, agrees: "An economy is nothing more than the voluntary exchange of goods and services between people" (interview). While he may at first propose confidently that "in a modern economy, we measure those voluntary transactions through dollars, OK?," when challenged about the complexity that is excluded from any economic theory, Marvin's tone shifts: "There's too much faith in the dollar assigned to something necessarily meaning there's value there. The classic case in economics is the homemaker versus a secretary. It could be the same person, but in one case they're at home with the children taking care of the household, but not getting paid for it, they're somehow less of a person than the secretary who *is* getting paid" (interview). One of Maine's prominent public advocates for capitalism, private enterprise, and the morality of market freedom is now speaking like a feminist economic critic of the invisibility and devaluation of unpaid housework (e.g., Waring 1988; Folbre 2001).

The economy, moreover, does not necessarily end with exchange. Carol, the director of another government department involved with social work, expands the economic domain further, distinguishing between "the for-profit money world" and something else altogether: "There are huge parts of this state where there *isn't* a cash economy, but there's an amazing, *thriving* economy" (interview). This other economy is characterized primarily by life-sustaining *labor*: "I think [this economy is defined by] *effort*, and contribution to some kind of a product, whether it's a tangible or it's a service. So whatever generates that. The world that I've lived in, pretty much since 1976, paid or unpaid has not been the issue. It's been the labor and the product of it" (interview) Carol proceeds to describe a whole web of underground monetary exchange, barter, sharing, self-provisioning, and volunteer work that sustains Maine families. For example:

> I'm thinking about a fellow who is quite an expert plumber, whose offspring have all gone to college. One's working in NYC as an architect. On the books [the plumber] is *unemployed*, because he barters. And that is the norm for, I'd say, 80 percent of that region. He gets paid in fish, he gets paid in firewood, he gets paid in [chuckles], you know . . . he gets paid in a lot of different things. (interview)

Nonmonetary and non-exchange activities, moreover, can amount to a significant displacement of the very need for money: "In the volunteer sector, for instance," Carol describes, "the *value* of Maine's volunteer labor is about $900 million. . . . That's a level of effort that towns, schools, hospitals, nonprofits could never actually pay for in cash" (interview). Community response to a fire in the rural Maine town of Pittsfield is a case in point:

> Did you see that in the news? Family of nine got burned out up there, and before they had a chance to even figure out where they were going next and have the ambulance deliver them to their brother-in-law's place, the community, that they were brand-new to, was calling them and saying, "What can we do?" And I'm sure there's going to be a rebuild their house effort. That's the neighboring kind of volunteering. (interview)

Resonances with Carol's formulation were echoed in many conversations, affirming a stream of sociological and geographical scholarship that has repositioned market exchange within a much larger sphere of activity. From the "substantive economy" of Karl Polanyi (1977), the "whole economy" of Barbara Brandt (1995), and the "total productive system" of Hazel Henderson (1995) to the "diverse economy" of J. K. Gibson-Graham (2006a), the domain of economy is expanded to include all the ways that "human beings make their living, whether or not this entails rational decision-making or economizing behavior and whether or not production is for use or exchange" (Dale 2010, 110).

The expansion does not end here, however, for some Maine development professionals also acknowledge a larger set of relations that must be included in any articulation of the economy: our constitutive relations with nonhuman forces, or "nature." We might be tempted to call this "the environment," and to repeat the conventional "nested spheres" formulation of an ecological economics discussed in chapter 1. Indeed, this is precisely where some of my interviewees go: "We've sort of lost the connection between the fact that all of this economic activity takes place *within* an environment," says Kathleen, the government statistician (interview). But for others, the lines are more blurred. When Oscar, an economic development director for a sub-regional planning agency, describes the object of economic development, it is about the creation of and care for *infrastructure*: "roads, bridges, highways, sewage systems, lighting, the capacity to sustain social interaction . . . [and this] would *include* ecology" (interview). To further elaborate the relation between economy and ecology, he resorts to a pseudo-historical mythologization reminiscent of many "just so" stories in economics (Rapport 1991), yet not in the service of the usual teleological narrative of Development:[1] "I think if we look at prehistory and history, economy was derived from the ecology. I mean if you were a Bushman in the Kalahari, your economy was about whether you could find water and grubs that day, and the guy who found more grubs had a surplus and so on and so forth. I don't think a lot of people keep that in mind" (interview). However problematic this rendering of indigenous San people as part of a lost past despite their continued struggles for survival and justice (Sylvain 2002), the "primitive" serves here not to demonstrate an evolution of economy *from* ecology, but rather to remind us that an ecological core remains present even in modern, industrialized, economic assemblages. I am hard pressed to find Oscar speaking of anything like an "environment" (except with reference to "environmental groups" as political entities), since all infrastructural elements that sustain human life are included as part of a now quite-nebulous economy. Furthermore, these are not referenced in terms of "ecosystem services" or any clearly quantifiable value, but are subsumed as part of an also-vague and inclusive notion of "quality of place" and "quality of life."

Although such "quality" is, for many development professionals who speak of it, primarily about *humans*, there are exceptions to this that push the definition of the economic domain to its very limits. For Sandra, the director of a sub-regional economic growth council (of all people to say this, given the hegemonic expectations of her role), quality of life "needs to be for our rivers and for our fish and for the animals. Yeah. You can't exploit that at the cost of humans. You know, the old 'man at the top of the chain and everything under it just for man's use' is baloney, but that's kind of a cultural heritage that kind of came down. I hope and think that's changing" (interview). What has "the economy" now become? More than a domain of monetary transactions, of exchange in general, or even of human provisioning labor, it morphs into something that involves *the entirety of constitutive relationships that make life possible*. Can this even be called an "economy"? Can it reasonably be seen to constitute a "domain" of any kind?

This expansive multiplication is only part of the picture, however, for the economy described by many of my interviewees is also *divided*. In one sense, it is divided in terms of a localization of articulations. If the hegemonic formation of the economy appears as a kind of universal knowledge—a "major" category constituted via an objective "view from nowhere" (Nagel 1989) associated with modernist epistemologies—a number of interviewees sought to *specify* and *locate* this knowledge. Such an approach is reminiscent of anthropologist Stephen Gudeman's contrast between "universal models," which assume a singular reality underlying all variations, and "local models," which constitute contextual, provisional, and heterogeneous sets of knowledge practices (2008, 17). According to Arnold, the director of a sub-regional economic growth council in Maine, the definition of "the economy" depends entirely on where one is standing. For a municipality, "the economy is property taxes" (interview), and therefore any activities that enhance that revenue stream are likely to be desired. For a business, it is about income and profit, which may include the minimization of property tax payments. For a chamber of commerce, it is about the number of enterprises, "how many ribbon-cuttings they go to" (interview), since its goal is increased membership. For Arnold, as an economic developer, the economy is about not only job creation policies, but also the attraction of young people: "We're really focusing in on demographics as our measurement. Would we not want a business that would hire people of my age category? Of course we would. . . . But a company that says I'm going to hire people seventeen to twenty-four, here's the kinds of skills that we want. *That's* it" (interview). What is so often viewed as a single "domain" of measurement becomes a series of *distinct* domains, each overlapping but not coextensive, and each potentially in tension with the others.

Nora, a researcher with a Maine environmental nonprofit, suggests something similar from a different angle. For her, there is no single "economy"; rather, there are multiple economies centered around different industries, interests, geographies, and time-frames. "I'm not sure there's just one economy, either," she says. "There's short-term and long-term. There's with externalities, without externalities. There's direct and indirect costs" (interview). Nora rejects the GDP as a simple measure of economic health, since it tends to obscure complex questions of cost and benefit: "You know, look at a residential subdivision. Is that good for the economy or not? It's good for the developer, and it probably puts up the GDP, but then it burdens the town schools, you know, water and sewer. And we are told that development can cost more than the revenues it creates, so, you know, is it good? For the economy?" (interview). The answer is complex, since in every situation, "You've got to define the economy. . . . *Whose* economy?" (interview). Nora proposes an answer: "There's going to be a different answer based on whose ox is being gored" (interview). The CEO of a large social service organization in Maine agrees. For Richard, "the economy" does not always refer to everyone in a given place: "Some of the decisions that are made in Washington," he says, "really have very little to do with community and environment, and have a whole hell of a lot more to do with economics and really the economics of *a certain group of people* (interview, emphasis added).

Is there ever *really* a conflict, in fact, between "the economy" and "the environment"? Might such conflicts be viewed, instead, as struggles between *different economies* or divergent economic articulations? If the economy can refer to all the ways in which human beings produce and receive livelihoods, then "environmentalists" would simply be economic developers with a wider frame of analysis. Witness this conversation with Elizabeth, a policy advocate for a major Maine environmental nonprofit:

> EM: [Your organization] is arguably focused on protecting the foundations of what makes life possible . . .
> ELIZABETH: Land, air, water!
> EM: . . . in a place.
> ELIZABETH: Right.
> EM: And yet somehow there's this thing called "the economy" . . . which *also* seems to be a thing that provides people with what they need. And the politics plays out in such a way that there are some people who are "for the economy," . . . and somehow would then see [your] work as marginal to what's really important.
> ELIZABETH: I think it totally depends on your time-frame. If all you're worried about is jobs next year, or profits next year, you can ignore the environment. You can abuse it. You can dump anything you want in the rivers, you can dump anything you want in the air, you can cut down all the

trees. . . . And the kind of work that we do, especially when we're talking about land and water ecosystems, is much longer term.

EM: So is [this] really a long-term economic development organization with a more-than-human constituency? [chuckles]

ELIZABETH: I mean, *yeah*! You could say that! To the extent that the environment is the basis of our entire world and society, of *course* it's economic. (interview)

Rather than "environment versus economy," it is a matter of multiple and contested economies, articulated around different populations, places, temporalities, and matters of concern. In what ways, and for whose benefit, will we care for our collective means of sustenance? Which of these means will be rendered visible within a given frame, and which will remain hidden?

The division between multiple economies is made quite clear in a surprisingly common binary articulation among economic, social, and environmental professionals alike. There are *two economies*, I have been told in various ways: the economy of measurement, money, and profit; and the economy of need, well-being, and sustenance. Kathleen, the government statistician, expresses this clearly:

Whether you're talking about the economy as a measurement . . . or as a driver of well-being, they're really two different conversations. We really don't tend to talk about everything all at once. We either talk about the economy because we want to know how things are doing and measuring it, or we're talking about the economy in terms of, OK, people are more educated, they're doing better in those senses. And so I think we've got sort of two different economies, where it's, yeah, it's the economy that's about *people*, and the economy that's about *numbers and statistics*. (interview, emphasis added)

Dorothy, the community health agency director, speaks simultaneously about the economy as a monstrous force, "all about the almighty *dollar*" (interview), and about the economy as *community itself*, all the ways—material and nonmaterial—that we meet our needs. "Are there other ways we can improve the health of the economy without spending money?" she asks in the context of a broader conversation about the rise of consumerism and its effects on younger generations and community coherence (interview). Such a question would be incoherent in terms of her first notion of economy. Travis, the director of an environmental health nonprofit, consciously specifies the division: "In one sense we could say that the economy is the way that we organize how we trade stuff with each other, right? Whereas in another sense, you could say the economy . . . isn't fundamentally about money and exchange, but the economy is about the way that we produce and provide things that we need. Other people might call that society or community or something else" (interview). In one economy—what I will call the *economy of accumulation*—the focus is on the endless expansion of exchange and money, measured in terms of GDP growth and other conventional (hegemonic) metrics. In the other economy—*the economy of sustenance*—the focus is on the healthy reproduction of human lives and communities, the meeting of needs through various means, which may or may not include monetary activity.

The separation of an economy of accumulation from one of sustenance helps to make sense out of a seeming-paradox that emerges from many of my conversations. Why, despite a pervasive sense that "economy" and "environment" are often in conflict, do so many people tell me that this is most assuredly *not* the case? "Inherently I would say no, there isn't [such a conflict]," says Marvin, the economic think-tank director (interview). People talk about conflict "because it sells, not because it's real," says Carol, the director of a government social services department (interview). "I don't think there's *any* conflict between the environment or the economy," says the environmental activist David. "There shouldn't be. It's a myth" (interview). David's rapid movement from the descriptive ("there isn't") to the normative ("there shouldn't") is telling. Two things are articulated at the same time: on one hand, there is no distinction, since the "environment" is clearly a fundamental part of what we need to survive—that is, a key dimension of an economy of sustenance. On the other hand, there *is* a distinction, since "the economy" also refers to a domain or process that is systematically undermining the ecological conditions of well-being—the economy of accumulation. Thus Elizabeth, the environmental policy advocate, can say in the same breath:

> I don't think of it as economy versus environment. I think that the economy and the environment are totally intertwined and you can't separate them. . . . Which is why, when I get depressed about my work, the reason I get depressed is because I feel like there's an economic system that we're never going to tame, so to speak, that's a little more powerful than the environmental system. (interview)

"You can't separate them," and yet one is utterly subjected to the other. What's the deal?

The problem appears to be that there is *only one word* to refer to two radically distinct—and, in fact, often opposed—realities. "We really have two different concepts and we're just calling them the same thing," proposes Kathleen (interview). Given that this "same thing" so often refers only to the contours of the hegemonic articulation, the *other* "economy" remains nearly impossible to speak of. Dorothy expresses the lack of language in this way:

> DOROTHY: I mean, economics are jobs, and we have an economic development group, and . . . what they seem to be focusing on is jobs, jobs, jobs. It doesn't matter what the jobs are and what they do, it's jobs. And when people have jobs, then they can shop . . .
> EM: But you seem to think differently about it.
> DOROTHY: I do, but I can't . . . *I don't know quite how to describe it.* . . . It's, it's just . . . I guess getting back to basics. Somewhere along the line, we've lost that. (interview)

Two zones of articulation, one word: this is both a symptom of hegemony and a mark of its ongoing destabilization. We have no language to refer to the work of life sustenance that is not always already bound up in the power-laden baggage of the hegemonic economy of accumulation, and thus many attempts to articulate something outside of the dominant assemblage are easily recaptured by it. This also suggests, however, that other articulations continually *haunt* the hegemonic formation, shaping its conditions of existence while also threatening its attempt to stand alone as the singular name of reality.

Multiplying the Social

While the hegemonic articulation of economy includes a narrow set of mostly private, market-based monetary transactions, its accompanying category of "society" captures much more. It is, in its hegemonic forms, both the totality of human non-economic relationships in a given place (whether in the larger aggregate of "society" or the smaller of "community") and the domesticated exclusion of those who fail to conform to its economically dominated modes of subjectification. One might wonder, at first glance, how such an expansive articulation could be widened or multiplied. Yet there is room to grow.

The first unraveling move is to refuse a distinction between activity that is strictly "economic" and that which is "social," thus collapsing the two into a general domain of human relationships and sustenance activities in a bounded space. I have already described the expansion of the economy into a broad zone of human sustenance activity; in the way Dorothy the community health director describes things, these domains are wholly merged. When asked, at separate moments, how she defines a "healthy community" and a "healthy economy," her answers were nearly identical. In an effective community "people's needs are met. They're in safe housing. They have access to healthy foods. Access to physical activity, even if it's just safe sidewalks, safe walking opportunities. . . . You know, it's *safe*. Think of the lead issues. And environmental issues, safe as far as the water is safe to drink, the air is safe to breathe. . . . People are supportive of each other" (interview). In a "healthy economy," Dorothy describes later, "I'm not seeing that there isn't any *want*. There's always want, but it would be nice if there wasn't *need*. You know? There are things that people need. Safe housing, good food, you know, a safe environment, opportunities to stay healthy, you know, good medical care" (interview). Community is economy is community, at least when both are "healthy." One could interpret government statistician Kathleen's proposal similarly: "The economy is about how *people* are doing. . . . It all comes down to *people*" (interview).

In these cases, an expanded or blurred socioeconomic domain can easily remain restricted to a particular bounded location: a "society" or a "community," now constituted by a more integrated measure yet nonetheless separated from other societies or communities. One can still speak, here, of Maine's collective, competitive dynamic with other states, and this risks three problems. First, it may reproduce a dimension of the hegemonic articulation by which one place is pitted against another, even if their measures are now "quality of life" rather than simply a rate of GDP growth. Second, it can all too easily erase the complex ethical questions that arise between places in a globally connected sustenance network. This is a key danger (though not an inevitability) of the activist vision of "local economies" that has arisen in Maine and many other places in recent years: a holistic parochialism articulated in what Doreen Massey calls "a hegemonic geography of care and responsibility which takes the form of a nested set of Russian dolls" (2004), with ethical concern strongest at the local level and then dissipating at ever-wider scales. Finally, the continuation of a clearly bounded socioeconomic articulation risks strengthening dangerous neoliberal trends around the devolution of collective responsibility from larger aggregates (most often the state) to "communities" (Rose and Miller 2008), a problematic process that Ash Amin refers to as the "localization of the social" (2005).

But Matthew, an economist focused on forest policy, challenges the tendency to eclipse complex interconnectivity in the name of one's own "place." Referring to a recent controversy over a proposed copper mine in Maine's northernmost county, he observes:

> Environmentalists used this convenient argument: They said, "We're absolutely opposed. We couldn't possibly have a copper mine in Aroostook County. Look at all those copper mines in Bolivia, and how they've wrecked the place." [This] basically says, "Well . . . we're fine with buying all of our copper from the mines in Bolivia, that are wrecking Bolivia. But we will not allow them in our state." This is one of those attitudes that needs a little bit of unpacking. That's the idea: save *my* environment, as long as I can buy my copper or bring my electricity from somewhere else. (interview)

While Matthew did not explicitly rearticulate the social in terms of global connection, this is the implication of his critique of localist environmental politics in Maine. Society can be seen to expand beyond place-bound aggregates of human activity to something more like a *global* aggregate: the social as the interconnectedness of humanity. "To address these big gigantic subject matters like energy, food supply, water supply in the age of a global economy," says Dennis, the alternative energy business owner cited in chapter 5, "you're going to have humans deciding whether they're going to cooperate or if they're going to compete" (interview).

Does society end, then, at the boundaries of humanity? In even the most radical of articulations, this is often the case, for here the diagrammatic boundary between (nonsocial) Nature and (social) Culture is reached. But the economic growth council director Sandra's extension of "quality of life" to include rivers, fish, and other animals gestures toward a radical rupture in this boundary (interview). Dorothy, the community health director, also—even if more indirectly—affirms a kind of more-than-human social ethic:

> EM: One last question. Healthy people, healthy communities: Does that also include other species?
> DOROTHY: Oh yeah! You're talking animals and . . . and, yeah, like pets . . . well, yeah. I mean, we all should live together in harmony [chuckles] and . . . I'm not *thrilled* about hornets by any means, but I won't kill one if I don't have to! [chuckles] . . . I have houseplants that I've had for forty-five

years. . . . And you look at the social factor, how important pets are to
people . . . that *connection*. . . . (interview)

Donna Haraway (2008) would not be surprised to find "companion
species" mediating and challenging the line between the social and the
environmental, opening a door that will then be difficult to close. As
soon as intimate nonhuman cohabitants are brought into the fold of
community, she writes, "the Great Divides of animal/human, nature/
culture, organic/technical, and wild/domesticated flatten into mundane
differences—the kind that have consequences and demand respect and
response" (2008, 15).

What *does* demand response? For Jeff Popke (2009), drawing
together threads from Emmanuel Levinas, Jacques Derrida, Jean-
Luc Nancy, and others, this is the fundamental question of ethical
practice. Rather than encountering a predefined space in which care
is to be enacted, the "community without essence" (Watkin 2007; discussing Nancy 2000) or the "being-in-common" (Nancy 1991) that is
our shared condition of existence calls us to continually ask and struggle over questions of *who* to care for and *how*. "What we deem 'the
social,'" writes Popke, "should thus be seen as an agonistic space of
negotiation over the very meaning and contours of the in-common"
(2009, 18). The social comes to signify, in this articulation, an ever-
open sphere of possible relations to which we might be responsible.[2]
"For me," says Brenda, the nonprofit youth advocate, "I think of community as being, 'What is our interconnectedness?' And that occurs in
all kinds of different ways, not just relationships but through our taxes
and through our commerce and through our . . . So all of that coming together creates community" (interview). Brenda resists a notion
of community or sociality that demands a definition of who is "in" and
who is "out" and instead begins with a fundamental question: "How
do we all be together in that space of community, and *help* each other?"
(interview). In a different but complementary vein, the director of a
statewide community health organization (Grace) suggests that "community" is commonly defined in terms of specific—often marginalized—
groups, as when an outreach effort seeks to encourage "participation
from the community" or get "community voices" involved in decision-
making (interview). But rather than affirming the social as a domain
of the (partially) excluded, Grace aspires to view the definitional dimension of "community" as an ethical and political *tool*: "I sometimes think

community allows you to frame your work in a way that you're being really intentional about the *who* and the *where* and the *why*, like why are we engaging or interacting?" (interview).

The social has now expanded well beyond the bounded, located space of non-economic human activity. As with the economy, such an expansion also constitutes a decomposition away from the very notion of a "domain" toward something much more fluid. Thus I can hear in my interviews a set of articulations that constitute society and community as continual *processes* of negotiation and decision-making. Trevor, the director of a sub-regional planning agency, describes tensions between different visions of economic development in these very terms. Bethel, a small rural town adjacent to a large ski resort, does not have to follow in the footsteps of North Conway, a highly developed and commercialized tourist hub in New Hampshire's White Mountains:

> They have different sets of opportunities to either seize or not seize, depending on what they want to see their community aspire to. Now, that's where community comes in. *It's a decision-making process.* Bethel does not want to be North Conway. Ask them! Now, is North Conway economic development? Yeah. Is that what you want? No. That balance of quality of life, not just place, the quality of life, the experience of people that live in Bethel and whatever they're going to say yes, we want a piece of pie, but we don't want *that* pie. (interview, emphasis added)

Community is formulated here not only as the open question of interdependence but also as the very *process of negotiating* this interdependence and making decisions about the kinds of futures we wish to collectively construct. The social becomes, in the words of the environmental nonprofit director Paula, the very work of imagining and crafting a collective future: "Fundamentally what I think we're trying to do is figure out how we're going to share this planet together, and what are going to be the rules of the game" (interview).

Multiplying the Environment

"What *is* the environment?" I asked. Nora, the environmental nonprofit researcher, described the complexity of the category: "There are a lot of environments," she said. "There's the *natural* environment, the *political* environment, there's the *social* environment. . . . [And] obviously climate change is much bigger than the natural environment, it's the *economic* environment" (interview). For Harold, the economic development consultant, "You have to look at the context; it can mean *built* environment, *political* environment, [or] you know, the *green* environment" (interview). If, in the hegemonic articulation of the previous chapters, the environment was an objective, nonhuman space from which resources can be extracted and amenities mobilized, it now begins to multiply into something nearly unrecognizable. But this decomposition is more complex and strange than that of the economy or society; as the paradigmatic figure of the "outside," the environment cannot *expand* in the same way, adding dimensions like layers of an onion. Its multiplication moves in the other direction: it appears *inside* the very places where it should not be, it appears *everywhere*, and at the very same time it disappears *as an environment* when one tries to actually locate it.

Indeed, for something ostensibly so large, important, and pervasive, "the environment" seems to appear primarily in very small and local forms. When asked to define it, many of the people I spoke with would describe only *particular* challenges, threats, or commitments. Witness Dorothy, the community health director, with a common style of response:

> EM: When you think about the environment, what is that for you?
> DOROTHY: I'm concerned about my neighbors' outside wood boiler, when I can smell plastic burning in it. I'm concerned about the river that used to run clear, now there's a campground with a hundred sites up it, and now it's green. Algae, green, slimy stuff because more and more people are using it. I'm concerned about the person whose culvert keeps washing out and they keep dumping more and more dirt into it and all that gravel is working its way down the river. (interview)

None of Maine's "environmental" organizations, in fact, can truly be said to focus on protecting, conserving, stewarding, or healing an "environment." Everything comes down to a specific project in a specific place, a particular species or watershed, a chemical, a toxic production process, a particular causal chain that leads from a specific human (often industrial) action to a specific harm. Despite its name, the statewide coalition called Environment Maine does not have "the environment" as its object at all, but rather (among other things): a proposed oil pipeline along the shores of Sebago Lake, "130 tracts of land within [Acadia National Park] that are privately owned and at risk of being developed," the Atlantic Salmon population of the Kennebec and Androscoggin Rivers, and the carbon pollution from coal-fired power plants in the midwestern United States (Environment Maine 2014). In Bruno Latour's terms, "it is always *this* invertebrate, *this* branch of a river, *this* rubbish dump or *this* land-use plan which finds itself the subject of concern, protection, criticism or demonstration" (1998, 221).

The environment is, effectively, a "floating signifier" (Laclau 2005, 131) that links together otherwise disparate matters of concern into something that can be articulated as a seeming whole. "The environment as a problem," write Phil Macnaghten and John Urry, "came to be created or 'invented' through issues and politics which were apparently not directly concerned with a single unambiguous environment as such" (1998, 21). As Dana, the director of a statewide environmental organization, describes, "I think [the environment is] a catch-all term for a variety of things. I think it means . . . a *lot* [laughs] the way I would define it. It's our air, our land, our water, our energy future, the health of our families, our healthy food [chuckles]" (interview). The environment as a whole must be produced as such, or, in Dana's self-conscious terms, "captured": "So in this . . . [points to a recent report by her organization] . . . this is the best job that we've done to capture [laughs] . . . *capture* the environment" (interview). But look too closely at this wide-meshed net, and its contents will escape right through the holes.

Even in articulations where "the environment" is taken as an actual object or domain by my interviewees, it appears in places where its presence disrupts altogether possibility of discrete domains. The discourse of "environmental health," located at the intersection of an external context and the intimate space of the human body, is a case in point. As Bradley, the director of a nonprofit conservation collaborative, asks, "Is lead paint an environmental issue or not? Certain environmentalists would say, 'No, that's not the environment.' And yet what could be more 'environment' than the place you live?" (interview). The place one lives—the household—is *not* the environment of the hegemonic articulation, since it is ostensibly a *human* space, a civilized space, an "inside" space of culture as opposed to an "outside" of nature. But when the outside turns out to be *inside*, what does the environment become? What remains that is *not* the environment? Brenda, the nonprofit youth advocate, initially responded to my queries about her organization's approach to "the environment" with a distancing move: "We don't talk about the environment here enough, I think. We don't talk about the natural resources of Maine here, but that is as impactful on children as anything else, as market forces! [chuckles]. Their water, the air that they breathe, their access to food that's locally grown and healthy versus processed" (interview). Yet she quickly caught herself in her own assumptions, stumbling on her words as she spoke: "In terms of the health of children, we don't . . . We've done papers on lead poisoning, but even then, that's man-created poison in the house, rather than out . . . although that's man-created, too, so never mind" (interview). She doesn't work on the environment, since that term indicates an *outside*; but she *does* work on lead poisoning, which is about an *inside*. Perhaps it is the *source* of the poisoning that makes something "environmental"? Thus creation by humans would indicate a social problem and creation by nonhumans would be environmental. Yet environmental problems on the "outside" are precisely problems *created by humans*! (Is an earthquake an "environmental problem"?) Brenda found herself in a mire of circular definitions, the sum total of which seemed to indicate that "the environment" might, in fact, be *everywhere*, and thus already a concern of her "social" organization despite the lack of overt recognition.

The inclusion of human health in "the environment" can also be awkward for conventional environmental organizations. Elizabeth, the environmental nonprofit policy advocate, describes her organization's move *away* from a focus on toxic accumulations in human bodies:

> One of the things that we've struggled with is human health. Because historically we didn't really do a lot of human-health-related things. And then in our toxics project, we did get into issues that, while they have what I would call environmental impacts, the primary impacts are human health issues. . . . But at this point in time we're saying to ourselves, well, there are other groups that focus primarily or exclusively on human health, and maybe this is the time for us to shift some of our resources from something that's purely a human health issue to something that seems to have more interaction with the environment. (interview)

It is difficult to decide: are toxins adequately "environmental"? Is the environment about nonhumans or about humans? If it is about both, then what does the term even *mean*? The Maine Environmental Priorities Coalition's *Investing in Maine's Environment* report (Kelley 2010) is awkward when it attempts to place the goal of "healthy people" amid a discursive context in which "the environment" has been defined primarily as a production-oriented resource and an aesthetically pleasing amenity. The text carries us, without transition, from the goal of "maintaining our solid roots in the beautiful environment we call home" (2010, 2) to the disturbing revelation that "too many Maine babies are born polluted from toxic chemicals" (2010, 3). Can we have it both ways? The very nature of the environment shifts in these pages: it was our paradise; now it is the poison inside of us. It was the nonhuman world beyond us; now, since "environment-related chronic disease" is a product of "toxic chemicals . . . found in workplaces and community environments" (2010, 4), it is a product of human beings. The environment is what we (some of "us" more than others) have wrought.

The internalized environment blurs into the very tissue of the human body, for the environment as a source of lead and other toxins is an environment that exists for humans only in its active *circulation*. Lead in raw form, buried as ore in the ground and interacting with no human, is not the environment. Lead mixed into a matrix of paint on an old windowsill, peeling, flaking, entering bodies and lodging itself there: *this* is the environment. This environment is what we breathe and what we eat, and since breathing and eating are acts of intimate ingestion—in which air and food enter us and touch us from the inside—the environment is inevitably located *within* our bodies. Humans make "the environment," eat "the environment," and *are* "the environment." What is *not* the environment?

This confusing tangle of articulations can be approached from another angle. In my conversation with the environmental activist David, the environment was initially described as "the place that all living things reside, this planet" (interview). Here we see a conventional sense of environment as a bounded space. This space is, moreover, the source of all sustenance: "I think that every organism needs to utilize the environment in order to survive" (interview). The environment might still be constituted here as a passive resource, a singular domain of "stuff" relative to a world of self-preserving organisms. But David's next statement seemed to pull the rug out from any hegemonic stability: "Whether you're a fungus in the soil or you're a human being, you're going to alter the environment in order to survive" (interview). For a human, the fungus in the soil is "the environment," one element of that which is necessary for survival, and one element that will be inevitably altered by the work of making a living (at least under any agricultural regime of subsistence). For a fungus, the *human* might be "the environment," as one dimension of the space of subsistence that must be navigated and negotiated, perhaps even altered. If all living beings thus alter "the environment," then this term can refer only to the entirety of complex interpenetrating processes of life-negotiation through which all "insides" and "outsides" are constituted relative to others. Far from being the "place" where "all living things reside" (interview), the environment in its absolute sense names the very *process* of this residence and the sum total of its ongoing effects. In its relative sense, the environment is—for humans or any other organism—that which we use and alter and that which uses and alters *us*. "There is no environment as such," writes Timothy Morton, quoting Darwin. "It's all 'distinct organic beings'" (2010, 60).

The environment opens here into what Morton calls "the ecological thought" (2010). With whom is our fate interdependent? "Who or what is interconnected with what or with whom?" (2010, 15). The ecological thought is the notion—terrifying when taken seriously—that *everything is connected to everything else.* "The ecological thought surpasses what passes for environmentalism," proposes Morton (2010, 3), because it destabilizes "the environment" as a domain of resources and amenities and indicates, instead, a set of complex and unsettling questions about what it means to be alive with others in an interconnected pluriverse. Latour makes a similar move when he defines "ecology" not as a science of certainty, but as a site of radical questioning. Ecology "does not know what makes and does not make up a system. It does not know what is and is not connected" (1998, 228). A Maine ecologist affirmed this definition, suggesting that ecology is the very *opposite* of the identification of the "laws" of nature:

> There's too many interacting factors, and they are never the same in every place. And ones that you think might not be that important send a trajectory off this way—a different species, a different history, a different geology, a different precipitation—and all of a sudden it doesn't work that way anymore. . . . The details really matter. You can't specify a couple of things [and say], "*That* governs everything." (Greg, interview)

Dennis, the business owner, describes the immensity of the *experience* of this kind of ecology: "When you turn the ignition on an internal combustion engine, you impact every human on the planet. When you have a child, you do the same thing" (interview). Economy, society, and environment all collapse here into a space of questions. This complexity, as Latour points out, "suspends our certainties with regard to the sovereign good of human and non-human beings, of ends and means"

(1998, 228). It opens a radical space of *ethics*: "The ecological thought," writes Morton, "thinks big and joins the dots. It comes as close as possible to the strange stranger, generating care and concern for beings, no matter how uncertain we are of their identity, no matter how afraid we are of their existence" (2010, 19). This destabilization of certainties and solidities is radically different than the deterritorializing forces of Capital and State described in chapter 4. Rather than rendering a world in which "all that is solid melts into air" (Marx and Engels 2012), the environment in the form of the ecological thought suggests that all that is solid may in fact be *connected* to air in ways that we can barely imagine.

Into the Fog Bank

In *The Natural Contract*, Michel Serres describes a painting by Goya in which "a pair of enemies brandishing sticks is fighting in the midst of a patch of quicksand" (1995, 1). While the viewer's initial focus may be drawn to the combatants—the obvious "agents" of the image— a third party asserts itself. "We can identify a third position outside their squabble: the marsh into which the struggle is sinking" (1995, 1). This marsh, for Serres, is that which we sometimes call "nature," and sometimes "the environment." But it is not the hegemonic version of these terms, neither the force of law that settles all disputes nor the domain to be managed. It is something wilder and much more dangerous, and it appears among, between, and beneath the duo of economy and society to foreshadow their potential end. It is what "environmentalism," in its most powerful forms, has tried to address even as it has often been thwarted by its own framing. *Something asserts itself*, without ever becoming sovereign, that demands new kinds of attention. I only hinted at it in the genealogy of chapter 1: while various articulations of economy, society, and environment circulated from the nineteenth century on, the *trio itself* was not born until the beginning of the end of the twentieth century. It was the crisis-inspired emergence of "the environment" as a generalized and politicized domain in the late 1960s that produced the full shape of today's hegemonic problem-space, and it was this emergence that simultaneously signaled its limits. The environment is a "third wheel" added to the dysfunctional couple of economy and society that triggers a desperate attempt toward domestication (call it "sustainable development") while at the same time destabilizing the whole configuration.

The hegemonic trio, produced by the addition of the environment, is thus at once a marker of modernity's diagram of power and a gravestone marking its imminent end. There can be no "harmonization," "integration," or "balancing" of economy, society, and environment, since the trio's first term (economy) is hell-bent on proliferating connections while denying interdependence and its third term (environment) will always threaten to break the entire configuration into an indefinite set of ethical questions about cause and effect, interdependence, and responsibility. This is not a "dialectic," it's a *mess*.[3] And if it is "the environment" that appears to mark the kinds of collective concerns that circulate at the emergence of the so-called Anthropocene, this is not because the parochial (albeit universalized) images of "nature" perpetuated by European colonizers have reached ascendancy in the collective consciousness, but rather because widespread recognitions of interdependence have undermined the viability of such images in favor of radical openings to the ethics of being-in-common (Roelvink and Gibson-Graham 2009; Gibson-Graham 2011).

If confronting such complexity is unsettling, and productive of more confusion than clarity, this is precisely the point. I have intended to show in this and the previous chapter that the hegemonic articulation of economy, society, and environment is only one particularly potent reality that coexists with—and is, in fact, continually challenged and threatened by—a multiplicity of hesitations, cracks, and proliferations that emerge from its very heart. The multiplication of *economy* blurs this domain from market exchange to human provisioning and into the indefinite zone of all that constitutes and sustains life. The multiplication of *society* blurs from a non-economic space of relation into the open question of interdependence—the very place where the *environment* as "the ecological thought" also takes us. Are we left with nothing but fog? And is there any point in redrawing these lines? One could say, for example, that economy should be defined in its broadest sense as humanity's "interchange with [its] natural and social environment, in so far as this results in supplying . . . the means of material want satisfaction" (Polanyi 1992, 29). But why the line between the material and the immaterial? Since when has human need, which clearly includes more than material dimensions, been truly captured by such a distinction? Perhaps, then, economy should signify any activity or process that meets human needs, in whatever form. But where is *this* line drawn? Are geologic processes not then included? Is economy the space of human *agency* acting to meet these needs? Is an incapacitated elder receiving care from younger generations not then excluded from the economic? Have we then returned to the social as the economic abject? Such lines of questioning could go on, and could follow the threads of possible alternative articulations of society and environment well. In all of these cases, we will find ourselves continually both *inside* and *outside* the very categories we had been trying to define the others against.

What, then, *remains* of economy, society, and environment? What *should* remain? Eric, the regional development economist, suggests a provocative image: "We draw neat little Venn diagrams that imply that the boundaries are crisp and clean," he describes, "but in fact it would probably be more accurate to say that you have *three fog banks of different densities colliding with one another*" (interview, emphasis added). Economy, society, and environment are no longer stable domains with defined boundaries but diffused clouds of intensity, clusters of wild particles converging, mixing, combining, diverging. When fog banks collide, what is left of each bank? Are we not faced with a *single cloud*, a nebula, itself demarcated from the surrounding air only by diffuse gradients? Environment becomes society becomes economy, and back again, their shapes merging, breaking, and shifting like wraiths in the mist. The question of what to *do* in such a nebulous and unsettling place—of what we might strategically make and remake of this daunting mess—is what the final part of this book will begin to pursue.

Part IV. (Re)composing Livelihoods

The problem . . . is not to put up bridges between already fully
constituted and fully delimited domains, but to put in place new
theoretical and practical machines, capable of sweeping away the
old stratifications, and of establishing the condition for a new
exercise of desire.

—Félix Guattari, *Chaosophy*

MY TASK NOW IS TO STEP into the space of converging fog banks and
compose something new from the "continuum of intensities" (Deleuze
and Guattari 1987, 70) into which the hegemonic trio is continually
decomposed. It is crucial that this fog bank image not be reduced to
one of simple blurring and confusion, to a mess that must be contained
or cleaned up, and certainly not to an undifferentiated "whole" in which
difference blurs into a seamless unity. Gilles Deleuze and Félix Guattari provide a different figure for thinking and encountering the fog
bank, namely the "body without organs" or "BwO" (1987, 153). Closely
related to the "virtual," the concept of the BwO is another strategy for
refusing a reductive ontology of *being* and the inevitability of whatever *is* in the world, in favor of an ontology of *becoming*—without, that
is, also rejecting the possibility of new forms of stabilization. If "organs"
are understood as discrete zones of ordering and territorialization that
render a body into an organism, an identity, or a subject, then the BwO
is the virtual zone of endless becoming that simultaneously renders all
forms of organization possible and continually threatens them to the
core. The BwO is always *virtually* present at the heart of every assemblage, yet can never be encountered as such since its virtuality is always
actualized in particular form. At the same time, its presence forms the

condition of possibility for the transformation and becoming-otherwise of all assemblages. The BwO is the limit of all diagrams, the zone at which diagrams come undone and open toward other configurations. As a strategic ontological figure of thought, the BwO reminds us that the assemblages of the present are only one possible way that reality can be composed and that other possibilities—including deep diagrammatic transformations—await actualization "below the surface," so to speak, of any given formation.

If the fog bank of chapter 6 is viewed as a BwO, then it no longer has to appear as a zone of pure confusion, a space that might otherwise evoke the panic that so often accompanies radical destabilization.[1] Indeed, as much as Deleuze and Guattari would see the movement toward the BwO as a precondition of revolutionary transformation, the point is never to finally reach it or to dwell eternally in its movement of "absolute deterritorialization" (1987, 55). Rather, to "become a body without organs" is to learn to experiment continually with what the presence of the BwO might enable to emerge anew. "Dismantling the organism," they write, "has never meant killing yourself, but rather opening the body to connections that presuppose an entire assemblage, circuits, conjunctions, levels and thresholds, passages and distributions of intensity" (1987, 160). The fog bank as BwO thus designates a zone of virtual affirmation, a movement toward other possible modes of becoming, and a site for careful, collective experimentation. I say *careful* because there is nothing inherently liberating about the BwO. One must actively work to craft the new that emerges, and to side with some emergences over others. We need to move beyond (or, perhaps, more accurately *through*) the Nietzschean imperative to "push that which is falling." If the categories of the hegemonic articulation are in crisis, and if our task is, in part, to amplify this crisis, then we must also be committed to the work of actively affirming new possibilities that emerge from the space of dissolution (Braidotti 2013).[2] What can be (re)composed from the fog bank? How might we follow fruitful lines of flight, connect with others along the way, hold on to just enough of the old that the new may be made more viable, and at the same time experiment with innovative articulations toward new politics and new forms of life?[3]

7 ECOPOIESIS

Making Habitats and Inhabitants

Composing the Oikos

Let us face the fog bank. To experience the dissolution of powerful articulations into a space of molecular becoming—a space of the very question of how we might live together and who "we" in fact might be or become—is to be definitively reminded that there is no economy, society, or environment to be negotiated or struggled over unless and to the extent that these categories have been *produced* as components of a particular assemblage. I have not intended to imply that the hegemonic trio is "actually" false, nonexistent, or unimportant, but rather that it must be seen as one constellation of (particularly powerful) articulations among many that are continually emerging and becoming-undone relative to a virtual zone of potential. When one advocates for economy, society, or environment, it is not a struggle on behalf of already-unified domains but rather a struggle *to compose* such domains as unities. One does not begin with the categories of the trio, but rather *ends up* with them if, and only if, a particular articulatory process is successful. Economy, society, and environment are, in fact, particular ways of *composing habitat(s)* for (certain) humans and for more-than-human others.

While I have thus far used the language of the "articulation of assemblages" to designate processes of composition, I can now speak more precisely and name the process by which particular modes of life are actualized from the fog bank as *ecopoiesis*. The *eco* is derived from the Greek *oikos*, variously translated as "house," "household," or "habitat," and serves as the common root of both economy and ecology. The term *poiesis* (also from the Greek) refers to the ongoing making of worlds, the process of "creation and ontological genesis" (Castoriadis 1998, 3). "Ecopoiesis" was first used as a term by astrobiologists (e.g., Lovelock 1987; Haynes 1990) to refer to the purposeful construction of viable habitat for terrestrial life on other planets, and I expand its meaning to indicate more generally the multidimensional composition of life and its conditions of viability wherever these may emerge.[1] Similar in spirit to Jason Moore's concept of the *oikeion*, focusing analysis on the "relation of life making" and refusing any a priori conceptual separation between "humanity" and "nature" (2015, 8), ecopoiesis names the process by which habitats and their inhabitants are coproduced (see also Grinspoon 2016, 75).[2]

The term may, at first glance, appear to resonate with Humberto Maturana and Francisco Varela's (1980) notion of "autopoiesis," in which porously bounded dynamic living systems transform flows of energy, matter, and meaning to continually produce and conserve their own internal organization.[3] I will discuss this concept appreciatively in chapter 9, but here it is crucial to clarify that ecopoiesis does not name such a "system dynamic." There are, in fact, no "ecopoietic systems," as if a system could preexist its ontological composition. There is, rather, an ecopoiesis *from which all systems—and their failures—emerge*. Ecopoiesis is characterized neither by boundaries or their absence, for it is the very *question* of the composition of such closing and opening that it seeks to address. It thus aims to continually shift the emphasis from product to process, and to the potentials that creation might open or close.

If *poiesis* is about creative *becoming*, then *oikos* is about *belonging*.[4] Ecopoiesis, we might say, is the becoming of belonging.[5] This belonging, this notion of habitat, should not be confused with anything resembling an external "environment," a passive "context," a fixed locale or resource pool, or a community consisting of a stable essence. Habitat, as I intend it here, names the web of constitutive interrelationships from which assemblages—communities, regions, institutions, concepts, families, individuals—emerge as singularities and which these assemblages, in turn, participate in composing. "Living beings," writes Brett Buchanan, "do not simply 'have' milieus as a location in which they live, but *are* a composition of these milieus" (2008, 175). Contrary to some of its common mobilizations in ecological science (e.g., Kearney 2006), I conceptualize habitat as a *relational* rather than a location-specific category.[6] It is not simply the collection of resources, in a particular place, that an entity needs for sustenance; it is the web of constitutive relations—always translocal and trans-temporal—that make a given life possible. In Gilles Deleuze and Félix Guattari's terms, we "cease to be subjects [and] become *events*, in assemblages that are inseparable from an hour, a season, an atmo-sphere, an air, a life. . . . Climate, wind, season, hour are not of another nature than the things, animals, or people that populate them, follow them, sleep and awaken within them" (1987, 263).

It is important not to render this interdependence of habitat and inhabitant in terms of a simple unity or even a codetermination. The relation is much more complex, and thus difficult to describe and to think: in one sense, "we" are nothing but the ongoing, emergent effect of particular actualizations of an *oikos*. As Bruno Latour writes: "What would a human be without elephants, plants, lions, cereals, oceans, ozone, or plankton? A human alone, much more alone even than Rob-inson Crusoe on his island. Less than a human. Certainly not a human" (1998, 230). At the same time, particular habitats make possible new forms of identity and action. An emergent assemblage thus becomes active *in* and *as* its own habitat, participating in the very relations that make this participation possible, and at times (sometimes radically) transforming them (Odling-Smee 1996). The hegemonic trio, as one constellation of ecopoietic articulations, makes us (partly) who we are and presides over the emergence of particular forms of agency, subjec-tivity, and imagination that (again, in part) continually affirm and sus-tain this habitat.

This notion of *oikos* shares some affinities with Jakob von Uexküll's early twentieth-century concept of *umwelt* (Uexküll 2010), which has seen a recent revival among biosemioticians (e.g., Hoffmeyer 1996; Sebeok 2001). Uexküll's ambition was to shift from a biology that viewed organisms as machinelike objects to be studied from the "outside," toward a "biology of subjects" (A. Weber 2010) in which liv-ing beings would be understood to co-compose their own worlds of significance. The *umwelt* is the totality of that which living subjects perceive and produce (Uexküll 2010, 42), the habitat within which they find themselves, which constitutes their sphere of agency, and which they, in turn, continually construct. The *poiesis* of *umwelt* is not just a matter of perception, but unfolds via a double "pincer move-ment" between the ascription of meaning and the enactment of mate-rial effects (Uexküll 2010, 48–49). The structure of the eye and the visualizations it is capable of producing, for example, are just as crucial as the significance such effects are given by perception. Each organism—and more important for Uexküll, each species—composes its own unique *umwelt* within which life unfolds. *Umwelt*, like *oikos*, is entirely relative to that which composes it and is, in turn, composed by it. This is a radical inversion of the notion of an "external environment," where externality is now constituted only in relation to a particular, embodied subjective center. There are as many environments as there are beings capable of engaging and composing meaningful worlds.

I diverge from Uexküll, however, on two key fronts. First, as an unrepentant Kantian (Deely 2004), Uexküll maintains a strong divide between the subjective and the objective, and poses a world of inaccessible and passively constitutive objects as distinct from worlds of action and meaning. "The object only takes part in . . . action," he writes, "to the extent that it must possess the necessary properties [to enable this action]" (2010, 49). This is a problematic distinction that only serves to amplify the hegemonic diagram. I do not know what "objects" can or cannot do, where the line between subjects and objects—if any— might lie, and what active role nonliving entities might play in the action of world-making. I resonate with the "vital materialism" of Jane Bennett (2010), in which the "pluriverse is traversed by heterogeneities that are continually doing things," and which seeks to "chasten . . . fantasies of human mastery, highlight the common materiality of all that is, expose a wider distribution of agency, and reshape the self and its interests" (2010, 122). The *poiesis* of habitat is never simply an act of subjects upon objects, but rather the very materialization of such a possibility in and through an agential field of forces that is always not-yet fully or finally decided.

My second divergence (in this case more qualified than the first) is in regard to the relation between *umwelten*. At some key moments in Uexküll's work, subjective worlds are figured in fundamental isolation from one another, each *umwelt* constituting a kind of self-enclosed phenomenological sphere cut off from access to a noumenal world beyond. A key image is that of a soap bubble: "The birds that flutter about, the squirrels hopping from branch to branch, or the cows grazing in the meadow, all remain permanently enclosed in the bubble that encloses their space" (Uexküll 2010, 69). While these bubbles can coexist in the same objective space—for example, in a field in which flowers (as objects) can enter into multiple *umwelten* in distinct and incommensurate ways—they cannot fundamentally overlap or meet. Each being or species, even while co-evolutionarily entwined, is cut off from others by a wall of subjectivity, and we thus move from the modernist image of a single world to a prefiguratively postmodern image of a proliferation of isolated worlds that cannot communicate.

Deleuze and Guattari, who draw on Uexküll in a variety of ways, counter this isolationist tendency by highlighting and transforming another of the biologist's images: *umwelten* as relational compositions of *point and counterpoint* (Uexküll 2010, 190). Invoking a musical metaphor, Uexküll bursts his own soap bubble image by proposing a mode of inter-*umwelten* "communication" in the form of a dynamic, embodied evolutionary dance between mutually co-constitutive beings: "The fly-likeness of the spider means that it has taken up certain motifs of the fly melody in its bodily composition" (2010, 191). In the hands of Deleuze and Guattari, this means that *umwelten* are never isolated but in fact are always emergent in/as processes of inter-becoming (1987, 314). This relationality must extend to the coproduction of subjectivity itself as an emergent property of relationship. Habitat is composed *as* the habitat of a particular being, a species, a community (or any other singularity), but also via the ways in which this being is continually territorialized and deterritorialized in relation with other beings and other habitats. Ecopoiesis is never the *poiesis* of a single *oikos*, but rather the ongoing, negotiated, agonistic co-composition of multiple habitats and their inhabitants.

Ecopoiesis beyond the Trio

What difference, in practice, does the concept of ecopoiesis make? First and foremost, it serves as conceptual tool to bring focus to the *processes* of composing habitat without already deciding on their outcomes (e.g., economy, society, and environment). It thus names, in one sense, the space of ontological politics where the materialization of habitat plays out—the myriad practices of language, representation, corporeal expression and assembly, quantitative and qualitative transformation, adaptive and dynamic response, and evolutionary negotiation that compose the *oikoi* of particular beings and communities. Returning to my conversations in Maine, I can reread hesitations, uncertainties, and acknowledgments of contingency and construction as sites of ecopoietic opening and contestation. Far from simply being "economic developers," "social workers," and "environmental advocates," my interviewees are active agents in ecopoiesis, composing and decomposing various forms of habitat that are not wholly reducible to the hegemonic trio. "Economic" developers continually (often to their chagrin) navigate and intervene in the dynamics of wetland hydrology, songbird nesting, predator ranges, climate regulation, and more. "Social" workers, meanwhile, confront questions about the importance of companion species, the need to expose children to the "natural world," and the ways in which the sustenance of some Maine people depends on the well-being of the deer they hunt for food. Environmentalists seeking to enact non-instrumental solidarity with nonhuman species always find themselves in the midst of struggles over the habitats of fellow humans. What kinds of conversations and transformations might open if all of these professionals were to recognize themselves as habitat-makers, as people participating not only in responding to the dynamics of preexisting domains but in fact working (along with many other forces) to produce particular habitats in which some forms of life are enabled and others rendered impossible?

This question points toward a second implication of ecopoiesis. The problem-space of the hegemonic trio and the modern diagram of power constrains us to developing "practical solutions" to apparent challenges, the nature of which remain themselves unchallenged. There is a field of *practicality* that corresponds to the field of *hegemony*, and this renders a whole host of possibilities apparently "impractical." The perspective of ecopoiesis challenges us to ask about the very conditions of possibility that undergird a given problem-space and its practical solutions. What new forms of practicality might a different *oikos* make possible? Ecopoiesis here serves as a tool for sensitizing us to the ethico-political stakes of what Isabelle Stengers (2005b) calls an "etho-ecology." For Stengers, one cannot separate the *ethos*, "the way of behaving particular to a being," from this being's *oikos*, "the habitat of that being and the way in which that habitat satisfies or opposes the demands associated with the ethos or affords opportunities for an original ethos to risk itself" (2005b, 997).[7]

If Maine's policy professionals cannot wholly break out of the hegemonic formation they also resist, this is not simply because of a lack of "will," of "consciousness," or of "courage" on their part, but because the particular etho-ecology within which they subsist has rendered deviations from hegemony profoundly difficult. One would have to risk what one *is*—and thus risk a certain form of extinction—to go against one's habitat. The political question, then, becomes not simply that of cultivating courage and dissent but also of *constituting different habitats* in which other forms of action and relation become more possible. This entails experimentation with transformations of both inhabitants and habitats, engaging the generative capacities of cohabitation, and asking questions of what particular relationalities can *do*: "We can never know," writes Stengers, echoing Deleuze's reading of Spinoza, "what a being is capable of or can become capable of" (2005b, 997). And neither can we know what a habitat is capable of being or becoming. Focusing on the becoming of various modes of belonging, on ecopoiesis and its constitutive effects, is a way of sustaining an attentiveness not only to that which sustains "us" (whoever that may be) but also to that which we have not yet become and to the always-emerging conditions of possibility for cultivating such becoming.

Ecopoiesis, finally, enables a crucial and related move in the realm of critical and performative scholarship. As I noted in chapter 1, various scholars have worked to trace the historical and ongoing production of particular hegemonic categories, and Koray Çaliskan and Michel Callon's "economization" approach (2009, 2010) is a prime example. These are crucial interventions that challenge the seeming-inevitability and self-evidence of hegemonic categories and thus open space for their contestation and transformation. Callon, for one, certainly intends for his work to help "produce the conditions in which new emerging forces are offered the possibility of becoming stronger [and] to limit the grip of established forces" (2005, 18). By itself, however, a tracing of the ongoing composition of hegemonic categories runs a profound risk: focusing on economy, society, and environment—even as verbs rather than nouns—may performatively reaffirm that which it purports to call into question. "We must ask ourselves," cautions Michel Foucault with regard to all such genealogical strategies, "what purpose is ultimately served by this suspension of all the accepted unities, if, in the end, we return to the unities that we pretended to question at the outset" (2007b, 28). In seeking an "economy," for example, the economization approach will always find one. Or it will find many. In either case, it risks tacitly reinforcing the problematic assumption that the composition of habitat does (and perhaps must) take the ultimate form of an "economy." This is clearly not the case.

The key to fulfilling the transformative aspirations of such genea-logical approaches, I believe, is to remain vigilantly clear that econo-mization, socialization, and environmentalization are only particular and partial *instances* of an ecopoiesis that always exceeds them. This is distinct from Callon's (1998) argument, elaborated in chap-ter 3, that economization proceeds by a "framing and overflowing." Ecopoiesis draws attention not to the constitutive overflow *of* the frame, but rather toward the virtual molecularities and the actualized becomings-otherwise that escape and constitute the frame/overflow system altogether. It is to recognize—and to encourage a vigilance in remembering—that there are always multiple articulations of collective life that escape the grip of the hegemonic formations that genealogy traces, and even more articulations "waiting," virtually, to be actualized.

Ethical Negotiation(s)

What, then, might we make of these lines of flight? This much should be clear: standing amid the fog bank of colliding intensities, in the space where the voices of Maine's economic, social, and environmental pro-fessionals fracture, multiply, and dissolve the hegemonic categories, we encounter a set of diverse and complex ethico-political questions about what it means to be alive with others to whom we are connected and to whom we are responsible, what such responsibility might mean, and who this "we," in fact, *is* and might *become*. To reiterate the pow-erful summary offered by the environmental nonprofit director Paula: "Fundamentally what I think we're trying to do is figure out *how we're going to share this planet together, and what are going to be the rules of the game*" (interview, emphasis added). Far from being the place where all meaning is lost, where differences are dissolved, and where possibilities end, the fog bank is the fertile space of ecopoiesis from which everything (potentially) multiplies and opens. Recalling the mul-tiplications of chapter 6 that expanded ever-outward, we find that at the "end" of the economy we arrive at the broad and open question of what sustains human and more-than-human life; that at the "end" of the social we arrive at the ethical question of our interdependence with others and its implications; and that the "end" of the environment car-ries us to this very same interconnectedness, only placed into a context well beyond the domain of the human and rendered radically con-tingent and complex. What remains is not a zone of confusion, but a proliferation of specific ethical questions and struggles that the articulation of economy, society, and environment often serves only to contain, obscure, or domesticate.

What are these struggles? They are negotiations over specific attachments between humans and other species, humans and particular forms of life and habit, humans and particular places; over different frames and experiences of time; over different desires and aspirations; over clashing values and regimes of care; over questions of measurement and (in)commensurability; over which constituencies may appear as legitimate participants in a given struggle; over the structure and implementation of decision-making processes; over different "geographies of responsibility" (Massey 2004), the scope and scale of the places people are ethically connected with; over clashing notions of causality and connection; over languages and styles of articulation; over differential power relations composed my multiple patterns of inequality and oppression. And there are more. I will illustrate and elaborate a number of these in chapter 10. For now, it is sufficient to say that amid this proliferation we leave the space of the hegemonic articulation and enter the space of *ethical negotiation*.

I define "ethical negotiation" as all the ways in which questions of belonging—of the composition and coexistence of habitats and their inhabitants—are negotiated, struggled over, and provisionally answered (for better or worse) by vulnerable, mutually exposed beings. I draw this term specifically from the work of J. K. Gibson-Graham and her elaboration of the concept of "community economy" (2006a). Despite its construction from two keywords that I have thus far associated with the hegemonic assemblage, community economy in the hands of Gibson-Graham and her collaborators is a radical resignification, a transversal articulation that cuts across and through the conventional categories it invokes. First, the term "economy" here does not signify a domain, a system, or a force, but rather suggests an open and contested site "emptied of any essential identity, logic, organizing principle, or determinant" (Cameron and Gibson-Graham 2003, 152). Stretched as far as the term can go without breaking entirely, "economy" becomes little more than the site of struggle over the *question* of how collective and individual life is—and might be—sustained. "Community" refers to the "sociality and interdependence" (Gibson-Graham 2006a, 83) in and through which such sustenance takes place. Gibson-Graham resists the positive determinations—essence, identity, locality, shared values, or traditions—that are often associated with community, drawing instead on Jean-Luc Nancy's (1991) theorization of an "inoperative community," a minimal ontological being-in-common that refuses reduction to a common-being. Community is nothing more or less than the exposure of beings to each other and to each other's finitude, the inescapable sociality that precedes and renders possible all existence.

Community economy is the ethical negotiation of livelihood amid "the sociality of all relations" (Gibson-Graham 2006a, 82).[8] More verb than noun, it names the specificities of dynamic encounter through which myriad interdependent beings negotiate the appropriation, production, circulation, and use of the means of life—the fraught, fragile, and fertile "commerce of being-in-common" (Nancy 2000, 74). Exactly how this negotiation is to be accomplished cannot be specified beforehand; only the dynamic of negotiation itself can be named. As Gibson-Graham describes, "what interdependence might mean, how it might look in any particular setting . . . are not questions [we] can answer in the abstract" (2005, 121). Community economy is a vague and open term because it names that which can never be generalized: the particular, local, "minor" negotiations of collective life that escape full capture by the hegemonic trio.

This specificity is what Nora, an environmental nonprofit researcher, intuits when she says that the environment can never be reduced to one thing because "there are lots of environments"; and, moreover, she reflects, "I'm not sure there's just one economy, either" (interview). Nora sees, instead, a multiplicity of distinctions and dynamics: not only does it depend on the locality and the specific actors involved, but "there's short-term and long-term. There's with externalities, without externalities. There's direct and indirect costs . . . there's going to be a different answer based on whose ox is being gored" (interview). Is building a pipeline to transport Canadian tar sands oil through southern Maine, she asks, good for "the economy"? It is good for the bottom line of some, and potentially destructive to the livelihoods of many others: "It's a question of winners and losers" (interview). "The economy" does little more, from this minoritizing perspective, than cover up the specificities of ethical negotiation.

While this formulation of community economy may be purposefully open, it is by no means a neutral description. At the core of Gibson-Graham's articulation of community economy is what can be called a "meta-normative" ethical demand: a call for the *exposure of exposure*, the imperative to render explicit the contours and stakes of the already-present being-in-common with others that makes our lives possible (Miller 2013b). Gibson-Graham resists any kind of specified *morality*—a list of things that we all "should" do or be—while at the same time calling for a commitment to the ongoing opening of *ethical* negotiation. There is, in particular, "a truly salient distinction . . . between whether interdependence is *recognized and acted upon* or whether it is *obscured or perhaps denied*" (2006a, 84, emphasis added).[9] Community economy names, therefore, not simply *any* space of interdependence and interaction but specifically those spaces in which the ethical dynamics of sociality have in some way been opened for negotiation, contestation, and transformation. How will we live together? Who counts as part of the in-common that "we" are composing and that, in turn, composes this "we"? What relations are rendered invisible or seemingly immune to contestation and change, and what relations are enabled to become sites of creative experimentation and articulation? Community economy is the mutual exposure of and to such questions.

By "exposure," I do not mean to imply privileged access to an underlying "reality" (*the Truth, at last, revealed!*); instead, I draw on the word's other valences: the way one is exposed to new events or experiences, exposed to the queries and demands of others, or perhaps exposed to harsh weather (one can even *die of exposure*). Exposure is not revelation, but *vulnerability*—the becoming-open that might ultimately force one to become otherwise. It is the very opposite of what Stengers calls "anesthetics" (2005b, 997), that is, the composition of an *oikos* in which encounters that might render one vulnerable to transformation are cut off through various modes of distancing.[10] Ethical negotiation is about exposure in the sense of an anti-anesthetics, the ongoing composition of etho-ecologies that refuse easy closures, majoritarian generalizations, and categorical predeterminations. It is in this sense that ethical negotiation names a whole array of ecopoietic relations and dynamics beyond the major molarities of economy, society, and environment. These are dynamics that some of my interviewees are already engaging.

Harriet, for example, the director of a statewide rural development network, describes her "economic development" work in terms of a grassroots, democratic process—an ethical praxis. "We want the community to own the economy, if that's possible," she says, at the same time refusing to give this "economy" any systemic integrity. For her, development cannot mean the alignment of community strategy with the demands of an abstracted economy, but must be a process through which "the community decide[s] what it wants to accomplish, and then you try and figure out how can we gauge where we are now and where we should go" (interview). Harriet and her coworkers are not compelled by a demand for competition or for more jobs at all costs: "It is about jobs, or is it about well-being and sufficient wherewithal to take care of yourself? What would you rather have—more jobs, or *enough* where you can enjoy your life?" (interview). She does not suggest that anything is possible, but rather shifts the emphasis of action from pre-determination by constraints to an exploration of possibilities based on democratically articulated need and vision—on ethical negotiation. If the economic has been hegemonically associated with a singular notion of quantitative "value," it now becomes the space of *values* (broadly understood) where individual and collective needs and aspirations are brought together in the form of collaborations or clashes. "There *is* conflict," says Dana, the director of an environmental non-profit, but she suggests that it is not between an "environment" and an "economy" per se. It is, rather, "between different values and priorities" (interview).

Breaking the "Golden Orbs of Value"

Gibson-Graham's radical theorization of community economy calls for a radical democratization of ecopoiesis, the creation of "acknowledged space[s] of social interdependency and self-formation . . . unmapped and uncertain terrain[s] that call forth exploratory conversation and political/ethical acts of decision" (2006a, 166). Such an approach is exemplified by an interviewee whom I have refrained from discussing thus far because her discourse and work challenge and escape even a multiplication of hegemonic categories. At the time of our interview, Irene was working for a statewide conservation organization, but her previous work included a significant stint in state government where she served—effectively, even if not officially—as a mediator, a *negotiator*, between parties involved in classic "economy versus environment" conflicts. For Irene, the core categories of the hegemonic articulation have little or no purchase: "I don't think 'economy, community, and environment.' It's my *life*. These are the things I care about, and they all mean a lot to me and I try to hold them all together at the same time when I do my work" (interview). It may be the case, suggests Irene, that people involved in various conflicts accept these categories and mobilize them in the process, but this is often only a problematic diversion from the crucial work of creative and transformative engagement. Responding affirmatively to my suggestion that the categories are frequently used to appeal to "laws of nature" (in various forms), Irene elaborates:

> People will use the economy as this sacred thing to close down a conversation, "Oh we can't do that." And likewise, the environmental community says, "Oh we can't do that, it would hurt the environment." And those are like these golden orbs of value that we can't hurt. That's the language. We have affinity to one or the other, more than the other. . . . [But] if we can avoid, at the outset, putting up one of those golden orbs of value, and focus less on the great value of the environment or the economy, not immediately say, "Well, this is about the environment, and this is about the economy," but [instead] sort of like: "*Here's a problem, what should we do about it?*" (interview, emphasis added)

Irene described her approach in detail, recounting numerous stories in which she played a role as a key convener and facilitator of negotiation.[11] In each case, numerous actors were in play: developers, corporations, employees of corporations, local citizens, scientists, conservationists, radical ecology activists, nonhuman species, tools of measurement, geological configurations, water currents, storm patterns, ecosystemic interdependencies, town governments, state regulations and regulators, tax codes, fossil fuel dependencies and consumption patterns, and more. In each case, Irene sought to open up questions about the actual needs and aspirations of all parties in ways that refused easy reductions to the hegemonic categories: "I hope you see a pattern here," she said after a number of stories. "You're listening to what the community *needs*. Is there a way to meet *their* needs *and* yours?" (interview).

"Need," in this case, does not mean articulations of generic slogans such as "economic growth" or "environmental protection," but rather the particular, detailed, and complex needs of people and institutions at a specific moment and in specific places: *this* species's habitat, *this* person's ability to contribute to the sustenance of his or her family, *this* town manager's concern for public safety, *this* company's claim that it won't be competitive under such-and-such circumstances, *this* configuration of rock, mud, vegetation, and water flow. There are no shortcuts here, and the term "negotiation" is shown to be true to its Latin roots: the negation (*neg-*) of leisure *(-otium)*, the *opposite* of freedom from labor.[12] Negotiation is the hard work of encountering others and attempting to compose a world together.[13] Irene would probably resonate with Latour when he writes: "Everywhere, every day, people are fighting over the very question of the good common world in which everyone—human and nonhuman—wants to live. Nothing and no one must come in to simplify, shorten, limit, or reduce the scope of this debate in advance" (2004a, 130). It does not "boil down," proposes Irene, to trade-offs between domains, to adjustments in the face of economic laws, or to prespecified and fixed realms of "interests." Rather, "it's about who you're working with. Are people into winning for their own pride or status? It takes courage to look weak, you know? So it does boil down to *people*" (interview). In Gerda Roelvink and J. K. Gibson-Graham's terms, it boils down to the "praxis of co-existence and interdependence" (2009, 147).

One might, of course, view Irene's work in terms of "compromise" and look for all the ways in which each of her stories reveals an ongoing maintenance of hegemony, a complicit actualization of dynamics of State or Capital, or a refusal to engage in "radical" critique. Indeed, Irene did not describe cases in which corporations were banished from Maine communities, "capitalism" was explicitly denounced, the "bad" was separated from the "good," or in which a great struggle culminated in systemic transformation. Yet neither did she describe situations in which things remained the same. If by "compromise" one means a settling for something "in-between" that neither party is wholly satisfied with, and that fails to enact creative transformation beyond the initial articulation of "camps" or "interests," then Irene is not at all in favor of this approach. For her, effective negotiation requires that all parties render vulnerable their own positions, realities, and modes of life to new learning. It is not about deciding what the other "must" become, but about a dance between holding one's values and opening to their transformation:

> You know, we don't all have to agree on our values to get along on this earth, but we should be able to find creative solutions to the problems that are vexing us. It would be boring if we all agreed! It isn't about changing each other, *it's about finding new ways of surviving.* . . . I don't have to convince everyone I meet that I'm right about my values, but I would like to be

able to have the chance to explore unique and creative strategies. And feel like they'd be open to that. And I want to retain openness in myself for that. (interview, emphasis added)

This "openness" is a movement of creativity enmeshed with acknowledged vulnerability, the cultivation of experimental engagements with reality that might compose new assemblages in which old problems and conflicts can be radically transformed. It is about refusing to accept the configurations of choices that emerge from the hegemonic assemblage and working, instead, to construct a new etho-ecology in which other ethico-political possibilities might emerge. Ossified generalities such as "jobs versus environment" might thus unfurl into dynamic specificities and open toward unexpected, transversal affinities. "What can a body do?" asks Deleuze (1990), following Spinoza. What can a community do or become? What can a particular complex regional assemblage of humans and nonhumans in Maine become? What is it already becoming, and how can these becomings be followed, amplified, and connected?

Nodal Points: Toward a New Ecopoiesis

One key strategy for amplifying and connecting multiple becomings of ethical negotiation in Maine is to develop new languages. While one can by no means simply "speak" a new reality into existence, language does enact a particular power with regard to ecopoietic processes involving humans. When the poet Muriel Rukeyser writes that "the universe is made of stories, not of atoms" (1968, 111), she names a crucial dynamic of material-semiotic performativity: one cannot simply encounter "atoms" without this encounter always already including the language by which it is (in part) made possible. It is not the case that language forms a wall between a (knowable) noumenon and an (unknowable) phenomenon as if some stable, objective world lay forever in Kantian suspension beyond us. Language, rather, is one dimension of a particular praxis of ecopoiesis, a technology of connection that produces new relations and affects (Latour 1988). If there is a separation enacted along with the connection, this is not simply because *language* fails to grasp a Real that always exceeds it, but because the actualization of a world never exhausts the virtual from which it is continually born (Deleuze 1994). Words, in and only in assemblage with other forces, may be potent actualizers, enabling the connection of myriad elements into widely circulating, widely reaching, and durable forms of life. Economy, society, and environment are cases in point. Seeking pathways for transformative action, one can, therefore, rightly place some emphasis on what Gibson-Graham calls a "language politics" (2006a, 54)—on the ways in which language can galvanize, organize, and incite new assemblages.

Following Ernesto Laclau and Chantal Mouffe (2001), Gibson-Graham conceptualizes such a politics in terms of "nodal points" (2006a, 55), representations that enable multiple differences to be assembled together in "chains of equivalence" (Laclau and Mouffe 2001, 144) without subordinating each element of the articulation to a totalizing unity. This is a useful concept, as long as we keep in mind (see chapter 1) that such assembly is always more than just linguistic, even if words are a strategic focus. It enables crucial questions: What ways of speaking might help to more potently express, connect, and strengthen ethical ecopoietic processes that escape capture by the hegemonic trio? Around what nodal point(s) might we attempt to organize new forms of ethico-political practice in Maine? What articulations might have the capacity to resist recapture by hegemonic diagrams, and yet also connect with a wide array of already-existing and emerging forces? Standing amid the fog bank as ecopoietic articulations and possibilities proliferate beyond the hegemonic formation, can (and should) we "salvage" the terms of this hegemony in a radically resignified form? Can economy, society, and environment be rearticulated and redeployed in ways that break with the hegemonic trio? Or have these terms themselves been irrevocably tainted by the power of this historical articulation?

Gibson-Graham offers a tentative and experimental answer to these questions of strategic resignification in her introduction to the second edition of *The End of Capitalism* (2006b). She describes why, in the face of critical concerns to the contrary, she retains the term "economy" even while seeking to break radically with previous conceptions:

> In the case of "economy," we are hoping to take advantage of the fact that a distinctive economic sphere has been performed and made "true," coming into existence as something widely acknowledged and socially consequential, something that participates in organizing life and things within and around it. . . . As a powerful everyday concept, "the economy" has libidinal and affective purchase; people pay attention when we start playing around with it. . . . If we abandon the concept, and resort (out of purism?) to an

ontology that doesn't involve an "economy," we are at risk of being ignored. (2006b, xxi)

The hegemonic articulation has conferred a certain power on the term "economy," yet this power does not inevitably serve hegemony. It can be turned against itself, away from itself, and can constitute a base of strength from which to articulate new assemblages. It is as if Gibson-Graham were intent on stealing some of the performative power of the category by dressing up in its clothes, putting on some of its airs, and sneaking into its meetings intent on hijacking the process for other purposes. On one level, this approach affirms the very thing it challenges: the power of a hegemonic articulation. Yet on another, it proposes to break this power off from the assemblage, carry it away, and join it with another set of transformative relations.

It is an important strategy, serving to remind us that even the most hegemonic of categories are sites of struggle that can be seized, mobilized, and turned against their inventors. Words and categories, like tools, do not have essences but are, rather, *relations*. One can thus imagine the entire trio delinked from the diagram of power and redeployed in a radically different set of connections. But this kind of re-articulation is also fraught with significant dangers and challenges. If the image of breaking off a part from the hegemonic assemblage and carrying it into another seems compelling (and it is, as Gibson-Graham suggests, an inspiring way to expand political possibility beyond the paralysis of purity), some mess must be added to the picture. What is broken off is a *node* in a web of relations, not all of which are themselves severed in the breaking. The term "economy," like its other hegemonic companions, comes away with multiple other things still attached, trailing behind: it is like trying to dig a single root from a rhizomic plant already interwoven with others in an impossible tangle. Put differently, terms are haunted by the assemblages from which they come and to which they remain (at least partially) attached. Any attempts to radically resignify "the economy" must run up against the multiple ways in which hegemony may be imported into the very heart of a new assemblage. We find ourselves suddenly, once again, talking about "the" alternative economy, seeking a blueprint for the new systematic economic domain, identifying new "laws" and forms of inevitability, constructing new enclosures. As I have already noted, even the kinds of careful, performative tracings enacted by concepts such as "economization" often end up reaffirming that which they sought to question.

Can one propose a new definition of, or add a new adjective (such as "community," "solidarity," or "ecological"), to powerful hegemonic words and effectively turn them from their conventional significations? Does this strategy underestimate the power of one assemblage to inhabit (even if by haunting) another? Does it remain too optimistic about breaking hegemonic habits of thought and feeling linked with hegemonic terms? On a more pragmatic note, might one tire of saying, "No, when I say 'economy' I don't mean what everyone else means, I mean . . ." or "No, it looks like a noun, but it's really a verb"? Or might we get mostly "laughed out of the snowmobile store" (Sandra, interview) when suggesting, "Maybe nonhumans have economies, too" or "Maybe we should think of the environment not as a domain, but as a *question*"? Meanwhile, remaining in the fog bank is of little help when trying to be useful to any on-the-ground struggle or policy debate.

My intention is not to propose a settlement to the strategic questions I have raised, nor to affirm them as two opposed sides from which one must inevitably choose. If Gibson-Graham has chosen at certain times to deploy the strategy of resignifying "economy," and to experiment with the possibilities and dangers such a move carries, then I will simply explore a *different* pathway for the purposes of further experimentation. What might it look like, I ask, to (re)compose articulations that *refuse* the categories of the hegemonic trio? At the same time, can this be done without mobilizing a language that is utterly alien to the daily conversations and struggles that now take place under the aegis of economy, society, and environment? How might I (re)compose in ways that have a chance of resisting easy recapture by the hegemonic assemblage while also not "leaving behind" possibilities of constructing meaningful alliances and connections with those whose institutional positions and daily exigencies continue to demand some connection with/in hegemony? This is the task to which I now turn.

8 ECOLOGICAL LIVELIHOODS

Beyond the Trio

From Quality of Life to Livelihoods

I showed Sandra, the regional economic development council director, the image of the three overlapping circles of economy, community, and environment published in the *Maine Measures of Growth in Focus* report (chapter 1, Figure 2). She essentially rejected these categories. I have already described, in chapter 6, how she challenged the notion of the social as a human-centered space, proposing that well-being must also be "for our rivers and for our fish and for the animals" (interview). She also sharply condemned conventional notions of the economy as "ethnocentric" and refused to accept a universal measure for the well-being of her rural community:

> People like to use Gross Domestic Product and all those ways to measure, and I don't pay much attention to those, because [sighs] . . . I think it's a bunch of baloney, frankly. I think you can't compare [this town] with a town of 4,200 in another state. . . . How would you compare that? Incomes? Median incomes? Maybe. The percentage of income in heating your house? Maybe, maybe you're getting closer to it? How much it costs to feed your family? Would you count the farmers' market then, or would you just count what's at the [supermarket]? You know? Would you count the tomatoes I ate this summer from my backyard, you know? So really, no. I don't think you can compare. (interview)

The regime of measurement enforced by economic hegemony is, for Sandra, a ridiculous game: "You measure up and you measure down and there are winners and, you know, that whole winners and losers [thing] . . . and, is that really . . . *really* . . . ? [exasperated laugh] (interview). Each place, rather, is a unique context in which a particular community strives to realize its own version of a good life that can never be rendered commensurate with the aspirations of another or with a generic model. "When you live here you've got to *get* it," she told me, "You've got to get that you can't run out to Starbucks for your morning coffee. . . . I mean you've got to appreciate what is here and not compare to the rest of the world, because it really is . . . Well, *you* know!" (interview).

Sandra's notion of economic development challenged some of the most central elements of the hegemonic articulation even while appearing as common sense. Development is, for her, a local, collective process of constituting sufficiency and well-being: "I think that wherever you are, it's having people work together as a community to get their needs met, and some of their wants and desires . . . as many as *possible* [laughs] (interview). This is not just about employment, income, or growth; it is a multidimensional process that includes these elements and much more:

> Economic development is taking what we have here and building upon it. Taking the natural beauty that we have here, the open spaces that we have here, the vistas, the downtowns, beautiful villages, and building upon that because it's unique and different from a lot of the world, a lot of the United States. And different again from other places in Maine. . . . Everything you do to strengthen a community, a downtown, strengthens the economy. Anything you do to make it attractive for people to want to visit, or a better place to live; anything you can do to be as self-sufficient as you can in a community, *that's* building the economy to me. (Sandra, interview)

"The economy" here is neither a force nor a domain, but rather a relational space of sustenance, a normative aspiration built around the specificities of people and place. It is the composition of habitat, the enactment of *livelihoods*.

When I showed Sandra the Maine Development Foundation's image of triple circles, I intended to spark a reaction relative to its clear representation of the hegemonic trio: Does she buy into it? Does she resist it? But Sandra's reaction swerved in a different direction, finding something new (or *becoming*) at the heart of hegemony. She looked at the triple circles with a furrowed brow, paused, and then proposed, "It's almost like you want to start in the *center*, you want to start with *quality of life*. What's the most important thing? What makes your quality of life good?" (interview). And, moreover, whose quality of life is this? That of humans, to be sure, but also "for our rivers and for our fish and for the animals" (interview). Sandra proceeded to describe this quality of life using the terms of the hegemonic trio, but with a difference:

> I think it's community that makes your quality of life good. And the environment, *literally* in terms of your health, makes your quality of life, but the *beauty* can also enhance your quality of life, you know. Peacefulness. And then economy, you have to have the means to, you know, put a roof over your head. You have to have some means to keep that roof over your head, whatever that is and whatever your *idea* of that is. (interview)

What is different here—what *escapes capture*—is that, with the exception of "community" (which can be read as indicating a broad notion of sociality and solidarity), the hegemonic terms are *superfluous to the argument*. One can, in fact, remove these words entirely from Sandra's statement without losing any substance. This is because "quality of life" has effectively *hollowed out* and marginalized the hegemonic trio by claiming its place in the middle of the diagram.

I had indeed neglected to notice a key dynamic at play where the three circles of the Maine Development Foundation's image meet, the central space in which the circles coincide and blur. In a hegemonic reading of the diagram—a tracing—"quality of life" appears as little more than a quaint marketing phrase, something to fill the middle space where the three ruling categories overlap. In Sandra's reading, however, economy, society (community), and environment are utterly peripheral to the action. With "quality of life" as the normative heart of the diagram, one can see the center not as a space where three still-stable categories meet and interact, but rather as a space of their radical *destabilization*—the space of the *fog bank*. Standing in the middle, so to speak, and looking outward, the hegemonic trio begins to appear not as a set of necessary conditions for life, but as three distinct yet interrelated ways to discipline, colonize, and capture life-forces into the hegemonic diagram. Shorn of their foundational status by this new view, they each appear hollow, pale, sickly—spaces of *non-quality* of life, perhaps even zones of death. Economy, society, and environment shrivel up as freestanding domains, capable of sustaining their own logics, values, interests, or needs. The only space that remains is that into which the trio has dissolved: the space of the very question of *life* itself.

"It's almost like you want to start in the center": Sandra's proposition can be read as a call for what Gilles Deleuze and Félix Guattari refer to as thinking *par le milieu,* or "through the middle" (1987, 25). This is the very opposite of a compromise seeking "balance" between stable elements; it is, rather, a movement that sweeps away the terms within which such trade-offs had been posed. "Between things," write Deleuze and Guattari, "does not designate a localizable relation going from one thing to the other and back again, but a perpendicular direction, a transversal movement that sweeps one and the other away, a stream without beginning or end that undermines its banks and picks up speed in the middle" (1987, 25). Sandra's articulation of quality of life shifts us from the major and molar categories of the hegemonic trio while also refusing a complete deterritorialization that would lead to despair or paralysis. We find ourselves, instead, in a space of active becoming, of vital questions, where life is lived neither in subordination to a hegemonic capture nor as a fragmented (in)difference. Taken as a transversal call to ethical negotiation, quality of life becomes a "meso device" in what Isabelle Stengers calls "mesopolitics": "The typical success of a meso device," she writes, "would be to confer upon a situation the power to make those who are attached to it, in an *a priori* conflictual manner, think together. Not overcome the conflict, but transversalize its terms" (2009, 5).

"Quality of life," of course, is not itself a radical term, and is rarely associated with radical politics. In Maine, it has become a common rallying point around which economic developers, social workers, and environmental advocates gather. It is often mobilized to serve the vague goal of "balancing" the three categories, and therefore stabilizes and legitimates the hegemonic configuration of power. Yet Sandra's articulation points toward a crucial underside to this formation: the quality of life discourse is also popular, I believe, because it offers a language with which policy professionals can speak of their work without immediate recourse to the categories they know (even if tacitly) are problematic. Thus, even as it appears to serve hegemony, it opens up new lines of flight. "It's not just how big is the pile of money you get," says Calvin, the director of an economic development think-tank, "but what is the quality of life you have? That's a much larger conversation" (interview). In the end, suggests Paul, the social worker, employment is only one small dimension of social service. "What we really do is try to bring resources together . . . to try to make . . . things better for everybody. It's quality of life, basically, is what it amounts to" (interview).

Bradley, the conservation collaborative director, makes the point even more boldly: "The economy is a tool, it's not an end. . . . I don't care if people have jobs, I care that people have quality *lives*. And jobs are a route toward generating a quality of life" (interview). Quality of life is a dynamic middle space that might serve as a key entry point into a different kind of politics in Maine. To ask the question of this "quality"—to take it seriously—is to open a space that economy, society, and environment cannot assimilate or contain. It is this open space that I propose to speak of in terms of "livelihoods."

Livelihood(s)

"Livelihood" is a common word, widely used in Maine and elsewhere to refer generally to the making and procuring of a living, the enacting of sustenance. It has been used in English, via a variety of spellings (*lifelode*, *liflade*, *lyvelode*, *lyveliod*, *livelyhoode*, and others) since at least the thirteenth century and, unlike the three terms of the hegemonic trio, it has meant roughly the same thing for all of this time, weathering the fall of feudalism and the rise of industrial modernity.[1] Alongside and transversal to the various articulations of economy, society, and environment, livelihood has subsisted beneath the surface through multiple historical eras as a kind of people's discourse—a term of *practice*, of experience, of complex lives lived and negotiated from the inside, *par le milieu*, rather than categorized from without. Livelihood is what unfolds in the space of life's action, the middle space in which the hegemonic trio blurs and dissolves into the power-laden specificities of encounter and (sometimes ethical) negotiation. Having not been wholly captured by a particular hegemonic metrology, it indicates a diversity of activities, a variety of skills and knowledges, a plethora of possible sites of action, and multiple configurations of ever-changing relations and processes that cannot be captured by a generality. Livelihood is, in this way, a *minor* (as opposed to a major) category: it resists unification under a singular standard of measure, image of action, or domain of life (Deleuze and Guattari 1987, 105). When invoked, it most often comes linked to particular contexts, stories, and strategies: How do people make a living in Maine? As Mainers well know, we do it in all kinds of ways. Moreover, livelihood also has the nice resonance of "lively," beckoning toward an affirmation of joy in the Deleuzian/Spinozan sense of enhancing a body's capacities through connection (Deleuze 1990), and it serves to remind us of the "lively matter" in which we participate and from which we continually emerge (Bennett 2010).

The Transversal Language of Livelihood

"Yes! *Livelihoods*! That's right!" exclaimed Richard, the CEO of a major Maine social service nonprofit, when I proposed the term toward the end our interview. We were talking about the profound shortcomings of the hegemonic trio and its associated divisions. Richard had expressed his frustration, throughout our conversation, at the various ways in which the "social" is marginalized relative to the "economic," and he made clear his desire for the hegemonic separation between humans and "the environment" to be overcome. Yet he lacked a language to speak otherwise. "I'm not sure you can talk about one without talking about the other," he proposed initially. "So in some way they are linked. . . . I'm not necessarily sure it matters which is first or second or third. One doesn't have more importance than the other" (interview). Later, he opted for a wonderful new turn of phrase: "All three *swarm*," he suggested (interview, emphasis added), invoking the image of multiple concerns buzzing around, inside and out.

In a subsequent array of personal stories, Richard invoked the hegemonic categories in overlapping "fog bank" senses to describe key concerns that face Maine people: "Do you have enough money to live on? Do you have a way to produce something in order to make a living? Does my family have enough? And do they have opportunities to create their own . . . economy?" (interview). Community, he suggested, is the space of care and support that sustains us beyond the money economy, and it too constitutes "economy": "I also see a different set of economies, and that is outside of the money-generating economy, and that is people's *talents* economy. And that *works* in neighborhoods. We have people who barter their time, their talents. They volunteer. . . . There's *that* economy" (interview). The environment as well, for Richard, is a site of sustenance and collectivity, and it is not external to our participation in it:

> What I think helps wrap the community in a nice neat little bow is the environment. And maybe it's because we live here [in Maine], because it's important to us, because . . . I don't know how you separate it out. It's a *fabric*

of . . . Here, you don't just talk about the environment, you *actualize* it in all kinds of different ways, whether it's garbage to gardens, composting, or recycling . . . or community gardens or caring for open spaces. (interview)

The categories of the trio clearly did not work to articulate or contain Richard's notions, yet he had no other way to describe things. Livelihood appeared for him as a term that was at once familiar and transversal, already cutting across the dividing lines of the trio.

Richard is not alone. "I don't really care about the quality of the economy—that's an abstract thing! I care about people's *lives*," says Bradley, the conservation collaborative director (interview). This is not an expression of callousness toward the hard realities of making ends meet, but an expression of frustration at the ways in which the hegemonic categories reduce well-being to "economic" measures. Frank, a department director at a large nonprofit social service agency, shares this sentiment. When he proposed that the economy was fundamentally about "employment" (interview), I asked him to clarify. "Maybe my use of the word 'employment' is less narrow than what you're taking it to be," he explained. "It's about livelihood. You can be self-employed, you can be gainfully . . . you know, pursuing your own *livelihood*. . . . But it's being able to make ends meet. It's being able to generate what you *need*, put food on the table . . . and *more*, right?" (interview). Livelihood, in everyday conversation, commonly refers not just to paid employment, but to all the diverse means by which Mainers (and others) "piece together lives" (Greg, interview) from multiple sources and through multiple activities and relations.

Such an articulation clearly cuts across and through the conventional economic, social, and environmental distinctions. Lives are composed from and emerge from all kinds of elements that cannot be contained by the hegemonic trio. As Paula, for example, the director of a statewide conservation organization, suggests: "You can't talk about livelihoods without talking about taking care of the environment as well, you know. It's all connected. We're talking planetary imbalances that are coming from climate change, and sea-level rise and all different kinds of things that are going to have potentially disastrous results for us from a health perspective and a livelihoods perspective" (interview). To make a living, and to have a living made for us by others, is necessarily to be bound up in multispecies socialities, to engage complex ethical questions of interdependence and responsibility, to mobilize strategies that cannot be categorized in conventional terms, and to participate in relations that are beyond accounting and beyond total capture by Capital or State. Moreover, it is not just *humans* who enact livelihoods. Consider, for example, the title of a letter to the *Maine Sunday Telegram*, challenging industrial forestry practices: "Cutting damages deer livelihoods" (Ritchie 2006).

One can, of course, find many mobilizations of "livelihood" that are far from revolutionary articulations beyond the hegemonic trio. People in Maine do sometimes speak of paid employment in terms of "earning a livelihood," or of livelihoods being "dependent" on a particular industry or resource. Of any environmental protection proposal, for example, one can find people asking about the livelihoods of those in directly impacted industries: "How is this going to affect their job, their livelihood, their paycheck?" (Stephen, environmental advocate, interview). But even these articulations fail to fully enroll livelihood into the hegemonic formation, for there is always the possibility that this livelihood could take another form, unfold via a different set of strategies, or appear wholly transformed within an altogether distinct assemblage. Take, for example, the definition of "economy" given by Eric, the regional economist: "By the economy I basically mean some system of primarily voluntary exchange of goods and services and money that people undertake as their means of livelihood" (interview). Livelihood is, indeed, hitched here to a classic assemblage of market exchange; yet there is nothing necessary about this relationship. Such exchange is, after all, only a *means* of livelihood, and there are many others. One might "earn" a livelihood (as a common hegemonic phrasing would have it), but it may also be given, shared, stolen, scavenged, gleaned, or inherited. Because livelihood refers to *life*, and because life is a force of wildness that always escapes complete capture, domestication, domination, or objectification, livelihood remains a fertile articulation for composing habitats and inhabitants anew.

Approaches to Livelihood

The language of livelihood as a strategy for overcoming hegemonic articulations is not new. At least since Karl Polanyi (1977), the term has been linked with various efforts to challenge orthodoxies of economic theory and international development. In particular, it is most often used to displace the hegemony of paid work and monetary exchange via capitalist markets: humans make livings, various theorizations suggest, through multiple activities and in relation to numerous kinds of institutions, motivations, and contexts. Moreover, the term tends to indicate a broad set of practices and values oriented toward the reproduction of life rather than the accumulation of capital, similar to the "economy of sustenance" described in chapter 6. In my own theorization of livelihoods, I seek to affirm and amplify these two dimensions while challenging others. Many existing approaches tend, in particular, to merge aspects of the *economic* and *social* without challenging an articulation of "the environment" as a domain of resources. The *human* continues to stand alone at the center of action and navigates—even "optimizes"— a world of objects or resources. A radically *ecological* notion of livelihoods, located within a broader ecopoiesis, remains to be elaborated.

Substantivism and Social Provisioning

For Polanyi, livelihood marks out a specifically "economic" space, but in a manner much more inclusive than the conventional economic theory he contests. What often passes for economics in general, he argues, is actually "an ingrained habit of thought peculiar to conditions of life under that type of economy the nineteenth century created throughout all industrialized societies" (1977, 5). In what Polanyi calls "formal economics," the economy is reduced to market exchange and its associated optimizing rationality operating under conditions of scarcity— a problematic conflation of "the human economy in general with its market form" (1977, 6). Contrasting the formal with the "substantive economy," Polanyi proposes that a true empirical economics must examine all the diverse ways in which human beings generate *livelihoods*, myriad "instituted process[es] of interaction serving the satisfaction of material wants" (1977, 31). As he describes:

> The substantive meaning [of economy] implies neither choice nor insufficiency of means; man's livelihood may or may not involve the necessity of choice and, if choice there be, it need not be induced by the limiting effect of 'scarcity' of the means; indeed, some of the most important physical and social conditions of livelihood such as the availability of air and water or a loving mother's devotion to her infant are not, as a rule, so limiting. (1992, 29)

Livelihood thus radically expands the economic to include all forms of human material sustenance, secured via "interchange with [the] natural and social environment" (1992, 29).

A foundational distinction operates in Polanyi's work, however, between "man" as active agent and "nature" (or "environment") as a relatively passive—though crucial—source of sustenance. The social, too, is distinct enough that he can speak of the "disembedding" of the economic—however ultimately impossible (Block 2001, xxv)—from the society it both serves and dominates (Polanyi 2001).[2] Additionally, as Koray Çaliskan and Michel Callon (2009) argue, Polanyi's articulation remains tied to the assumption of an "economic" whose definitional contents need only be transformed. Formalists and substantivists, in fact, share a common epistemology: they both "draw their attention towards that which is economic, what we have called the economic X. The salient difference between formalism and substantivism involves the identity of the X " (2009, 377). In other words, and despite Polanyi's profound contributions to the genealogy of "economy" (2001), his substantivism is still bound up with key elements of the articulation it ostensibly seeks to challenge. The language of livelihoods continues to hold out the possibility of something beyond these divides, but is not yet able to actualize such a movement.

Polanyi's notion of livelihood has been taken up, expanded, and transformed in a variety of ways, yet none of these explicitly challenge its hegemonic remainders. Economic anthropologist Rhoda Halperin (1994), for example, elaborates a Marxian-Polanyian approach to livelihoods that is tied to a clear distinction between "ecology" and "economy." Ecology, for Halperin, refers to the movement and transformation of matter and energy, and is distinct from "institutional" factors involving modes of social organization (1994, 59). Economy emerges at the intersection of the two in what should now be a familiar triangulation. Although Halperin's intention is to avoid the environmental determinism associated with certain strands of economic anthropology, and thus to assert a space of cultural agency, her formulation nonetheless affirms an objective nature upon which culture can and must act. Economy becomes "the material-means provisioning process in cultural systems" (1994, 83), the site of interface between culture and materiality, a mediation between a subjective humanity and an objective nature. Key elements of the diagram of power remain intact.

Feminist economic literature on "social provisioning," exemplified by the work of Marilyn Power (2004) and Julie Nelson (2009b) among others, does not enact such a clear distinction between ecology and economy, yet nonetheless does little to challenge the Nature–Culture divide that haunts even the most substantive versions of economics. Social provisioning, like Polanyi's substantivism, begins from a rejection of economic articulations that reduce livelihood to dynamics of market exchange and utility-maximizing rationality:

> Social provisioning need not be done through the market; it need not be done for selfish or self-interested reasons, although neither of these is inconsistent with social provisioning, either. Thus, the concept allows for a broader understanding of economic activity that includes women's unpaid and non-market activities and for understandings of motivation that don't fall under narrow or tautological notions of self-interest. The term also emphasizes process as well as outcomes. The manners in which we provide for ourselves, both paid and unpaid, are included in the analysis. (Power 2004, 6)

A strength of this approach is its emphasis (not unlike in Polanyi, but here amplified) on *process*. Rather than constituting a system or logic of organization, social provisioning "illuminates the ways a society *organizes* itself to produce and reproduce material life" (Power 2004, 7, emphasis added). Additionally, and similarly to the language of livelihoods, provisioning focuses on life lived from the *inside*: "The term 'provisioning' directs attention to the purpose of economic activity. Passive images of workers and consumers are replaced with those of people facing challenges around how to meet their needs and obligations" (Neysmith and Reitsma-Street 2005, 382). Again, however, key aspects of the ontological structure of the hegemonic articulation stand relatively intact: humans navigate (now collectively and institutionally rather than just as individual workers and consumers) as agents (variously constrained or empowered) in a sustaining yet distinct domain of "natural resources" (Power 2004, 15).

The Sustainable Livelihoods Approach

Perhaps the most elaborated notions of livelihood have been developed in the field of development theory and practice, in the form of the "sustainable livelihoods approach" (SLA). Variably drawing on and transforming many of the insights of Polanyi and subsequent substantivists, and taken up by both activist scholars and international development institutions, SLA is a complex zone of converging and conflicting articulations. The language of "livelihoods" first entered the sphere of development discourse in the famous Brundtland report, as a straightforward reproduction of the hegemonic assemblage: "The most basic of all needs is for a livelihood: that is, employment" (WCED 1987b, 49–50). Another WCED report of the same year, *Food 2000* (1987a), expanded the definition slightly, but rendered it synonymous with a generic set of resources: "Livelihood is defined as adequate stocks and flows of food and cash to meet basic needs" (qtd. in Chambers and Conway 1991, 5). It was Robert Chambers and Gordon Conway, in a widely cited working paper, who transformed the term into a foundational articulation for a new practice of development. In their definition:

> A livelihood comprises the capabilities, assets (stores, resources, claims, and access) and activities required for a means of living: a livelihood is sustainable which can cope with and recover from stress and shocks, maintain or enhance its capabilities and assets, and provide sustainable livelihood opportunities for the next generation; and which contributes net benefits to other livelihoods at the local and global levels and in the short and long term. (1991, 6)

Livelihood, for Chambers and Conway, is not reducible either to "employment" or to "stocks and flows"; rather, it is a power-laden field of relations in which lives are made and unmade. There is a radical dynamism in their articulation that goes well beyond the simple image of the more or less agential human standing amid a world of resources to be managed, protected, or mobilized. The reciprocal relation of habitat and inhabitant, of agency and the etho-ecology that renders it possible (or impossible), is particularly apparent in their understanding of the dynamics of "means" and "ends":

> A livelihood in its simplest sense is the means of gaining a living. Capabilities are both an end and means of livelihood: a livelihood provides the support for the enhancement and exercise of capabilities (an end); and capabilities (a means) enable livelihood to be gained. Equity is both an end and a means: any minimum definition of equity must include adequate and decent livelihoods for all (an end); and equity in assets and access are preconditions (means) for gaining adequate and decent livelihoods. Sustainability, too, is both end and means: sustainable stewardship of resources is a value (or end) in itself; and it provides conditions (a means) for livelihood to be sustained for future generations. (1991, 5)

In a radical reading of this passage, livelihood can be understood as both the process of enacting life sustenance and the processes by which one is rendered capable of such enactment by the other beings and forces that compose one's *oikos*. This is always a matter of negotiation, of agonistic encounters between multiple transient and durable forces, both human and more-than-human. We begin to approach a notion of livelihoods here that truly opens questions of ecopoietic becoming.

Following this fertile work by Chambers and Conway, SLA has moved in a number of directions at once. On one hand, it has been elaborated to deepen and expand the insights of its originators. Leo De Haan and Annelies Zoomers, for example, delink livelihood from its Polanyian articulation as *material* sustenance to include a much wider array of relations: "This is not to say that livelihood is not a matter of material well-being," they write, "but rather that it also includes non-material aspects of well-being. Livelihood should be seen as a dynamic and holistic concept" (2005, 32). Anthony Bebbington construes "assets" not just in terms of passive resources, but as relational connections that enable new forms of action and new etho-ecologies to emerge: "Assets should not be understood only as things that allow survival, adaptation and poverty alleviation: they are also the basis of agents' power to act and to reproduce, challenge or change the rules that govern the control, use and transformation of resources" (1999, 2022).

On the other hand, SLA has moved in a direction that is significantly narrower and more technocratic than the intentions of Chambers and Conway. In the work of Ian Scoones, for example, who developed a key diagram (1998, 4) that was subsequently adopted and modified by numerous development agencies (e.g., DFiD 2001; NZAID 2006), the "assets" dimension of livelihoods is converted to the language of "capitals" (Scoones 1998). Far from opening the question of assets as a site of multiple ecopoietic articulations, Scoones shrinks the field: "Drawing on an economic metaphor . . . livelihood resources may be seen as the 'capital' base from which different productive streams are derived from which livelihoods are constructed" (1998, 7). Myriad living relations are thus uncritically reduced to "natural capital," "financial capital," "human capital," and "social capital" (1998, 7–8).[3] No amount of Bourdieuian apologetics can avoid the sense in which this language is bound up with a hegemonic, economistic articulation that renders complex, dynamic relations into bundles of objects, potential commodity values, conceptual oversimplifications, and quantities to be counted and assessed by external standards (Mdee 2002; Fine 2010).

True to the ethico-political content of the "capitals" notion, a whole field of professional development intervention literature has subsequently developed around SLA in which we are once again presented with individual humans and human "households" navigating—indeed, quite often even rationally *optimizing*—"opportunities" via various strategies in a field of variably accessible "resources."[4] Narrowed, in particular, to application among "the poor," livelihood becomes a term for various modes of "coping" (Rakodi 2002) in the face of limited access to capital. As a practice of technocratic intervention, it becomes a particular style of government, a coded colonialism that can now intervene in the name of "people-centered development" (DFiD 2001) to implement a particular, morally infused vision of the good life in which the primacy of capitalist markets and human exploitation of a distinct "environment" remain unquestioned. Indeed, one gets two strong impressions while reading the bulk of mainstream SLA literature: first, that it is only "poor" people who have and make livelihoods, only "poor" people who are vulnerable, and only "poor" people who must change (Mdee 2002; Brocklesby and Fisher 2003); and, second, that some people's livelihoods are more "dependent" on "natural resources" than others (Scoones 1998, 6)—as if some human communities were exempted from a total dependence on earthly habitat.

SLA thus appears to take at least two radically distinct forms: a technocratic developmentalism closely aligned with the hegemonic formation I have sought to challenge throughout this book and a more radically democratic expression that beckons toward an undoing of modernist, capitalist, and (perhaps) even humanist hegemony. Rather than simply dismiss SLA for its first form, as a hopelessly co-opted and corrupted field, I want to build on my (selective, performative) reading of Chambers and Conway and develop some key threads of what can be called the "minor" becomings of SLA. First, however, I turn to one final set of theorizations that offer crucial elements to a theory of livelihoods.

The Subsistence Perspective, or Livelihood versus Accumulation

While not explicitly elaborating the language of livelihoods, Veronica Bennholdt-Thomsen and Maria Mies's "subsistence perspective" (1999) is a powerful Marxian-feminist attempt to acknowledge, strengthen, and cultivate diverse, non-exploitative practices of life-sustenance. For Bennholdt-Thomsen and Mies, as with Polanyi, there are two fundamentally incompatible notions of "economy." Their bifurcation does not rest, however, on a formal/substantive distinction, but one much closer to what I proposed in chapter 6 between the economy of accumulation and the economy of sustenance. As Bennholdt-Thomsen and Mies describe:

> There exists a different conception of "economy," which is both older and younger than the capitalist patriarchal one . . . based on the ongoing colonisation of women, of other peoples and nature. This "other" economy puts life and everything necessary to produce and maintain life on this planet at the center of economic and social activity [rather than] the never-ending accumulation of dead money. (1999, 5)

"Subsistence" is their name for this other economy, that which is fundamentally oriented toward the sustenance of human and more-than-human communities.

The use of the term "perspective" is quite intentional in their formulation. As with J. K. Gibson-Graham's notion of "community economy," Bennholdt-Thomsen and Mies are not proposing a "new economic model" in place of the old (1999, 7), but rather seeking to render more visible and viable a host of practices, traditions, and aspirations that are already present yet often marginalized or weakened by hegemonic power. "Subsistence" is thus not a *domain*; it does not map onto either the hegemonic "economy" or "society" (despite Bennholdt-Thomsen and Mies's use of these terms) but rather cuts across both transversally. It is a set of productive and reproductive practices, "all work that is expended on the creation, re-creation and maintenance of immediate life and which has no other purpose [such as, for example, commodity production and private profit]" (1999, 20). Subsistence, the work of life itself, is what animates Capital's "dead money" (1999, 21) as the force of living labor, yet it is also what Capital exploits, denies, and degrades. A politics of subsistence recognizes that "without subsistence production, no commodity production; yet without commodity production, definitely, subsistence production" (1999, 20). Practices of noncapitalist livelihood must be valorized and organized to enact revolutionary delinkages from Capital and thereby render its force increasingly impotent.

The subsistence perspective embraces the Polanyian and feminist economic views of livelihood as a complex and diverse array of practices, rationalities, and relations, but adds a more explicit emphasis on the structures of *value* that animate various regimes of sustenance. "In non-capitalist subsistence," write Bennholdt-Thomsen and Mies, "use-values are produced for the satisfaction of limited human needs"

(1999, 57). These use-values are equated with Marx's concept of "simple exchange" (C-M-C: commodity-money-commodity) in which "use value is exchanged for use value" (1999, 57). Exchange-value production, in contrast, is associated with Marx's notation of M-C-M' (money-commodity-more money) and generates commodities that have "no other purpose than to be exchanged in the market for a higher price than their production costs" (1999, 57). On one side we have a regime of production, circulation, and value articulation oriented toward life and its sustenance; on the other side, a regime oriented toward endless profit.

It is not clear to me, however, that this distinction is most effectively expressed via Marx's two circuits, since C-M-C is only one possible (monetized) instance of a much wider array of livelihood practices. In his work on theorizing postcapitalist practices of "commoning," Massimo De Angelis (2017) suggests an approach that serves to clarify and extend the distinction. While the C-M-C movement does suggest a different value orientation to that of capitalist accumulation, it becomes a mere subset of a wider and more fundamental process that De Angelis calls "the circuit of the commons" (2017, 193). Here, both common wealth (shared "resources") and collectivity (or "community") are reproduced through the ongoing work of commoning, of "life activity through which common wealth is reproduced and comes to serve as the basis for a new cycle of commons (re)production" (2017, 200). Commons and Capital/State thus represent two radically distinct—and often opposed—value orientations: "Commoning is a social labor flow pushed by needs, attracted by desires and oriented by sense horizon and aspirations; it is a life flow in which money, if necessary, is only a means to a human end—unlike capital flows whose only rationale for moving is a . . . quantitative increase in money" (2017, 206). De Angelis thus carries the subsistence approach in a direction that breaks definitively from the grip of a commodity-centric view. The operative distinction here is not between circuits of exchange, but between regimes of value: it is the difference between having "enough" and having "too much," between livelihood maintenance and a drive toward accumulation (Davis 1991; St. Martin 2009). It is the difference between *making a living* and *making a killing*.

As I have already suggested, people in Maine *know* this distinction at an intuitive level, and this knowledge is not necessarily divided along partisan lines or even (at least sometimes) class lines. To be sure, there is a widely circulating ideology that seeks to pose extractive profit and endless accumulation as *necessary* for the livelihoods of the general populace. But despite Fox News, the actual practice of people's daily sustenance exceeds such stories. In some cases, I can speak to my right-wing, Christian fundamentalist neighbors about nonmarket subsistence practices more easily than I can with suburban liberals. It was not the radical left that opposed a recent bill in the Maine legislature (LD 218) to restrict access to private land for foraging, but rather a host of libertarian voices from the rural "right."[5] Moreover, while a conventional Marxian view might suggest that the fundamental divisions between a livelihood and accumulation orientation is about *class* (with C-M-C on the side of the workers), it should be clear that subsistence cuts across all such divisions even as it marks them *as* divisions. Wage labor may be oriented toward sustenance rather than accumulation, and accumulation may indeed mark those subjected to its violence as "dependent" or "poor," but no capitalist could ever be found who does not also enact subsistence values and practices in some core dimension of their lives. Either class must be viewed here as a *process* that can be enacted multiply (Gibson-Graham, Resnick, and Wolff 2001) or non-accumulative, sustaining livelihood practices must be understood as *transversal* to class distinction, therefore opening up (potentially, at least) a field of crosscutting possibilities for transformative collective action.

Whether framed in terms of subsistence or commoning, these are powerful perspectives that open up the terrain for amplifying diverse modes of livelihood while also foregrounding historical and ongoing relations of enclosure, colonization, and exploitation. In many ways, my approach to theorizing livelihood owes much of its substance to Bennholdt-Thomsen, Mies, and De Angelis (not to mention, of course, Gibson-Graham, discussed elsewhere). But I respectfully depart from them in two key ways. First, and most superficially, I seek different terms to do similar work. The language of "subsistence" runs up against strategic difficulties in its common association with bare-bones survival. One is hard pressed to avoid reading the prefix *sub-* without thinking of something *beneath* or *below*, as in "substandard" or "subhuman." In Maine, subsistence is likely to invoke images of poverty, hunger, vulnerability, living on the edge.[6] I seek, in the language of livelihoods, something more affirmative and widely connective. Regarding De Angelis's language of commoning, I mobilize this term for slightly different (though resonant) purposes in the next chapter, challenging the identity he asserts between livelihood and commoning. One can, I will argue, enact livelihood values without engaging in explicit commoning, and the distinction between the two is politically crucial.

My second and more substantive challenge to both approaches is against their shared emphasis on "autonomy." For Bennholdt-Thomsen and Mies, subsistence is equated with "independence," "self-sufficiency," and "self-reliance" (1999, 21), where one pictures—as in so many radical left economic visions—powerful humans standing at the center of a world that is now, finally, at their command (albeit to care for and "sustain"). For De Angelis, a similar emphasis emerges from his notions of "autonomy" and "autopoiesis": an "organic unity controlled only by its own laws and not subject to any other" (2017, 226). The problem here is not the political affirmation of human freedom or the self-conscious construction of boundaries. Rather, it is the absence of an accompanying acknowledgment of the necessary, constitutive limits of autonomy and of the dangers of inscribing it as the sole focus of radical transformation. As I will elaborate, we are also *made by others* (allopoiesis) and this making is not always a matter of oppression but may also be the very condition of possibility for freedom. This is where, once again, the "ecological thought" is crucial, for even De Angelis will speak of the nonhuman living world as a collection of "resources" to be commoned (2017, 126) rather than as a realm of (potential) ethical relations, or a web of beings *with* whom we might become co-commoners.

The Ecology of Livelihoods

In order to move beyond the limitations of the various articulations outlined above, while building on their strengths, a conceptualization of *ecological livelihoods* is essential. I do not intend the term "ecological" here as a synonym for "environmental"; nor as designating a scientific holism or a definite unity that subsumes all; nor is it a site of knowledge about an objective set of dynamics and laws to which one might appeal. "Ecological" in the sense I wish to mobilize it has little to do even with a notion of "nature." I follow, instead, a thread of ecological thought described briefly toward the end of chapter 6. Ecology can be understood as that which *cannot* be reduced to an environment or nature, contained by a unity, transformed into an object, or mobilized as an ontological court of appeal. It is, in Jean-François

Lyotard's terms, "the discourse of the secluded . . . the thing that has not become public, that has not become communicational, that has not become systemic, and that can never become any of these things" (1993, 202). Or, as Bronislaw Szerszynski summarizes, ecology is "not the name of a totality but of the impossibility of any such totality" (2010, 14). Such a notion is present in Bruno Latour's work as well, where "political ecology" designates the very *failure* to "defin[e] the common good of a dehumanized nature" (1998, 228) and instead becomes a site of uncertainty regarding questions of interconnection and ethics. "Is everything interrelated?" he asks, subsequently answering, "Not necessarily. We do not know what is interconnected and woven together" (1998, 232). This is also Timothy Morton's "ecological thought," the mind-boggling interdependence that we can never master, never know, and that beckons toward an ethics we have only begun to explore. Ecology is not "a picture of some bounded object," but rather "a vast, sprawling mesh of interconnection without any definite center or edge. It is radical intimacy, co-existence with other beings, sentient and otherwise—and how can we so clearly tell the difference?" (2010, 8).

Ecology, therefore, as the linkage of *oikos* (habitat) to *logos* (reasoned speech), comes to name both an ethical demand and its ultimate (infinite) impossibility. Because our constitutive connections to others proliferate wildly, we are called toward the ethical exposure of these connections and their effects. "The ecological thought," writes Morton, "thinks big and joins the dots. It comes as close as possible to the strange stranger, generating care and concern for beings, no matter how uncertain we are of their identity, no matter how afraid we are of their existence" (2010, 19). This is the demand of *community* in Jean-Luc Nancy's and J. K. Gibson-Graham's sense described in chapter 7, and it is what much of the science of ecology—in its practiced specificities rather than in its popularized, holistic generalization—has in fact responded to. What *is* my connection to the small frog that is threatened by the development of a new big-box store in my town? What *is* my connection to mercury accumulating in Maine's freshwater ecosystems from rainwater carrying midwestern power-plant emissions? What *is* the connection between coal-fired electric generators, people turning on coffee-grinders in Chicago, smallmouth bass laden with toxins in a Maine pond, and communities (human and nonhuman) devastated by mountaintop removal in Appalachia? We must attempt to trace all of these relations and more, because they are all constitutive moments from which our agency emerges and to which it must respond. And yet this is an *impossible task to complete*: it is the very nature of interconnected habitats and their inhabitants that the totality of connections can never be traced or known, much less faced with wholly adequate responses. The *logos* of the *oikos* will be forever present as an active ethical demand and yet also will be forever crossed out as an impossible one in its totality: ~~ecology~~![7]

Elements of Ecological Livelihood

A new articulation of livelihoods must carry forward some of the key insights of the previous formulations discussed above: an emphasis on the multiple forms of practice, institution, motivation, and (non) calculation through which humans compose livelihoods; an analysis of the ways in which particular ecopoietic articulations compose and sustain relations of exploitation and oppression; a focus on enhancing human agency in the face of these destructive forces, and on constituting the wider institutional and cultural conditions of possibility for the flourishing of multiple forms of freedom; and a recognition of the more-than-material (in its crude sense of "material base") nature of livelihoods—highlighting relational, emotional, and spiritual dimensions. Additionally, it must add some key elements that the radically democratic force of ecology calls forth. I will briefly sketch five of these.

First, livelihoods must apply to *everyone*—not only to the "rural poor" and to people and communities generally located in the majority world (as "targets" of development), and not only to humans—but to all living singularities (including collectivities).[8] Even Chambers's attempt, in SLA theory, to develop an ethical articulation of livelihoods needs to be challenged here, for when he proposes that "a sustainable livelihood should not damage but enhance the livelihoods of others . . . now and/or in the future" (2005, 202), livelihood remains a human affair. If all living beings compose (and are composed by) livelihoods, then no heterotroph, at least, can avoid damaging the livelihoods of others.[9] As "mortal beings," writes Donna Haraway, we "live in and through the use of one another's bodies" (2008, 79). No one, honestly at least, can "pretend to live outside killing" (2008, 79). Thus the simplistic normative demand for the non-degradation of others' livelihoods cannot be sustained. It must be shifted, rather, to the level of Stengers's "etho-ecology" (2005b), to the space in which we confront questions about the kinds of anesthetizations and anti-anesthetizations that disable or enable ethical negotiation. This is Haraway's move when she proposes that the problem is not to impose a moral ban on all killing (an impossible demand), but rather to "learn to live responsibly within the multiplicitous necessity and labor of killing, so as to be in the open, in quest of the capacity to respond in relentless historical, nonteleological, multispecies contingency" (2008, 80). We might alter Chambers's proposal, then, to say that an ethical livelihood (and perhaps a "sustainable" one as well) should not damage but enhance the sensitivity and capacity of singularities to encounter and respond gracefully to the multiple interrelations and interdependencies that compose them.

Second, while it may at first appear paradoxical given the previous requirement of a livelihoods articulation applying to "everyone," ethical conceptualizations of livelihood must avoid generalizations or "major" articulations that attempt to capture and domesticate specificity, difference, and becoming into frames of predesignated or determined causality and structure. This is to say that "everyone"—every living singularity—enacts a livelihood, but the specificity of this enacting cannot be determined a priori or in general. Even Scoones can see that livelihoods requires such localization: "The appeal is simple," he writes of SLA in its best moments of practice, "look at the real world, and try and understand things from local perspectives. Responses that follow should work with such realities and not try and impose artificial categories and divides on complex realities" (2009, 172). This is not to say that we cannot or should not sometimes attempt to develop accounts of particular patterns, tendencies, or "habits" (Latour 2004a, 86) that unfold in livelihood practice, but simply that these accounts can never constitute wholes of which particular instances are mere "examples." They are, rather, *added to* particular assemblages as one more connection that might make a difference (Deleuze and Guattari 1987; Latour 2005).[10] The notion that human beings enact particular optimizing rationalities when confronted with scarcity, for example, cannot insert itself at the level of ontology—as "the way things really are"—but rather must always remain a performative proposition in which its claims cannot be separated from the "reality" they may help to compose. This is because, as William Connolly reminds us, "it is likely that every confident articulation of stable human interests in a specific historical context inadvertently naturalizes some contingent features of the present by treating them as if they conformed to the universal as such" (1995, 33–34). We return, once again then, to ontological politics, where a suspension of certainty and universality may serve to continually open up space for new becomings.

Third, not only must the dimensions and dynamics of livelihood always escape complete capture by generalization, but they must also refuse totalizations or reductions via *measurement* or representation more generally. As Chambers and Conway make clear, livelihoods must be recognized as ultimately incommensurable and immeasurable:

> Concepts of wellbeing or deprivation have often been determined by their measureability. Convenience of measuring income or consumption has reinforced the definitions of deprivation as poverty, and of poverty as low income or low consumption. The ideas of employment, a job and a workplace are reinforced by the relative ease with which these can be identified and counted. . . . As professionals, we define as significant whatever we capture and can count in our crude and standard nets. . . . [Livelihoods] are not easy to measure or estimate; and any attempt to reduce measurement to a single scale or indicator risks doing violence to precisely the complexity and diversity which many rural livelihoods manifest. (1991, 18)

Once again, this does not mean that one cannot or should not ever measure, as measurement can be a crucial performative strategy for rendering particular assemblages more visible, durable, and (for better or worse, depending on the case) manageable. It implies, however, that such measurement can never be confused for a "whole" it may claim to represent, and the violence enacted by any measurement and subsequent comparison must always be a site of active ethical response. For every measurement produced and every comparison made, one must make a countermove following Sandra, the economic growth council director in insisting that something has been lost, something violated, and that "really, no. I don't think you can compare" (interview).

Fourth, and in a related fashion, livelihood theorizations must refuse to accept, a priori, the necessity of particular forms, modes, or trajectories of development. One cannot know if livelihoods must involve overcoming something called "poverty" that is granted a seemingly objective and universal status. One must problematize any discourses and strategies that imply necessary or normatively asserted movements of *particular* living assemblages in general (abstract) directions: growth, improvement, resilience, sustainability. Each of these may all too easily code for reproductions of hegemony or, in Vassos

Argyrou's terms, "the ability of a group of societies to define the meaning of the world for *everyone, yet again*" (2005, ix). If development is
to be thought at all within a livelihoods frame, it must be thought as
an *event*: "I think we're seeing a new development here." This event
has nothing to do with the teleological movement of progress that animates the central axis of the hegemonic diagram of power; rather, it
indicates the very moment of *ecopoiesis*, the eruption of creation, the
actualization of a virtual that is never exhausted (Deleuze and Guattari
1994, 156). Let us, indeed, become advocates for this kind of development—the very opposite of what development in the West has most
often been. Development as event is the enactment of radical democracy, a refusal to compromise the force of desire (De Vries 2007), the
opening of possibility for collectivities to conserve or transform livelihoods and habitats according to processes in which the outcomes of
such composition have not already been determined or decided.

Finally, in the spirit of such a radically democratic movement, livelihood must be taken out of a techno-managerial frame and transformed into an open-ended, always-revisable, experimental set of tools
for enhancing the capacities of collectives to enact forms of life beyond
the entrapments of the hegemonic trio. Livelihood frameworks and
approaches must, like Bennholdt-Thomsen and Mies's intentions for
the subsistence perspective, "enable people to produce and reproduce
their own life, to stand on their own feet and to speak in their own
voice" (1999, 3). This is not just a conceptual move; nor is it a move
only "on behalf of" those who have been silenced in development, for
it entails a fundamental transformation of the relationships between
those who would "develop" (or support "development") and those who
would be the subjects of such intervention. Livelihood will cease to
be a techno-managerial practice only when it is recognized that the
professionals who are paid to "develop" *must themselves become subjects and participants of development* as much as, and perhaps even
more than, those they work with. Indeed, it would be comic if the
tragedy were not so profound: so many professional "developers," having decided that it was *others* who needed to change, have used their
high salaries to participate as good citizens in the most destructive and
ethically anesthetized culture of consumption and waste our species
has ever enacted. Who *truly* needs "development"?

To bring this back to Maine: those of us who are concerned about
enacting other futures and escaping the clutches of the hegemonic

articulation must participate in the development of new livelihoods as members of a collective (or multiple collectives) engaged in self-transformation. To experiment with undoing "poverty" in Maine cannot simply be a matter of examining "measures of economic distress" and developing policies that "target" poor people for "improvement" (e.g., Acheson 2007), but must involve experimentation with undoing the relations of exploitation from which extractive affluence emerges and that form poverty's conditions of existence. This is to say: those who have the ability to think, write, and act via access to significant wealth and privilege (I am speaking of myself here, among others) must ourselves become sites for intervention. Professional "development" work would thus entail a becoming-vulnerable to the very questions and challenges we are promoting, an *unbecoming-professional* toward a becoming-community in new ways with/as those we work with. This is not a community that would present "us" as a unified or undifferentiated group—one in which we would say "we're all in the same boat"—but rather a community of exposure to the asymmetrical in-common of power relations, exploitations, interdependencies, and intercomplicities. Affluent developers and people struggling for daily subsistence are not in-community as part of a "human family," but rather in-community as effectuations of a common diagram of power, participants in a shared assemblage for which all must take radically differential responsibility. Perhaps more important for this project, we are also participants in an assemblage that is becoming-undone, traveling on lines of flight toward other forms of life that we must now struggle, variously yet collectively, to actualize: ecological livelihoods.

9 TOOLS FOR A POLITICS OF ECOLOGICAL LIVELIHOOD

Diverse Economies and Beyond

The construction of a politics of ecological livelihood capable of challenging and displacing the centrality of the hegemonic trio is no easy task, and it entails multiple dimensions. First and foremost it involves the work of rendering visible the many practices of ethical livelihood that are already unfolding in Maine communities—acknowledging them, strengthening them, and linking them together in webs of mutual recognition and support (Miller 2010). Efforts such as the Maine Co-operative Business Alliance, the Center for Ecology-Based Economy, and the Maine Federation of Community Food Councils (among many others) are already enacting this work in unique and powerful ways, seeking not only to support and connect that which exists, but to render innovative ethical livelihood practices accessible to ever-wider communities of people.[1] Engaging this on-the-ground organizing work with the amplifying power of activist-scholarship is crucial, and deserves its own book (or two or three). In the present project, I am focused on another important—albeit more "abstract"—dimension of transformation: how to challenge the *frames of reference* within which these efforts are commonly assembled. The language of ecological livelihoods is a starting point for this work, but it calls for further elaboration and specification. What particular conceptual tools might help to make new kinds of sense out of the complexities of livelihood negotiation?

This task of developing alternative frameworks for thinking and enacting livelihood has already been taken up robustly in one form by J. K. Gibson-Graham and other members of the Community Economies Collective. As a kind of empirical grid or prompt to explore potential spaces for the construction of community economies (chapter 7), the "diverse economies framework" proposes that conventionally recognized and celebrated activities such as paid work for a capitalist firm and capitalist market exchange are only the tip of the proverbial iceberg of livelihood practices and relations (Figure 9). A whole host of noncapitalist and "alternative" forms of labor, enterprise, transaction, finance, and property are alive and well below the waterline, sustaining us even while not being recognized as such by standard metrics and institutions (Gibson-Graham, Cameron, and Healy 2013). This is a powerful image and approach that has inspired and animated numerous action research and organizing projects around the world and has shaped my own thinking and work profoundly.[2] It enables me now to ask questions that push *beyond* it: What if we cease

Figure 9. The diverse economies iceberg. Image by Adam Turnbull, used with permission.

to talk about an "economy"? What happens when those things labeled "economic" can no longer be separated from those labeled "ecological"? What is called forth when, in a rapidly warming world, the iceberg *melts* (Figure 10) and we are confronted with a breakdown of the line between the *inside* and the *outside* of that which sustains us?

My task in this chapter is to initiate a project of transposing the connective and proliferative intuitions of diverse economies theory into a new key, one in which the separations between elements of the hegemonic trio are no longer implied or even possible. This entails the development of new frameworks for conceptualizing the nature of our interdependencies. "A *new mode of distinguishing* is necessary," writes Jason Moore (2015, 22). How do we begin to articulate—while acknowledging inevitable heuristic simplification—a way to talk

Figure 10. The iceberg, melting. Original image by Adam Turnbull, modified with permission by Ethan Miller.

about the dimensions of ecological livelihood without recourse to the old categories of the trio or their surrogates? Elizabeth Barron's notion of "econo-ecologies," articulating human and more-than-human livelihoods together to "make clear the intimate and heterogeneous relationships that exist among biota (human and nonhuman)" (2015, 174) is one such allied beginning, and I experiment in this chapter with co-resonant directions that such a development might take. I weave together here a constellation of concepts to prompt further work and thinking in Maine and beyond: a *livelihoods triad*, which elaborates a relational approach to thinking beyond the simple notion of "making a living"; a fleshed-out conceptualization of *habitat* and its many dimensions; an ethico-political approach to the *commoning* and *uncommoning* of livelihood practice; and, finally, a framework for mapping and amplifying cross-fertilizing and synergy-building practices of *trans-commoning*. Taken together, these various concepts might begin to constitute a rudimentary "toolbox" for an experimental political praxis of ecological livelihood.

Making, Receiving, Providing: The Triad of Livelihood

How are livelihoods made? A classic answer in many strains of social theory is that they are made through human labor. We work for our livings. Whether built on the assumption of a fickle nature from which life must be wrested or on a paradigm of abundant resources upon which human creativity can work its world-shaping magic, the core focus remains the same: on the myriad ways in which human beings "set[ ] in motion the natural forces which belong to [their] own body, [their] arms, legs, head, and hands, in order to appropriate the materials of nature in a form adapted to [their] own needs" (Marx 1992, 283). In such a frame, it is almost inevitable that something like an "environment" will emerge as an externalized source and sink, and that a "society" will continue to stand as an aggregate catch-all for those nonenvironmental dynamics that exceed the individual or household but cannot be reduced to an environment or "nature." Moreover, the image associated with livelihoods as (only) *making* a living remains tied to images of autonomous, rational, optimizing individuals that have caused so much trouble in the history of Western industrialism, patriarchy, and colonialism (Whatmore 1997). To ward off these forms of recapture, we need to be able to speak of livelihood in ways that acknowledge and expand possibilities for agency while also refusing to affirm a lone human subject as standing, premade and presumed, at the center of a world of objects and objective dynamics.

What stands at the center instead, I propose, is not a subject or an object—indeed, not a thing of any kind at all—but an *encounter*. Living singularities, in whatever forms they may take in different ecopoietic regimes, can be viewed as differential effects of the ongoing convergence of three relational dimensions or processes (Figure 11): *making* one's living (autopoiesis), having one's living *made* by others, human and nonhuman (allopoiesis), and making livings *for* others (alterpoiesis). From the standpoint of the singularity that emerges from this convergence, we can also refer to this trio in terms of *receiving, making,* and *providing*. I use the term "singularity" here once again as a way to remain open to a wide variety of possible entities to which this triadic relation can be applied. An "individual" is only one possible kind of being that might emerge, and we may just as effectively use this framework to explore the constitutive relations of an organization, a family, an identity group, a historical formation, a population, or a species. For all singularities, each of these moments is inescapable

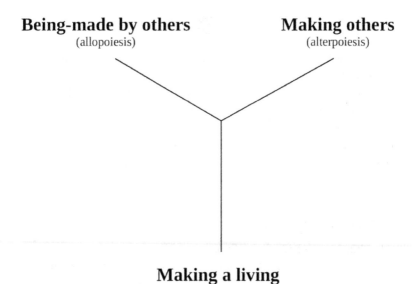

Being-made by others   **Making others**
(allopoiesis)   (alterpoiesis)

Making a living
(autopoiesis)

Figure 11. The livelihoods triad: Making, being-made, and making-others.

dimensions of ecopoiesis, and each is also split by the always-open questions of *that which can be known* (What makes us? Who do we make?), *that which can be engaged and transformed* (How can we compose this relation differently?), and *that which utterly exceeds us*.

This triad is not intended as ontological totalization that diagrams the structure of life itself. It is a *strategic* figure, a tool for generating questions and connections. In contrast with the ontologizing device of the prism (chapter 4), the livelihoods triad can be figured as a kaleidoscope. It is a machine designed, as its Greek etymology describes, to compose "beautiful forms" for a viewer. Rather than presenting things as they "really" are, as if from a "God's eye view" (Haraway 1991), the kaleidoscope is an overt assemblage of viewer-instrument-light-image-world that diffracts, simplifies, and multiplies all at once to transform a particular scene, for a particular participant, into a momentarily stabilized "beautiful form." In Gilles Deleuze and Félix Guattari's terms, the triad is a *map* rather than a tracing:

> [It] fosters connections between fields, the removal of blockages on bodies without organs, the maximum opening of bodies without organs. . . . The map is open and connectable in all of its dimensions; it is detachable, reversible, susceptible to constant modification. It can be torn, reversed, adapted to any kind of mounting, reworked by an individual, group, or social formation. . . . A map has multiple entryways, as opposed to the tracing, which always comes back "to the same." (1987, 13)

Unlike the molar categories of the hegemonic trio, which claim to subsume and explain the world by putting everything in its place, one can make no generalizations about the elements of the livelihoods triad. It is composed only by an act of situated engagement, always laden with the specificities of power and context, and it is meant to help us more effectively render visible the relations of livelihood in which we participate. The point, of course, as Marx always reminds us (1975, 423), is not just to see them, but to *change* them.

Autopoiesis, or Self-Making

The dimension of *making a living*, to which I have already referred, involves the active work of seeking, procuring, and producing the means of sustenance. At first glance, and with the weight of hegemony bearing down, one might be tempted to see this as just another way to talk about the economy. Recall, however, the multiplications of chapter 6: no such distinction can be sustained for long when we are speaking of all manifestations of life-making work. Making a living names all the dimensions of self-production or "autopoiesis" (Maturana and Varela 1980) in which all living beings engage; most fundamentally the ongoing construction and maintenance of relatively stable forms of living organization—including patterns of meaning—from flows of energy and matter. Some of this work (perhaps more than most freedom-loving humans would want to acknowledge) unfolds outside consciousness or intention as autonomic processes: a beating heart, a pulse of endocrine, a neural signal, a shift in temperature-regulation activity, a reflex. And some of this work is quite intentional: seeking, seizing, choosing, imagining, planning, altering, harvesting, catching, processing, collecting, saving, and persisting. Autopoeisis is the enactment of "living labor" in the Marxian sense, only extended beyond Marx's humanist conceits that would rob a bee of its dignity (Marx 1992, 284; see also Morton 2017). It is the site of agency in which a subject exercises particular forms of capacity, perception, skill, and knowledge to engage a world that it also participates in making.

Self-making is a matter of composing relations of and with "mediators," various forms of embodiment, capacitation, and enhancement that link one thing to another in chains of action (Latour 2005). To eat, for example, is a matter of particular perceptive apparatuses (eyes, noses, molecular receptors, cilia, etc.) forming and sustaining relations with other entities that may become "food" if other mediators of knowledge, memory, embodied response, and means of intake and digestion are all lined up (Farina 2011). To make a living is to assemble networks of mediators and to be assembled by and through them; to fail to make this assembly, or to be thwarted by other forces, is to risk suffering or death. This point is crucial to avoiding an affirmation of the diagrammatic distinction between subjects and objects, thus viewing life-making as a matter of a preformed agent (subject) doing things *to* and *on* a passive, stagelike world. As Haraway asserts, autopoiesis is always "sympoiesis," making-with (2016, 58). Agency might best be understood here as "distributed" (Bennett 2010)—an emergent property of a collective *making* that composes its own locus.

While deeply problematic when taken by itself as a definition of life or as a "model for living and dying worlds and their critters" (Haraway 2016, 33), autopoiesis is nonetheless a crucial dimension of livelihood that must be acknowledged, cultivated, and continually politicized. It is undoubtedly the dimension of livelihood that tends to receive the most attention amid a hegemonic assemblage focused so intently on the autonomous individual. And yet this attention often elides or obscures the many ethical and political questions that can be asked about the work we do to produce ourselves and our habitats: Who determines the conditions and trajectories of our self-making labor? How might we do this work differently? What actions and strategies become available to a self-making singularity (a Maine family, a rural Maine community, the state itself) in a given habitat (*oikos*)? How do desires for different forms of action emerge and how are they acted upon or thwarted? To what extent does a given relation or arrangement open up possibilities for the increase of agential expression, for whom, in what collective combinations, and at what costs to others?

Allopoiesis, or Being-Made by Others

While the agency and self-making power that emerges in the dimension of making a living is crucial, its overemphasis—as I have noted—risks reinscribing an impossible normative demand toward an autonomy that we need to confront and transform. As our increasingly visible interdependencies with a more-than-human living world make clear, we are all utterly dependent on beings and forces that exceed us. We are made by others in a dimension that can be called "allopoiesis" (*allo*, from the outside). I draw this term from Francisco Varela, Humberto Maturana, and Ricardo Uribe (1974), who define it in contrast with autopoiesis as the production and maintenance of a system's organization from forces beyond that system. Autopoiesis and allopoiesis are not, however, mutually exclusive dynamics. As microbiologist Scott Gilbert (2013) argues, building on the work of Lynn Margulis (e.g., 1999), dependence on relations with others is a constitutive property of life itself. No autopoiesis without allopoiesis: prior to any making of a living, we must be *given* one (Puig de la Bellacasa 2017, 70).[3] We are all on the dole. In one sense, being-made involves various relations by which others "provide" energy, matter, and meaning that sustain us. Prominent examples in the human domain include birth, parenting, language acquisition, support in times of sickness, physical nourishment, and our relations with those from whom our money comes (whether via simple exchange, redistribution, or the exploitation of others). The discourse of "ecosystem services," increasingly common

in Maine as an attempt to value more-than-human constitutive relations in terms amenable to the hegemonic articulation (Troy 2012),
also names key relations of being-made. Sue Jackson and Lisa Palmer
propose to resignify and reorient this discourse toward "a relational
ethic of care and responsibility" by focusing on concrete, constitutive
relations of "communicative reciprocity within and across human [and]
non-human realms" (2014, 2).[4]

Being-made is not just about the provision of materials that feed
autopoiesis; it also names what Elizabeth Grosz calls the "non-normative
imperatives of an outside that weighs on individuals and groups, in
ways that they cannot control but are implicated in and are effects of"
(2005, 51). The *allo* may be parents, friends, bosses, exploited employees, or the living beings who become our food, but it is also gravity,
genetic variety, the emergent properties of myriad forms of energy and
matter that not only produce limits to action but also incite it, provoke it, and constitute its conditions of possibility (Grosz 2005, 43–
44). To recognize our being-made, and the being-made of all that is
actualized in our world(s), is to foreground a constitutive dependence
that simultaneously demands reciprocity and exceeds any possibility
of it. What does it mean to be alive and capable of limited yet precious
action—that is, to embody *response-ability*—in the presence of a creation that can never be mastered?

At the interface between allopoiesis and autopoiesis, we can speak
of a host of actual and possible relations by which the work of self-
making encounters and incorporates its conditions of possibility: theft,
gift, borrowing, exchange. Each of these relations and their variations
are premised on, and constitutive of, a different set of habitat relations.
Are more-than-human lives and their labor understood as resources to
which (certain) humans are entitled via nonreciprocal appropriation?
Do the things that sustain us from beyond ourselves merit reciprocity or ongoing relations of responsibility? What kinds of institutions
(property relations, stories, rituals) do we institute in relation to the
myriad dimensions of allopoiesis in our lives and communities? What
modes of being-made must be struggled against, and which modes
embraced? These are ethical questions, and they open toward others,
since *we do not even know with whom we are connected* (Latour 1998).
How might we render our interdependencies more visible while also
recognizing the impossibility of any complete accounting? How do we
gain, as the well-known "serenity prayer" has it (Niebuhr 1987, 251),

the wisdom to discern the difference between those dependencies that can be transformed and at whose mercy we truly are?[5]

Alterpoiesis, or Making Others

The third dimension of the livelihoods triad, that of *making-others*, entails "us" (whoever we may be) standing in the very position of those others by whom we are made, acting ourselves as forces of creation. So much of the energy of self-making is, in fact, oriented toward making livings *for* others. I call this dimension "alterpoiesis" (*alter* as in "other"). In some cases, it takes the form of involuntary relations: exploitation by capitalist firms that provides surplus for owners at the expense of producers, playing host to various (other kinds of) parasites, or becoming compost when we die. In other cases, alterpoiesis forms a core part of the intention or vector of a living being: giving birth, raising children, contributing to the composition and sustenance of various collectivities, caring for places and things, supporting elders and others. And many relations are complexly ambiguous, fraught with power and struggle: the sense in which the capitalist firms noted above do provide essential wages and benefits amid (and because of) exploitation; ways in which women have so often unevenly borne the weight of care work; the complex dynamics of state-enforced social redistribution; and the vexing problem of our responsibility to future generations for things like climate stability, habitat toxicity, and the inheritance of profound inequality.

The making of others is clearly not reducible either to altruism—"because I care"—or to instrumentalism—"if I care for you, you'll care for me"—precisely because of the ecological nature of livelihood relations. One may not ever know if one's making of others will help to make oneself in turn; and indeed, where are the boundaries of this self in a context in which we emerge at the very intersection of an *auto*, an *allo*, and an *alter*? As Scott Gilbert, Jan Sapp, and Alfred Tauber (2012) remind us in their work on the pervasive nature of organismal symbiosis, "we have never been individuals." Key ethical questions in this dimension of making-others include: To whom are we obliged or called to offer our energies, our lives, and ourselves? To what extent are these relations shaped by forms of coercion and violence, and to what extent can we transform such relations? How are our makings-of-others connected with our being-made, recirculating energies and matter in ways that maintain our habitats and those of others, and to what extent is this connection severed by various extractive mediations? What habitats, what worlds, do we participate in producing for others—now and in generations to come?

Habitat

This schema of making, being-made, and making-others is, ironically, another trio, but as a *triadic relation* it is radically different from the geometry that characterizes the hegemonic formation. This livelihoods triad cannot be turned into a triangle, a Venn diagram, or a series of nested spheres without isolating, deanimating, or freezing the dynamic relations it is intended to foreground. Indeed, no term can stand alone; nor can it be connected to another without passing through the point of encounter and emergence at the heart of the triad. Making a living is possible only in its relation to being-made; making-others emerges only from making oneself. Making a living stands as a relational *relay* between two realms of making (poiesis) that require its connection or mediation (Figure 12). One's making of others becomes, for those others, the dynamic of being-made. In this sense, a triad can never stand alone and is always already on the way to becoming part of another triad. "I" and "we" emerge as nodes and relays in a complex ecological mesh, sites of continually enacted agential articulation between a habitat that makes us and the habitats of others that we participate in making (Figure 13). As the effects of multiple encounter(s) between being-made, making, and making others, we are this complex mesh of intersecting and overlapping livelihood assemblages, "a knot of species coshaping one another in layers of reciprocating complexity all the way down" (Haraway 2008, 42). As Timothy Morton puns, "*What a fine mesh we've gotten ourselves into*" (2010, 61). Since we cannot get ourselves out, we must, as the impossible and necessary task of ecology demands, go *in*.

I defined "habitat" in chapter 7 as a set of relations—which may or may not pertain to a single, discrete place—from which singularities emerge and upon which they act. It is, in Val Plumwood's words (drawing inspiration from Kakadu elder Bill Niedje), "that which grows us" (2008, 145) and that which we, in turn, grow and sustain (or undermine). This definition can be further elaborated in light of the relations of the triad: while autopoiesis, allopoiesis, and alterpoiesis name

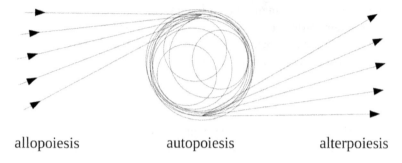

allopoiesis   autopoiesis   alterpoiesis

Figure 12. The relay of livelihoods.

Figure 13. The mesh of livelihood relations, webs of habitat.

processes and relations by which a singularity emerges, habitat is a
way to speak of the whole adjacent mesh that is differentially composed by, and in turn composes, these relations. It is, in a sense, the
sum total of that from which allopoiesis draws and that to which alterpoiesis contributes—the more or less durable *assemblage* of accumu-
lated, co-constitutive ecopoietic interrelations. This is difficult to think,
but crucial: habitat cannot be understood as an "environment" in the

hegemonic, passive sense of a pool of resources from which a particular being or population draws. It is always a realm of other beings, other relations, other triads operating at varying speeds and with varying durabilities. "Climate," for example, does not name a *thing* or substrate upon which millions of contemporary species rely, but rather an emergent property of a mesh of triadic relations within which all beings are differentially participating (Margulis 1999; Volk 2003; Harding 2006). Habitat is materialized as *habit* in the Deleuzian sense: "the way in which life accommodates materiality and brings its own materiality into coordination with [other] material forces" (Grosz 2013, 231).[6]

Habitat can and must, therefore, be conceptually distinguished from the three moments of the triad even if, in practice, they are inseparable. What *are* our habitats? How do our modes of life sustain or undermine them? How do we participate in caring for or destroying the habitats of others with which our own livelihood assemblages are intertwined?[7] Lest this sound, once again, like "environmentalism," I propose a rough schema for mapping key dimensions of human habitat (Figure 14).[8] We live, I suggest, in dynamic negotiation with and through *biosocial habitat* that involves the living labor of humans and nonhumans producing (or undermining) our bodily conditions of existence; *geosocial habitat* that is composed through nonliving agencies, often in negotiation with biosocial processes, on geological scales and temporalities— relations of earth, mineral, climate, cosmos; *technical habitat* that enables (or disables) the realization of particular forms of life; *institutional habitat* that structures life via durable forms of organization, governance, and rule; *cultural-conceptual habitat* through which foundational understandings of "the world" are generated, sustained, and transformed; and *emotional-affective* habitat through which patterns of affective resonance and structures of collective feeling and sense are composed and recomposed.[9]

These forms of habitat are impossibly blurred in practice, but their distinctions can be useful in generating analyses and strategies that resist the categories of the hegemonic trio while also moving beyond the "fog bank." Take the problem of poverty in Maine, for example. As I described in chapter 3, poverty is composed by the hegemonic assemblage in terms of a lack of monetary income and wealth, perhaps combined with an analysis of various "social" factors that generate and sustain such lack. But money, from the perspective of those needing it (quite distinct from the perspective of those accumulating it far beyond

Biosocial Habitat	Webs of human and more-than-human bodily sustenance; wider relations and processes of living ecological labor. This includes distant relations of production mediated by markets (migrant work, factory work, colonial exploitation, invisible labor) as well as the relations sometimes referred to as "ecosystem services."
Geosocial Habitat	Biosocial relations plus (though sometimes minus) the forces of nonliving matter, acting on geological scales and temporalities -- everything from the Earths' climate system, nutrient cycles, soil formation, and plate tectonics to interplanetary dynamics (moon cycles, seasons, etc).
Technical Habitat	Enabling tools and techniques that compose relations with other forms of habitat, including embodied skills, technical knowledge, processing systems ("software"), and various forms of "hardware."
Institutional Habitat	Forms of collective organization, governance, law and its enforcement structures; including multiple forms ranging from kinship, identity groupings, and modes of structured livelihood provisioning to durable organizations and state forms.
Cultural-Conceptual Habitat	Worldviews, stories, ontological accounts, frameworks, concepts, forms of circulating knowledge; hegemonic and counter-hegemonic diagrams that shape collective understandings and experiences of reality and its spaces of freedom and constraint.
Emotional-Affective Habitat	Patterns of circulating affect, feeling, collective energies or "vibes," rippling or cascading processes of trauma and healing, the often-invisible "baggage" of collective experience that shapes action and possibility.

Figure 14. Types of habitat.

any need), is one *habitat mediator* among many (Latour 2005, 37), and it renders only certain habitat relations into sites of sustenance (i.e., only those things it can purchase). From the perspective of ecological livelihoods, poverty takes on a radically different set of meanings. One can lack habitat—sustaining allopoietic sources—in multiple dimensions. Insufficient biosocial relations can compromise health and direct sustenance. Destabilized geosocial habitat (e.g., climate change) may change the rhythm of seasons, break sustaining precipitation and growth patterns, or flood homes. One can lack technical mediators that would render existing (possible) habitat relations useful: no skills for the available jobs, no knowledge of growing or foraging food, no ability to build and fix things in the absence of money to pay for it. The landscape of institutional habitat may be broken or destructive: rules about kinship that render nonheterosexual forms of love into sites of exclusion and struggle, policing practices that mark nonwhite bodies as targets of violence, or structures of decision-making that make no space for the agency of those most affected by rules and their implementations. I could go on, but the key point is that "poverty" can take many forms, and for each of these there is a corresponding set of possibilities for wealth and well-being. The mapping of such a landscape enables new kinds of empirical precision when it comes to engaging the details of sustenance, and it might also generate a radically different politics, with new possibilities for identity, alliance, and collective action.

Commoning and Uncommoning Livelihoods

Clearly, problems of politics confront us. It is one thing to map the diverse relations of livelihood and its habitats, and it is another thing to compose new sites of negotiation, struggle, and creation through which transformation might unfold. If the livelihoods triad and the concept of habitat can help to open up new experiences of ethical awareness and new possibilities for ethical encounter and negotiation, they do not yet constitute a set of tools for *politicizing* these openings. By "politics," I mean the process—often struggle—by which particular orders of life and power are produced, challenged, unmade, and remade. Ethics opens *questions* about how we should live together, while politics wrestles over the construction and institution of provisional *answers* (Miller 2013b). How should common worlds be instituted? Who gets to participate in this process? To begin engaging with the politics of ecological livelihood, we need a set of concepts that render visible the ways in which the various moments of ecopoiesis become sites for politics or are closed down as such. For this task, I propose the language of *commoning* and *uncommoning*.

A robust literature on the concept and practice of "commons" has flourished in recent years, most often focusing on the myriad ways in which human communities make, share, and care for pools of collective, material and immaterial resources.[10] This has tended to place emphasis on particular types of property relationships, contrasting the collectively managed and shared commons, for example, with regimes of private property and unmanaged open access. Historian Peter Linebaugh (2008) initiated a crucial shift in language and thinking when he introduced the term "commoning" to this conversation, focusing less on *things* in common and more on the complex *processes* of social labor through which the in-common is produced and reproduced. As Massimo De Angelis describes, "there are no commons without incessant activities of commoning, of (re)producing in common" (2010, 955).

Commoning, in this understanding, is the self-activity of a community of people who "make and share a commons" (Gibson-Graham, Cameron, and Healy 2013, 130), a continual practice of making-common and sustaining that which sustains. Commoning involves various forms of collective intervention in flows of matter, energy, and meaning that compose the commons community, and it entails the collective construction and maintenance of particular boundaries, values, habits, and institutions that enact ongoing care.

I wish to build on this notion, but with an important twist and clarification. As I noted in chapter 8, De Angelis articulates his elaboration of commoning in terms of a distinction between value orientations. "Commoning," he writes, "is a life flow in which money, if necessary, is only a means to a human end—unlike capital flows whose only rationale for moving is a gap, a delta . . . a quantitative increase in money" (2017, 206). Commons and commoning are equated here with what I have called livelihoods—a set of relations and practices oriented toward sustenance rather than accumulation. But not all forms of sustenance involve an explicit acknowledgment of or commitment to the in-common. Numerous Maine families engage with livelihood through institutions of exclusive private property ("This is *my* woodlot") and amid all kinds of refusals to acknowledge interdependence (denying reliance, for example, on the labor of undocumented migrants for food). While commoning is always about livelihood, livelihood is not always explicitly about commoning and can sometimes entail its denial. By merging his analysis of a life-value orientation with the concept of commoning, De Angelis renders it difficult to engage the many places where this disjunction appears. How do we understand and intervene in practices of noncapitalist livelihood that *do not* involve "modes of production, distribution and governance of the commons that are participatory and non-hierarchical, motivated by the values of the commons (re)production" (De Angelis 2017, 121)?

A similar blurring occurs in Michael Hardt and Antonio Negri's conception of the common, which can be viewed as a close analog to my notion of habitat. On one hand, the common is produced as the shared conditions through which all relation and communication are made possible (2004, xv). On the other hand, "the common marks a new form of sovereignty, a democratic sovereignty . . . in which the social singularities control through their own biopolitical activity those goods and services that allow for the reproduction of the multitude itself" (2004, 206). In its first version, the common marks an ontological condition, while in the second it describes the collective recognition of this shared life and thus an overt site for political organization and struggle. A continually produced ontological common (habitat) is, without a doubt, a necessary precondition for the common as a political struggle, but the use of the same term for both moments renders the possible disjunction between them—itself a key site of struggle—difficult to engage. There are forms of shared life, of habitat, that enable livelihoods in common while never facilitating anything resembling democratic sovereignty.

A distinction must be made, then, between relations of sustenance and the rendering of these relations as sites of explicit struggle and connection. This is how I propose to understand commoning: as the *ethico-political explicitation of habitat*. Commoning refers to the myriad ways in which livelihood relations are rendered into shared spaces of mutual exposure and negotiation through which living singularities actively respond to the ethical demands posed by specific instances of an ontological in-common. This is to say that commoning constitutes shared "matters of concern" (Latour 2005), or, better yet, "matters of care" (Puig de la Bellacasa 2017), where "matter" should be taken in both senses of the word at once. It is not that *all things shared* are commoned, but that all shared matters are commoned to the extent that they appear as active questions, concerns, or sites of struggle. Gravity, for example, is a shared condition of existence for all, but it would not (yet) constitute a site of commoning for beings other than certain physicists and their assemblages until such a time that someone were to develop an antigravity machine and open the common as a possible site of explicit negotiation. The climate of the planet has constituted a shared field of experience for humans and other organisms since their evolutionary emergence; yet the climate only becomes a site of potential commoning when certain humans become aware of their active role in undermining its recent, relative stability and begin to experience this climate as a site of ethical and political engagement (Gibson-Graham, Cameron, and Healy 2016).

Commoning unfolds, then, as the composition of an innumerable set of variable "spheres" of concern and negotiation that articulate livelihood triads together in explicitly common habitat assemblages. It is the site where *oikoi* overlap, converge, and enter into forms of material-semiotic negotiation. It is often a boundary-drawing site, an enclosure,

since it entails particular participants and not others, particular negotiated settlements and stalemates that must be bounded in order to
remain stable. Thus commoning cannot be contrasted—as it often
is—with enclosure.[11] This is to say that while some enclosures disrupt
and destroy commons, others actually *constitute* them. The ethico-
political question must shift from "commons versus enclosure" to *what
enclosure, for whom, for what purpose, and to what effect?* It matters a
great deal which *side* of a given enclosure one ends up standing on.

For clarity's sake, then, I suggest that we oppose processes of
commoning with those of *uncommoning*.[12] If commoning is a making-
explicit of the negotiations of the common (habitat), then uncommoning is an *anesthetization of the common*, its ethico-political closure, a
rendering-nonnegotiable of habitat relations.[13] Uncommoning is not
a *non*-common, since habitat itself cannot be undone as a shared
condition of existence, and nor does it always entail the destruction of
that which sustains us. Uncommoning is, in a strange way, also an
articulation of the ontological common and even a production of sustaining habitat, but this production is *alienated* or estranged in the
Marxian sense (Marx 1964)—dispossessed, in varying degrees, of the
means of encounter, negotiation, and response-ability. The conventional capitalist factory is a space of the common, of a shared existence
for those who work there; but until workers organize to challenge or
rupture capitalist discipline, it remains *uncommoned habitat*. To the
extent that the distancing relations of commodity exchange, combined
with etho-ecologies of resentment and fear, render migrant farm labor
into a site of unacknowledged interdependence and unrealized ethical responsibility, this dimension of biosocial habitat is uncommoned.
When farmworkers and consumers organize to construct new forms
of encounter and relation, opening up space for recognition and negotiation of interdependence—and perhaps mutual struggle in the face
of exploitation—this habitat becomes a site of commoning. As the de-
alienation of shared habitat relations, commoning is the politicization
of ecological livelihoods.

A crucial concern might be raised at this point. Is this notion of commoning, which foregrounds the opening of questions and the making-
explicit of negotiations, really another thinly disguised form of "human
exceptionalism"? Does it imply, with its apparent emphasis on conscious acknowledgment and representation, that "human communities [are] distinguished by an ethics and/or politics in which no beings

other than humans can possibly participate" (Smith 2013, 24)?[14] I
think not, and for two reasons. First, the human itself is already
understood—if we take ecological livelihood seriously—as a more-
than-human assemblage. There is no discrete zone of "humanity,"
separated from a zone of the "nonhuman" (as in Nature/Culture) from
which an exceptionalism could be sustained. "Human," as Morton
describes, "means me plus my nonhuman prostheses and symbionts,
such as my bacterial microbiome and my technological gadgets, an
entity that cannot be determined in advance within a thin, rigid outline"
(2017, 40). Even *if* only "humans" are commoning (and this is rarely
the case), then a multispecies collectivity is always already at the heart
of the negotiation. Second, there is no reason to believe that humans
are the only living beings capable of ethical encounter and therefore of
commoning. "If ethics," writes Mick Smith, "is . . . a mode in which communities can be created and constituted, a sensibility that allows things
to appear in an other-directed loving gaze, to affect events, hearts, and
minds, to open new fields of significance . . . then this is not a mode
that is in any sense co-extensive with the human species" (2013, 26).
The ethical and political explicitation I have associated with commoning need not take the form of words or of human-generated representation: the protesting cry of an entrapped monkey, breaking through
the anesthetizing assemblage of an experimental lab, is a call toward
commoning. So, too, is the response of an apple tree to practices of
care or abuse. If there is a human located as the recipient of such calls
in these cases, this is only because commoning never takes place *in
general*; it is always from a *particular* place, experience, and being. I
am writing primarily about the kinds of commoning—by far not the
only kinds—in which humans participate in some substantive way.

How does all of this relate to the hegemonic trio? While economy,
society, and environment do capture and constitute various dimensions of habitat—markets, regulatory institutions, social norms, statistical representations, social funds, pools of "natural resources" upon
which many rely—I have described in previous chapters many of the
ways in which these articulations enact uncommonings. Whether via
relations that subordinate Maine people and others to "market forces,"
enforce majoritarian norms of (economistic) human agency and subjectivity, or isolate human subjects from a more-than-human living world
rendered into objects or environment, these modes of the in-common
divide our constitutive interrelations against each other and render

their radically democratic ethical negotiation difficult. The political task, then, is to challenge all articulations that appear to determine beforehand what the shape of common habitat is and might become, and to open new spaces for shared recognition and negotiation of our actual, complex livelihood relations. "The only way to compose a common world," writes Latour, ". . . consists precisely in not dividing up at the outset and without due process what is common and what is private, what is objective and what is subjective" (2004a, 93). And, I would add, what is economic, social, environmental, or otherwise. A political praxis of ecological livelihoods begins with the work of mapping the contours of livelihood relations, assembling potential commoners, and then actively commoning these relations as sites of collective ethical action and transformation toward more just and viable shared worlds.

A powerful example of such a praxis in Maine is the story of the Port Clyde community-supported fisheries (CSF) project, sparked in part by an action research "counter-mapping" project seeking to render collective practices of fishing and ocean-care more visible. In the neo-liberal assemblage of commercial fishing practice, fishermen are articulated as "spatially mobile and competing individuals" (St. Martin 2009, 500), seeking to maximize their catches (and monetary returns) in an undifferentiated ocean resource space. But in 2002, Kevin St. Martin, Madeleine Hall-Arber, and other collaborators began a process of radically challenging this view. Using a large database of vessel trip reports from the National Marine Fisheries Service, and in collaboration with numerous fishers in the region, they produced a new cartographic representation that visually correlated the relationships between the home ports of fishing vessels and the particular ocean regions in which they were fishing. Instead of depicting a generic scattershot of individual boat trips, this map depicted discrete clusters of work—zones of shared activity linked with particular *communities* of fish and the people catching them. While the existence of such clusters was not unknown to those engaged in the work, seeing and discussing this map in participatory workshops helped some members of the Port Clyde fishing community to generate a fresh *recognition* of collectivity and interdependence (St. Martin 2009). A new commoning was initiated.

Seeing and interacting with these maps of a "community-at-sea," according to Robert Snyder and St. Martin, "resonated with the nascent group of concern forming in Port Clyde and complemented its emerging vision of a future fishing industry based on community and environmental well-being" (2015, 35). Sparked by a new sense of solidarity and collective responsibility for their part of the ocean, this group formed the Midcoast Fishermen's Association (MFA) as a vehicle through which to advocate for area-based fisheries management and develop new forms of mutual support. With assistance from the Northwest Atlantic Marine Alliance and the Island Institute, the MFA went on to create the Midcoast Fishermen's Cooperative and to build Port Clyde Fresh Catch—the world's first community-supported fisheries (CSF) program, modeled on the widely recognized practice of community-supported agriculture. Through the CSF, fishers were able to begin composing a new assemblage of concern and care among themselves, the ocean ecosystems they work with, and the communities of humans who are sustained by the fish they catch.[15] The uncommoning of the neoliberal fishery assemblage was radically challenged here, as multiple forms of commoning were consolidated and constructed through a shift in collective vision. What else can the work of commoning do?

Trans-Commoning: Articulating Community Livelihoods

If the hegemonic assemblage *assembles* via the composition of durable linkages across multiple domains—bodies, processes, ideas, subjectivities—then the work of composing new modes of life must do the same. Pervasive practices of uncommoning can be undone and transformed on wider scales only by practices of commoning that break their isolation from one another and together compose what De Angelis calls "commons ecologies" (2017, 287). These are webs or networks of commoning practices and sites, connected in ways that generate and sustain dynamics of mutual support and collective amplification. By linking together, constructing new forms of interdependence, and sharing resources and experiences, commoning communities become more durable and resilient in the face of multiple challenges. Indeed, they may also increase their capacities to expand and grow—thus commoning that which had been uncommoned in new ways and actively challenging and transforming hegemonic assemblages of livelihood. The active labor of constructing and maintaining such connections, of commoning between and across multiple commons, is what De Angelis (2017) calls "boundary commoning" and what I will call *trans-commoning*.[16]

This is precisely the strategy of change that has been proposed and developed within solidarity economy movements around the world over the past twenty years (Arruda 2009; Mance 2010; Miller 2010). Rather than viewing radical transformation as a matter of overthrowing a monolithic and all-encompassing "capitalist system" and imposing a new—ostensibly better—order in its place, solidarity economy efforts begin by recognizing the actually-existing diversity of cooperative, equitable, noncapitalist livelihood practices. Built from the creativity of communities responding to their own needs "from the bottom up," initiatives such as worker cooperatives, community land trusts, housing cooperatives, community currencies, solidarity markets, subsistence homesteads, community loan funds, and cooperative banks (among many others) can serve as locally rooted, democratically responsive elements from which wider webs of liberatory livelihood can be constructed. Solidarity economy organizing is, therefore, not about convincing people to adopt a particular economic model or vision; it is about generating new kinds of visibility for existing solidarity (commoning) practices and linking them together in dynamic networks. It is about trans-commoning practices of ecological livelihood.[17]

In 2006, I developed a graphical tool to help map existing practices of interconnection between solidarity economy initiatives and to enable new possibilities for such linkages (Miller 2006). This circle, which linked six livelihood "moments" of creation, production, transaction, consumption, surplus allocation, and governance has been mobilized in a variety of teaching and organizing contexts. I return to it now, modified and elaborated (Figure 15), in light of the project of ecological livelihoods. Transposed out of the key of economy, it serves as a tool for visualizing the landscape of actual and possible trans-commoning practices. It is a different "view" on livelihood than that of the triad: whereas the schema of receiving-making-providing centers a particular singularity at its point of ongoing emergence, the livelihood circle involves a stepping back to view an entire "local" web within the larger mesh of interdependence. It is a way to account for some of the many interconnected commonings through which multiple members of a collectivity are sustained. While perhaps appearing quite systematic, this circle in no way intends to represent a "system" in the sense of a unified, self-contained entity that can be characterized by generalizable dynamics or "laws." It is not an economy, a society, or an environment. It is, rather, a *strategic map of relations*, actual and possible.

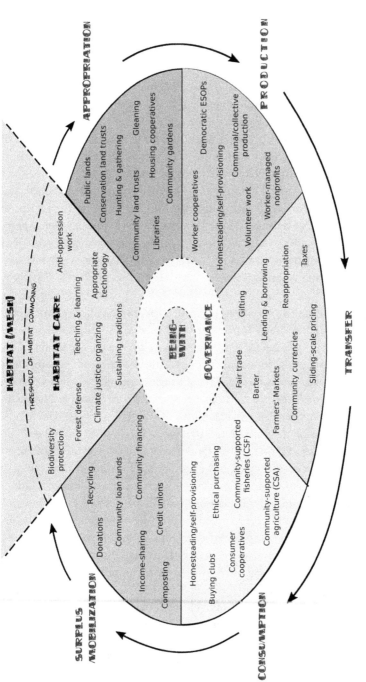

Figure 15. Circle of livelihood: Trans-commonings, actual or possible.

The circle "begins," and also opens or even ruptures, with the ecological mesh of habitat—the constitutive zone of allopoiesis beyond accounting. A line can be drawn here that marks the point at which particular dimensions of this habitat become common concerns, and the conscious, active work of *habitat care* begins. This livelihood "moment" includes all the ways that members of a given collectivity participate in maintaining or enhancing the health and resilience of the habitat relations upon which they and many others depend. While some of this work is currently the domain of conventional "environmentalism" (focused, perhaps, on biosocial and geosocial habitats), it also includes the work of caring for cultural-conceptual, institutional, technical, and emotional-affective habitat relations. Moving to the next moment of the circle, these habitat relations are realized only through their *appropriation* as such by those whom they sustain, and this includes relations of property and dynamics of procurement: Through what relations are particular habitat relations accessed and secured? This is where the "inputs" of *production* come from, where production refers to the myriad autopoietic processes by which the matter, energy, and meaning provided by others is transformed via labor into the refined "goods and services" needed for sustenance. Once produced, the things of the world must (except in the case of direct subsistence work) pass to others through some form of *transfer* or transaction (gift, theft, exchange) before they are used or *consumed* as sources of sustenance. These various moments generate diverse forms of excess or *surplus*, which must then be allocated—wasted, redistributed, or reinvested in either habitat care or production. All of these moments involve forms of *governance*, or the construction and negotiation of durable rules—not just via the state, but in multiple forms—that structure collective relations and dynamics. Finally, at the heart of it all are the processes by which "we" learn and unlearn how to live together—the practices of *being-with* that animate our daily relationships of love, friendship, cooperation, conflict, division, and collective learning.

The structure of the circle should be taken only as a rough guide and not as a claim to any absolute distinctions or to a fixed set of relations between the moments of livelihood. In practice, it is all in *motion*, with relations in each zone of the circle crossing over, blurring, linking, and even transgressing others. The point is not to place things into their "correct" location in an ontological schema, but rather to use this figure as a *starting point* for exploration, discussion, and strategy. Each localized mobilization of the circle will generate a distinct set of ele-ments within and across the various moments (Figure 15 is filled in, for illustrative purposes, with a range of practices currently enacted in Maine), and the image can serve a variety of distinct purposes. It can be used to map existing practices of trans-commoning, as when the Midcoast Fishermen's Association (production) mobilizes a form of community-supported market exchange (transfer) to connect with organized consumers in various churches and local buying clubs (con-sumption). It can be used to describe a particular configuration of cur-rently unconnected commoning practices and sites that might form new linkages in the future, strengthening ethical livelihood networks in new ways. And it might also be used to identify key gaps—and therefore key possibilities—of commoning practice, areas where new forms of commoning and trans-commoning might be imagined and constructed so as to render new linkages possible.

In a broader sense, the livelihoods circle and the concept of trans-commoning might serve to remind us that opposition to the hegemonic trio does not entail a binary choice between proposing a new blue-print or model for "life beyond," or sinking forever into the blurred embrace of the fog bank. A politics of ecological livelihood mobilizes strategic, transversal analytical categories to challenge the divisions of the hegemonic trio, to render existing practices of diverse liveli-hood composition and commoning more visible, and to catalyze new alliances—trans-commonings—that might be capable of composing more liberatory forms of life and new diagrams of power and possibil-ity. Thinking in terms of trans-commoning can affirm that we do not need to spend our time puzzling over how to "relink" or "harmonize" an economy, a society, and an environment; we can instead seek to make the connections that render such an effort increasingly obsolete.

10 ONTOPOLITICAL COORDINATES

Rearticulating Struggles in Maine

(Re)composing Conflict and Possibility

If the conceptual tools of the previous chapter enable us to see the contours of our interdependencies more clearly, and perhaps to participate more effectively in their composition, some crucial dimensions of ecopoiesis and ecological livelihood remain unaddressed. In particular, how do we rearticulate the nature of our *conflicts*? To challenge the ways in which the hegemonic trio has configured particular relationships as conflicts among economy, society, and environment is not to deny conflict in general. Ecopoiesis is no utopia of harmony and cooperation: we *struggle* over the composition of common worlds. But if we are no longer fighting over tensions between the forces and domains of the hegemonic trio, what are we fighting about? How might we (re)compose modes of conflict that map the lines of our interdependencies more clearly and generatively? How might we more effectively engage in *commoning* and *trans-commoning* at the sites of our conflicts? The ontological politics of ecopoiesis is a complex terrain, and a mapping of the myriad sites and processes by which collective worlds are made and unmade is a monumental and crucial task. If "ecopoietics" were a discipline, this would be its work. In this final chapter, I can only begin to sketch the faintest outlines of a few key ways in which struggles of (un)commoning might be more effectively posed in a politics of ecological livelihood.

Following Massimo De Angelis (2003) and J. K. Gibson-Graham (2006a), I propose that these struggles can be understood and engaged as ethico-political negotiations around particular "coordinates." They do not involve predetermined dynamics or "laws," and they cannot be measured according to their success or failure in realizing some imagined ideal (Gibson-Graham 2006a, 86). Coordinates are critical *questions* asked not only in words, but in the relations we participate in composing—questions about the most basic contours of our identities, collectivities, relations, and modes of life. They do not often appear overtly as public sites of struggle, since their contours remain in the background of a hegemonic, uncommoned ecopoiesis—presumed, taken for granted, naturalized, or hidden as world-making practices that could be composed otherwise. And yet it was in my conversations with Maine's economic, social, and environmental professionals that most these dimensions emerged clearly as sites of negotiation. Sometimes with intention and other times inadvertently, my conversations provoked conceptual commonings through which fundamental dimensions of life-making were momentarily opened up for contestation. With inspirations from Bruno Latour's (2004a) "tasks" for the composition of common worlds and Gibson-Graham's (2006a) "coordinates of ethical negotiation" in mind, I listened in my interviews for transversal articulations through which real conflicts and struggles in Maine could be discussed and negotiated without recourse to divisions among economy, society, and environment. These are *alternative practices of ecopoiesis*, emerging between the cracks to express something beyond the hegemonic trio. I will focus on eight—among many others—of what might be called "ontopolitical coordinates for commoning": constituency, value(s), measurement and comparison, performances of the "whole," knowledge and uncertainty, needs and strategies, surplus, and "incentives." These are just a few of the dimensions of world-making over which Mainers (and others) struggle and might yet struggle.

1. Constituency

When Sandra suggests that "quality of life" must be "for our rivers and for our fish and the animals" (interview), she scrambles the conventional solution to the question of who counts as part of "the economy" and who is relegated to an "environment." Similarly, when Oscar proposes that "economic infrastructure" must include not only "roads, bridges, highways, [and] sewage systems" but also "the capacity to sustain social interaction . . . which would include ecology" (interview), he introduces a profound instability to the heart of the hegemonic articulation. Livelihoods are constituted by *all kinds* of relations and

attachments, and no "economic," "social," or "environmental" controversy can avoid the emergence of multiple interested parties, attached
via myriad motivations and energies, to multiple common and obscure
beings. When asked, for example, about whether the widespread discourse of "quality of place" included elements that did not directly
contribute to scenic amenities for the creative class, Oscar noted that
"there are always smaller things. There's always a group of people
who are focused on the preservation of the small things, whether it's
birdwatchers or salamander preservers or people who want to harvest
the little ferns. . . . There's always a *constituency* for that" (interview,
emphasis added).[1]

While many were external to "the economy," these multiple constituencies are all *internal* to livelihood composition as key elements of
the triad of making, being-made, and making-others. The "little ferns"
to which Oscar referred, for example, are fiddleheads (*Matteuccia stru-
thiopteris*), an important traditional rural Maine food collected for subsistence and for market in the early spring. Are birds and salamanders
any less crucial? This is the very question at stake in the coordinate
of constituency: Given that we are constituted by immense and complex interdependencies, and that we do not really know who or what
we "really" need, *which* beings will be allowed to participate as crucial elements of public negotiations regarding the ongoing provisional
outcomes of a particular ecopoiesis? Who or what shall count as a
legitimate participant in the dynamics of livelihood and habitat composition? What beings will be excluded and why? This is one of the
most crucial points of (non)negotiation in debates over economic development projects and environmental protection initiatives, but one that
is often disguised by hegemonic framings. We can explore this coordinate more specifically in two dimensions: the question of *participants*
and that of *practices*.

Regarding participants, consider an example. Those fighting for "the
environment" in Maine are often contending that other species and
their ecosystems should be considered as legitimate participants in ecopoietic processes. In the struggle over the Plum Creek corporation's
rezoning proposal, one key dimension of conflict was whether entities such as the threatened Canada Lynx, the Least Bittern, the Rusty
Blackbird, the planet's changing climate system, the specter of peak
oil, and hikers in search of "primitive wilderness experience," among
other beings, should matter in public deliberation over economic

development. Some challenged such an inclusion as illegitimate over fears that this proliferation of recognized entities would eclipse the robust participation of "local people" who needed "jobs." Others feared more generally that the God-given rights of "private property owners" were threatened by the entire debate. In all cases, the struggle was at least in part about who or what gets to count in the composition of livelihoods—and, indeed, *whose livelihoods should matter*. It is not the case that, on one hand, there are certain things that provide "us" with what "we" need (Plum Creek offering employment), while, on the other, there are "mere preferences" (protecting Lynx habitat) or "special interests" (addressing climate change). It is a question of commoning and uncommoning, of whether a given process will open itself and its already-present participants toward the question of constituency, and then, of which constitutive beings will appear as viable *commoners*.

The question of practices is equally crucial. What activities, processes, and relationships are permitted to appear as legitimate contributors to livelihood composition in public debate? If a conventional articulation of "the economy" reduces livelihood to paid employment in capitalist firms, a whole host of other articulations that I have already described challenge this narrowing of the field of view. Maine people variously recognize the existence of hunting, fishing, trapping, foraging, home gardening, barter, gifting, parenting, housework, informal marketing of subsistence surplus, government redistributions, voluntary reduction of consumption needs, worker- and community-owned cooperative businesses, caring for land and waters, and the work of "ecosystem services" as just some of the many ways that livelihoods are composed. The key question, of course, is whether these practices are to be recognized as legitimate *enough* contributors to livelihood composition to appear as valuable, viable, or desirable dimensions of a transformative regional development process.

2. Value(s)

How do we decide, amid the proliferation of constituencies, what and who is important? The coordinate of value(s) involves an engagement with the multiple ways in which we generate and sustain relations of signification and care with regard to various elements of ecopoietic processes. What do we care about? And, at least in some cases, what do we care about *more* than other things? In the hegemonic frame of "the economy," valuation is enacted via a monetary index, a rendering-commensurable of all beings and relations in such a way that they can be ranked and compared. "You've got to be able to come up with some sort of apples-to-apples comparison to be able to make a valid decision," says Kathleen, the government statistician (interview). The problem, of course, is that livelihood is not reducible to these commensurate terms, and in order to make it appear as such it must be taken over via a kind of metrological colonization by conceptual, monetizing acrobatics such as "replacement value" appraisals, "willingness to pay" evaluations, or estimates of "existence value."[2] Kathleen recognizes that "it's hard to assign a dollar figure to 'I feel better when I have a pretty thing to look at'" (interview), and yet because the *question of value(s) itself* is not commonly viewed as a public coordinate of negotiation (rather, it is already decided that "economic value" is essential for rational decision-making), she remains trapped in a regime of quantitative cost-benefit analysis and, more generally, in the regime of "the economy" and its accompanying categories.

As John McMurty (1998) argues, economic value is not an objective, non-normative measure distinct from "social values" (as in, e.g., Blaug 1997), but is a particular "value practice" (De Angelis 2007, 24) through which social norms and power relations are continually instituted. As one ecopoietic articulation among others, the rendering of beings and relation in monetary terms is a question of *ethics and politics*: What does this practice (and institution) of making-valuable enable and foreclose? What does it common and uncommon? Even more important, what are other modes of valuation that are enacted within, alongside, and against it? What do (or might) they enable and foreclose? As Calvin, the director of an economic development think-tank, asserts: "I would maintain that if you use census data around poverty in Maine you're missing the point that there are a lot of people that might be considered to be in poverty who are actually living, not great lives, but they're not they don't consider themselves poor. Because they're living in a value system that's different than the national census value system, you know" (interview). Struggles posed as conflicts between the hegemonic categories may often, and perhaps *should* more often, be struggles over multiple modes of value: "There *is* conflict. Between different values and priorities," proposes Dana, the environmental non-profit director (interview). Linked with the coordinate of constituency, we can see that this is not a matter of prioritizing economy, society, or environment but rather of *valuing complex relations*. It is about the commoning of the three dimensions of the livelihoods triad and its habitats.

To return again to the example of Plum Creek: it is not at all the case that this struggle can be reduced to a battle between groups who placed "economy" and "environment" in different rank orders. Indeed, every party involved in the controversy took up as a core concern the creation of viable livelihoods in the region and enacted this concern via "economic" development proposals (e.g., Kellett and St. Pierre 1996; Didisheim and De Wan 2006; Colgan 2007). What was at issue, at least in part, were the radically different forms of valuation that these proposals demanded. While experts debated about whether the Plum Creek plan would be "good for the economy," a much more unsettling and fertile—yet much more marginalized—struggle was unfolding over *contending articulations and rankings of what truly matters*. What unexpected alliances and productive betrayals might have been enabled if spaces had been opened in which these complex value struggles were foregrounded, delinked from the "golden orbs of value" of the hegemonic categories (Irene, interview), and even scrambled? Might it have become clearer, for example, that some "environmental" groups were genuinely concerned about the most basic, practical, and immediate needs of human livelihood in northern Maine and that some "economic" groups were, in fact, most concerned about maintaining an allegiance to particular abstract causal models linking quantitative regional growth (and corporate profits) with aggregate income statistics?

3. Measurement and Comparison

The question of value(s) is intimately connected with another key coordinate: that of measurement and comparison. On one hand, I hear Kathleen, the statistician, asserting that standard measurement is necessary because we need to be able to compare things: "When people want to know how the economy is doing, it's either because they want to know how we compare to someone else, or they want to know how we're doing compared to a different point in time" (interview). An acknowledged simplification such as GDP is therefore justified "because we need to have something to look at" (interview). On the other hand, Sandra—the economic growth council director—forcefully expresses her opposition to such measurement and comparison: "So really, *no*. I don't think you can compare" (interview). Eric, the regional development economist, meanwhile reminds me that "measurement increases precision, but creates its own distortion" (interview). All of these articulations come from prominent experts in the field of economic development. What are we to make of this other than to say that it is not a matter of simply "looking at the hard numbers" (Owen, interview) to see what they "say," but of the very *question* of numbers and their mobilization as technologies of indexing, valuation, and comparison?

The first key struggle of this coordinate involves whether a measurement can even be produced, and, if it is, what forms of exclusion and violence this production entails. This is the question of the "value beyond measure" of natural beauty and the "services" that come to us from others (Maine Land Trust Network 2005, 2) and how it confronts demands for quantification. As Brenda, the social service researcher, describes Maine: "We have this natural beauty and a kid can go outside and be *healed* in a way, by taking a walk in the woods or on the beach. And so that piece, isn't measured, and it's not really measurable. We don't have an indicator for that" (interview). And yet people want "hard numbers," and many powerful institutions demand quantification as a strategy for governing people, things, and spaces (Rose and Miller 2008). A commoning of measurement would begin at the very site of its emergence: rendering visible the exclusions produced by existing measurements, opening possibilities for new practices of measurement, and *instituting the incommensurability* of multiple beings and becomings who should never be compared in quantitative terms. Indeed, in many cases, one must not simply seek to show that a given proposal to protect an ecosystem, save a population of endangered birds, or restrict the use of toxic chemicals can generate measurable "economic prosperity," but rather *one must fight for the space to refuse this standard.* In other cases, commoning at the coordinate of measurement and comparison is the work of composing new, collective mobilizations of numbers that can help give shape to other modes of ecopoietic becoming.

4. Performances of the Whole

Aside from rendering comparisons possible, measurement feeds into another key coordinate of livelihood negotiation: that of the articulation of "wholes," or the making of what Latour calls "scenarizations" (2004a) or "panoramas" (2005). Easily confused with the actual, impossible-to-capture "whole" that it purports to describe, scenarization is the process of producing a systematic account of reality via a nontotal representation. It enables a story about "the big picture," and thus serves particular processes of performative composition, while also cultivating awareness of itself *as a picture*. When Kathleen tells me that "there is no, sort of, 'economy' sitting under my desk" (interview), as a way to describe the economy as a mere accounting convention, she is missing the sense in which this economy *is*, in fact, under her desk—in boxes of printed reports generated by her department to show people what "the economy" is made of. She describes: "We've done some presentations where we try to boil it down to: OK, here's Maine's economy, and there's this little triangle of consumers, businesses, and government and, you know, directional arrows going back and forth" (interview). At the very same time, she acknowledges that such an image "leav[es] out all of the complicated bits" (interview). It helps to structure action, to advocate for certain strategies or pathways of composition and not others, but it is clearly limited. It shows the whole *only*, in fact, by leaving things out.

The coordinate of scenarization enables a shift from assuming a set of spheres to which various big-picture representations more or less correspond, to asking the very question of the partial composition of images of the whole. What is included and excluded in a given scenarization? What does a given scenarization enable us to do or to imagine, and what does it foreclose? The different scenarizations offered by both Kathleen and the Maine Economic Growth Council in the *Measures of Growth in Focus* report (Figure 2, chapter 1) are clearly problematic in the ways that they reinforce purified divisions and obscure important practices and interrelationships. My trans-commoning livelihood circle in the previous chapter (Figure 15) is an attempt to produce a very different kind of "whole," both in content and in function. What other scenarizations can be offered to the process of regional livelihood composition? Who gets to participate in performing the whole? Who appears in public as the expert capable of making such a scenarization?

Commoning at the coordinate of scenarization is not simply a matter of someone (like me) developing an image and then mobilizing it. It requires, ultimately, the mobilization of processes by which scenarizations themselves become sites of contestation and collective theorization. It requires "participatory theory" (Pain and Kindon 2007) through practices by which aspiring "scene-makers" enter into relations of accountability and mutual vulnerability with communities of practice. Imagine representations of Maine's "whole" emerging from bottom-up processes of knowledge-making in which multiple constituencies would negotiate complex values, measurements (and nonmeasurements), and visions to compose provisional scenarizations to enable strategic collective action. This has never happened, but it *could*. What would this look like? What might it generate? Who will initiate and organize such a process?

5. Knowledge and Uncertainty

What can we claim as knowledge, and where does this knowledge reach its limits? How are various forms of knowledge established, rendered valid, compelling, or obligatory in ecopoietic struggles? Who is able to participate and who is excluded? How are forms of knowledge constituted as durable habitats upon which other negotiations may then be founded? How is the constitutive uncertainty at the heart of all knowing acknowledged or suppressed? These are all key questions of a coordinate that rarely appears as such. Knowledge is often posed as that which dispels uncertainty and intervenes to settle negotiations: "The economic and social science arena, I don't know . . . ," says Dana, the environmental coalition director, "but geology, biology, chemistry, physics . . . these are actually things that are constant, that there's a *law* [laughs]. The *scientific laws*! They've been proven, and so I have less tolerance for people who argue that those facts [can be disputed]" (interview). It is clear, however, that these "laws" do not always settle disputes in the ways that Dana might hope for. Scientific facts are called into question, contradicted with other facts, replaced by new facts upon further investigation, unsettled as legitimate modes of knowing, or simply ignored altogether.

Much of what passes for disputes between economy, society, and environment can be articulated instead as conflicts over different knowledge claims, ways of knowing, and relations to uncertainty. It is the claim of a causal link between "productivity," business success, economic growth, and human well-being that enables the Maine Development Foundation and others (Chad, interview) to suggest that policy oriented around increasing worker output should become a priority to achieve "quality of life for all Maine people" (MEGC 2013). It is the often-assumed causal link between income levels and various health, education, and life satisfaction outcomes that renders social work into a project of economic assimilation. And it is the appeal to an incontestable, objective zone of Nature and the scientific facts that describe its laws that enable environmentalists to claim immunity to political contestations of knowledge. Yet for all the work to "short-circuit" political negotiation via appeals to "facts" (Latour 2004a), politics remains active at the very heart of debate because it is the nature of this knowledge itself that is never actually settled.

It was clear when I spoke with Dana that there is a significant difference between the *assertion* of indisputable fact and its actual role (or lack thereof) in an ecopoietic negotiation process. In contrast to the causal chain that is asserted when an economic developer claims that giving tax breaks to a large corporation leads to greater community well-being, Dana asserts that many causal chains in her own work are much simpler and clearer: "Pollution in water makes you sick. Pollution in air makes you sick. Right? . . . It has a very clear, direct arrow from here to here" (interview). Dana's claim may make for an effective organizational pamphlet phrase, but it elides the multiple complex mediations that are actually needed to establish such a link between pollution and sickness. I ask her about a different issue in which causation might be more difficult to simplify: "It strikes me that the climate change argument is just as long a chain of causation as the corporate profit argument," I propose. Her response is telling: "It shouldn't be! You know? It shouldn't be because it's so clearly . . . because it's science! *Science*, right? You pump too much carbon dioxide and other gases into the atmosphere, it traps heat, which . . . then . . . warms up the ocean, warms up global temperatures, causes the ice to melt. You know, creates more moisture in the air, creates more extreme weather" (interview). It "*shouldn't* be," since "science" ostensibly simplifies all complex claims into indisputable facts that are subsequently reducible to sound bites; but Dana's attempt to clearly distill these relations in this manner *fails* in an unfinished proliferation of elements and linkages, each of which is just as complex as the next. Can an environmentalist trump all other political claims with appeals to objective science? Can an economist do the same?

Rather than obscuring politics and ethics in the name of factual closure, or excluding certain beings and relations via a refusal of scientific evidence (think climate change denial), knowledge and uncertainty must itself be posed as a site of commoning. This is not to suggest that "facts" cannot be provisionally settled or that common "foundations" of knowledge should not be sought among particular collectives in order to work out the possible shapes of being-in-common. Rather, it is to follow Latour—and I allude here to his crucial and substantive work on the questions posed by this coordinate (Latour 1987, 1999, 2004a)—in proposing that "the deliberations of the collective must no longer be suspended or short-circuited by some definitive knowledge. . . . The collective does not claim to know, but it has to experiment in such a way that it can learn in the course of the trial" (2004a, 196).

6. Needs and Strategies

One can hardly talk of livelihoods without confronting the question of needs. "It boils down to *survival* at the end of the day," says Dennis, the renewable energy business owner (interview). "We're obliged to play [the game of market competition]," says Arnold, the regional development agency director, "not because the game's being played, but because you need to *survive*" (interview). "What are the needs?" asks Harriet, describing her bottom-up approach to rural economic development (interview). There is a widespread sense that when one peels back hegemonic discourses about jobs, income, productivity, and market competition, a kind of *essence* is revealed—that which is *necessary*, "basic needs" upon which all else depends and that ultimately drive the dynamics of livelihood. As Chad, the economic development agency director, describes: "Regardless of what you're doing or regardless how you value wealth or whatever, there is a bare minimum in there that would define some basic needs. Resources to . . . money enough for food, fuel, health, and other things" (interview). This, then, clearly constitutes a key coordinate: What do we *need*?

The question is not as simple as it may initially appear, for "need" is a tricky concept. It performatively names precisely that which it asserts: a necessity, an incontestability, those conditions that must be met in order to avoid suffering, undoing, or even death. To assert a need is, quite often, to make a demand: fulfill this *or else*. Thus the discourse of needs can appear with a great force of uncommoning. Recall Owen in chapter 3: "Those people need *jobs*. I mean, it's not even a question" (interview). And yet while needs are sometimes mobilized to stop conversation or contestation—closing off the possibility, for example, that "jobs" are not the only meaningful response to "poverty"—they are also key means of *challenging* hegemony. "We don't *need* more *stuff!*" proclaims Bradley, the conservation consortium director, challenging the supposed necessity of growth and the ongoing increase of commodity production and consumption (interview). To ask "What are the needs?" in a community development process is to raise the possibility that the hegemonic economy is not, in fact, meeting them or even engaging them. It is also, potentially, to draw on the seeming-incontestability and even "naturalness" of needs in order to gain an ontopolitical foothold in the face of a powerful assemblage.

Here, then, is a core challenge at the heart of this crucial coordinate of needs: we seem to *need* to speak of needs, and yet to do so risks participating in a naturalization or uncommoning by which particular relations are rendered seemingly inevitable or incontestable. Nego-tiation cannot simply unfold, then, around questions of "how to meet needs"; nor can it simply be founded on lists of "basic needs" (e.g., Max-Neef 1991; Noonan 2006; Rauschmayer, Omann, and Frühmann 2011) that would enable normative interventions or judgments upon existing relations of livelihood provision. It must involve the very ques-tions of what "needs" *are*, who gets to decide, on what basis they may be claimed, and who is constituted as their subject. What is going on when we assert that there is a *needer* who *needs*? Are there ways to think about this that might enable more robust commonings around struggles for sustenance? I will suggest three key areas in need of clar-ification: the distinction between "needs" and "strategies," the defini-tion of "need" itself, and the question of the subject of this need.

If needs tend to confront us as incontestable assertions, then an important distinction between "needs" and "strategies" might help to loosen the grip of this uncommoning. This is found in the theory and practice of nonviolent communication (Rosenberg 2003) as well as in the work of radical development theorist Manfred Max-Neef (1991, 1992).[3] It is also enacted in the complex mediation work described by my interviewee Irene, who seeks to break the "golden orbs of value" (chapter 7). In each of her examples of creative negotiation, the key move involves a recognition that the things appearing as immediate needs—building a road, developing a particular site, enacting a law, or even creating jobs—are, in fact, *strategies* intended to meet needs that are much less specific. "You have to go down," she suggests: "What's underneath the need, the *stated* need?" (interview). People need to be nourished, and getting a job to earn money to buy food is a strategy to achieve this nourishment. Town managers need to serve the diverse demands of their community, and promoting a particular development proposal is a strategy to accomplish this. By opening up a "deeper" conversation about needs and loosening the grip of that which appears—at first—as a "need," Irene enables a radically different negotiation to unfold. If people in rural Maine have needs for sustenance, health, and belonging, then "jobs" might appear as only one possible strategy to realize them. Another strategy might involve challenges to the very assemblages that have rendered jobs obligatory. Additionally, what kinds of new dynamics might be generated if the needs/strategies distinction were foregrounded in the struggle over Plum Creek's rezoning and the future of Moosehead Lake? Plum Creek's plan was a strategy to fulfill its need to maximize shareholder returns. Do local people require this strategy to meet needs of sustenance? Are there other strategies that might be mobilized? The uncommoning grip of "need" on collective imagination might be loosened here to make way for new forms of creative negotiation.

What, then, *is* a "need"? In one common form, it appears to be *that which is necessary given a refusal to question the hegemonic assemblage itself.* This is what allows Owen to assert the "need" for jobs as unquestionable: given isolated individuals captured by a coercive assemblage in which access to key means of sustenance have been privatized and monetized, then "jobs" will indeed appear as that which is utterly necessary. The other side of the same assemblage is the widespread assertion of *business* needs: an improved "business climate," a friendly "regulatory environment," favorable taxation policies, and "incentives" that allocate public funds to private ends. Yet even alternative formulations that would contest such articulations tend to draw on a naturalization of need. Rather than assume a hegemonic etho-ecology, various "basic needs" or "human needs" approaches in development theory assert an essence that lies beneath all variable assemblages. In Felix Rauschmayer, Ines Omann, and Johannes Frühmann's terms, needs are "the most fundamental dimension of human flourishing" (2011, 10). The danger here is that counterhegemonic discourses might end up actualizing the very same diagram of power that they purport to challenge: mobilizing a discourse of necessity and essence in the name of closing off ethico-political contestation and rendering the always-situated politics of knowledge production invisible.

Does the distinction between needs and strategies require a positing of need as foundational essence? I do not think so. An alternative is already present in the work of Max-Neef (1991; 1992), though perhaps underdeveloped. While Max-Neef often presents needs as objective forces or properties that subsist beneath the cultural variations of human life, he sometimes recognizes something more complex: *needs do not precede the strategies that fulfill them*. Because needs are inseparable from the ways in which they are addressed in concrete, historical experience, "it is inappropriate," he writes, "to speak of their being 'satisfied' or 'fulfilled.' . . . It may be better to speak of realizing, experiencing, or actualizing needs through time and space" (1991, 24). I want to amplify this direction of thought: needs, I propose, are not essences, properties, or even spaces of actual or potential lack within a living being or assemblage. They are, rather, *retroactively stabilized propositions* that enable us to loosen the grip of particular strategies. "Needs" are themselves discursive strategies for actualizing the virtual differently. If I "need" nutrition, for example, it is only because relations between my bodily assemblage and particular foods and nutrients have been articulated into the abstraction of "nutrition" so that I might explore the possibility that these constitutive relations might be assembled differently (i.e., eating various foods) as a means of sustaining my existence. A politics of needs must always foreground the sense in which one can never find a need except in abstraction: it is always *this* relation and *that* relation. Life is strategies "all the way down," and "need," in fact, constitutes yet another strategy to add to (and transform) the rest.

Finally, we come to the question of *who* or *what* is the subject of need (and strategy). In the hegemonic articulation, this is often answered in terms of an ecologically isolated human individual or family. This is what makes it possible for Eric, the regional economist, to repeat a classic assertion of economy over environment: "The environment as a subject gets far more attention from wealthy places than poor places, and it gets far more attention in good times than bad times. . . . It's related to the stresses on the hierarchy of needs" (interview). When a human can be presented as an isolated individual, with needs reduced to immediate bodily inputs that are ranked in hierarchical order (i.e., Maslow 1943), then all other constitutive relations can be relegated to the "social" and "environmental" as luxuries. Marxian economics partakes of a similar structure of thought when it views "necessary labor" as "the time-measured expenditure of human brain and muscle required to reproduce the performers of surplus labor" (Resnick and Wolff 2006, 93). Not only does this fall into the trap of focusing only on the "making a living" dimension of the triad discussed earlier; it also risks reducing necessity to the level of individual wage-earners and (perhaps) their immediate families.[4] In all of these cases, articulations of need are intimately linked to questions of identity, community, and ecology. If "to be one is always to *become with* many" (Haraway 2008, 4), then who is to say where the boundaries of the subject of a given articulation of "need" should be drawn? Indeed, it must be recognized that the assertion of needs and the composition of "self" and collectivity are intricately intertwined, actualized together in the ongoing encounter between making, being-made, and making others. To common at the coordinate of needs must also involve explicit negotiation of the very question of community and its boundaries.

7. Surplus

Never far from questions of need are struggles over the production, appropriation, and distribution of *surplus*. Something remains after need has been met; something has been produced over and above that which was required to sustain those who produce; something exceeds its immediate use and opens toward a different relation. What is this surplus? Who can claim it as their own to use or pass along? For what purpose or effect is it mobilized? These are some of the crucial questions that circulate around a coordinate that was *not* clearly or explicitly articulated in my conversations with Maine's economic, social, and environmental professionals, despite its centrality to so many of the relations they engage. Why is this the case? I suspect at least two reasons, and they both point toward the importance of amplifying surplus as a prominent coordinate in any work to develop a political praxis of ecological livelihoods.

One of the most potent sources of critical engagement with questions of surplus comes from the Marxian tradition. It is Marx and those who have built on his work who enable us to articulate an analysis of capitalist exploitation as the process of extracting surplus value from the labor of commodity-producing workers. Profit, that endless, addictive goal of the "economy of accumulation," comes from surplus—value over and above that which is needed to reproduce the producers—and this surplus arises, at least in part, from the *living labor* of those who must work for capitalists in order to live. Despite a widespread notion that each contributor to the process simply gets a fair return (wages to the workers, rent to the landlords, and profit to the capitalists); a Marxian frame suggests that workers are effectively extorted, in the very guise of "individual freedom," into handing over a portion of their life energy to those who claim to own it. Hence a vast, ongoing transfer of resources and wealth from the many to the few, and an obscene accumulation of surplus—and the power that it enables—on the part of these elites. How can this not be a site for widespread and explicit contestation? Because this analysis has been nearly erased from public discourse in Maine, as it has elsewhere in the United States. Beyond a deep, embodied sense that something is *not fair*, how many wage workers in Maine view themselves as producing surplus value that others appropriate while calling it a "fair exchange"? Not many. The surplus generated through paid labor is invisible as such: we just get a *wage* in exchange for a *job*. How many people view the wealth of the "1 percent" as a *collective product*, now uncommoned in private hands? Not enough. Where would anyone have learned these ideas? Hardly anywhere. The critical-analytical void produced by the wholesale marginalization of Marxian perspectives (along with others critical of Capital) has left "surplus" to those mainstream economists who would view it as nothing but a marginal benefit or loss generated by the supply-and-demand dynamic.[5] For many Mainers, this means that surplus—and certainly a collective "social surplus" (DeMartino 2003)—simply isn't a site for explicit contestation and struggle.

A second factor has also tended to eclipse surplus as an ethico-political coordinate: the widespread sense of *scarcity* experienced by so many people in Maine and elsewhere. If surplus refers to an amount left over after needs have been met, or a quantity of something that is extra, then very few people would tend to think that they have much surplus to struggle over. What is left over "at the end of the day," after all expenses have been paid, often seems like very little. This is in part because the match between the necessary costs of living and the prevailing rates of pay are so poor for so many Mainers: *less than half* of all people in the state earn a living wage for their work (Henry and Fredricksen 2014). Furthermore, the endless production of "needs," the relentless drive toward consumption as a mode of self-realization and belonging (Illich 1993), can quickly convert any potential surplus into the next round of necessity. To have "enough" is anathema to the demands of the growth machine. It is any wonder, then, that people rarely see taxation and public redistribution as a dynamic of "surplus"? And even if they do, is it any wonder that questions over its appropriation and distribution are so often infused with fear and scarcity-based dynamics of exclusion and resentment ("not for *those* people . . .")? And yet surplus persists: it is what enables alterpoiesis, the ongoing practices of care for others to which Maine people are in fact deeply committed. It funds our community organizations and their life-sustaining work, even if from sources whose right to make such decisions should be called into question. It is what sustains our bodies and communities in the form of nourishment produced by more-than-human others—the surplus of sunlight, photosynthesis, respiration, growth and life-giving decay. And, in the form of money and other modes of material power, it continues to accumulate in the hands of those who most definitively do *not* need it, while others can barely imagine what "having extra" might mean.

Surplus, in all of these senses, is a crucial coordinate precisely because it is so widely and profoundly *uncommoned*—rendered all-too-often invisible as a site for collective contestation and creative transformation. Much more can and must be said about this site of struggle (see Miller 2013a), but for now I raise some crucial questions that must emerge at this dimension of ecopoiesis: What practices of collective teaching and learning might render surplus more visible as an ethico-political coordinate? How might we more effectively conceptualize and map the myriad forms that surplus takes, and the multiple ways in which these forms are (and might be) mobilized? What does surplus look like from the perspective of a livelihoods triad (receiving, making, and providing) in which multispecies assemblages co-create worlds together? What tools and practices might help us to negotiate the difficult and ever-shifting lines between need and surplus? How can we more effectively foreground the ways in which struggles over surplus, as with those over need, are also struggles over *constituency* and *belonging?* Who counts as the "we" for whom something is extra, and can be shared? What kinds of worlds do we seek to build with such sharing? And what kinds of worlds are we *obligated* toward building by the calls that resound from our commoned interdependence?

8. "Incentives" and Ecologies of Practice

It is quite common in public policy circles to hear talk of "getting the incentives right." Whether in the realm of economic development, social service, or environmental protection, there is a hegemonic sense that the world is composed of rationally optimizing, self-interested individuals who will comply with policy aspirations only if presented with the proper array of "carrots and sticks." The problems with such an articulation should be clear after the critical tracings of Part II, and it might be tempting in this context to reject the very notion of "incentives" altogether. Is this not merely a mode of governmentality seeking to institute forms of rule in which authority has been internalized as the very desire of subjects themselves (Foucault 2010b; Rose 1999)? This may often be the case. But there is a broader and more ecological way to think about incentives that can configure them as a key coordinate of ethical livelihood negotiation and perhaps even enable different engagements with those invested in this language.

Take, for example, a moment in my conversation with the environmental business owner, Dennis. I asked him, "At what point are we trying to make a fundamentally problematic system sustainable by greening it, versus figuring out how to change our relationships?" (interview). His reply could, at first glance, be read as an instance of the hegemonic notion of incentives: "Yeah, it's a massive question," he responded. "I don't have the answer to it. . . . [pause] . . . That's where my optimism is challenged. Because I don't always trust the instincts in people to pursue good when the benefits of pursuing bad are so . . . *attractive*" (interview). One might picture here a set of preconstituted humans, acting out their "human nature" to pursue maximum personal benefit even at the cost of planetary destruction. But this is not the only way to read Dennis's response. What if the "attraction" he speaks of is not a matter of essential, individual propensities but rather the emergent property of a habitat, an *etho-ecology*, in Isabelle Stengers's (2005b) terms?

Incentives, following the work of Stengers described in chapter 7, can be understood as the name of particular kinds of obligating attachments within etho-ecologies that render them potent. I understood this during an interview with Bradley, the conservation consortium director. My warning flags went up when he used the word "incentives," but the more carefully I listened, the more I realized that he meant something quite different from the hegemonic version of the term. "Another theme in my work," he described, "is moving away from thinking about individuals and to thinking about what are the incentives that people work and live in" (interview). He continued:

> If you're an elected official, the rhetoric about jobs is absolutely important, but the other thing that's important is maintaining your tax revenue so that you don't go bankrupt. So you have somebody come in and say, "I'd like to replace that mill that just shut down, and I'm going to do it by doing something that's actually really bad for the environment, but it'll cover a lot of taxes," and you're immediately in a tough spot. That's not because there's an explicit conflict between nature and economy, it's because the people coming in aren't bringing in alternatives. The challenge is to figure out the alternatives, and to figure out how you build incentives to the various decision-makers. (interview)

Incentives here are a move away from questions of individual motivation and toward an "ecology of practices" (Stengers 2005a). It is not a matter of providing carrots and sticks to self-interested individuals, nor of assuming any particular essential motivation at the heart of practice; rather, it is about composing new relations and institutional configurations in which new forms of motivation and action become possible. "How," asks Bradley, "do you build incentives for them that favor decisions that see the broader range of implications, and don't always take the presented alternative as [inevitable]?" (interview).

Commoning at the coordinate of incentives is to open the question of what kinds of ecologies of practice might challenge and transform existing options, motivations, and desires, and what might be enacted in their place to offer new possibilities for action. Of *course* the Plum Creek struggle was polarizing: the ecologies of practice that composed it entailed a single proposal to which there was an institutionally mandated yes-or-no answer: "*That's* what creates these dichotomies," says Bradley, "is when you're given *a* proposal . . . and suddenly it's jobs versus the environment" (interview). It is the etho-ecology of this situation that must be transformed, made into a site of struggle, negotiation, and creative practice. In Bradley's terms: "One way you evade these dichotomies, is by simply *evading these dichotomies*—you just *do* things" (interview); that is, you just do things that compose a new ecology of practice and thus render a new habitat inhospitable to the dichotomies—or, in the frame of this book, to the *trio*.

Transversal Questions

"How can we get the economy going again?" "How can these social problems be solved?" "How are we going to balance protecting the environment with the need to grow our economy?" These are the kinds of questions—however difficult or controversial—that often seem to come with their answers prefabricated like a choose-your-own-adventure book. For all the fervor with which they are debated, they continue to lead us only into different variations of the same trap, the same narrow space of (im)possibilities. In any such situation, it seems wise to proceed by *asking different questions*. Things would look different if rather than asking how the economy or its companion categories are doing, we were asking about the relations of making, receiving, providing, and the co-constitutive habitats that sustain various collectivities. Or, if, rather than asking about how to balance economy and environment, we were asking: Who *constitutes* and gets to participate in a given world-making process? Whose *values* matter, and how are they to be *measured* and compared (or not)? What kinds of *wholes* should we represent to ourselves as tools for collective deliberation, and who gets to determine their shapes? Whose *knowledge* counts, and how do we acknowledge the limits at the heart of all knowing? (How do we compose a politics of *humility*?) What do various collectivities *need*, and how do we strategically separate need from strategy so that creative synergies might emerge? What forms of *surplus* are being produced, and how shall we mobilize them? How are our current behaviors, relationships, and modes of thinking shaped by their habitats, and how might these *ecologies of practice* be transformed to generate new becomings?

Asking these kinds of questions—and there are undoubtedly many more to be asked—is one key strategy for "breaking the golden orbs of value" (Irene, interview) and opening up new kinds of conversations and encounters. This is work that is already being done on many fronts and in many ways in Maine and beyond, but the assemblage of the hegemonic trio stands as an obstacle to valuing, amplifying, and expanding such transversal interventions. How might the Plum Creek struggle have been different if no "environmentalists" had showed up to (in the perceptions of some local people) spoil a good opportunity for economic development; instead, a process of critical and appreciative community-based inquiry—a process of true development as an *event*—had been launched around key questions of livelihood and its ethical coordinates? What if, rather than being set up to fight against environmentalists "from away" on behalf of a real estate investment trust from even *farther* away, people were encouraged to imagine and embrace the lives, landscapes, and communities that they *actually long for* or might *come to long for* if freed from various forms of imposed necessity? Any number of other such apparent conflicts between the elements of the hegemonic trio can be reformatted and reimagined in this way.

Such transformations of framing and thinking are, as I have emphasized, no substitute for the hard, grounded work of organizing collective energies and building new material relations and capacities. But they are also a form of transformative work that we ignore at our peril, particularly at a time when the landscape of values and public discourse is so deeply fractured and polarized. We *need* new modes of thought, encounter, conversation, and negotiation that resist pre-positioning their participants in the old, stale roles and caricatures of the hegemonic assemblage. We need politics that refuse the easy terms of established camps, left/right dichotomies, and divisions between critique and creation, while also opening up space for acknowledging interdependence and confronting its myriad relations of power with a commitment to challenging oppression while liberating imagination and collective creativity. We need a politics that can equip us for the emerging challenges of a climate-changing era, where lines blur and implications proliferate and where new categories will be needed to help us build new forms of life together. A politics of ecological livelihood and its many coordinates, which I have only begun to elaborate, is one experimental proposition for such a project. Dare we try it?

CONCLUSION

Becoming Otherwise

Economy, society, and environment: only the bizarre history of Western modernity, actualizing its particular diagram of power, could have produced such a strange and divisive way of articulating the relations that sustain us and to which we are responsible. Like so many grand and totalizing assemblages produced by a mess of desire, fear, creativity, and violence, this world-making trio is at once powerful and fragile. It structures and limits the horizons of imagination and possibility, and at the same time it cracks beneath its own weight and opens toward myriad "becomings-otherwise" that we are only beginning to engage. My goal in this book has been to loosen the grip of this hegemonic articulation while also tracing its effects, opening up space for imagining and enacting life beyond this trio and the forms of life it helps to compose. I have pursued this work not simply by opposing hegemony and demanding an "alternative" in its place or by proposing a utopian model for a future world, but by mobilizing a multimodal strategy of problematization, critical engagement (tracing), destabilization and multiplication (decomposition), and the articulation of concepts and strategies that might amplify the emergence of new assemblages (recomposition).

In so doing, I hope to have offered a possible pathway beyond the false choice of critique or creation. One cannot simply affirm possibility in the presence of actual(ized) forces of coercion that shape the space within which such possibility can unfold. And likewise, one cannot simply fixate upon a monolithic articulation of oppressive hegemony (and an equally potent resentment) in a world in which power is never total and difference proliferates. The task, instead, must be something like *creative critique* or *critical creation*, enacted through an understanding that hegemony is at once totalizing and nontotal, a recognition that acknowledging the potency of hegemonic assemblages does not necessarily imply a performative affirmation of their grip and that it is both possible and necessary to *oppose* and *compose* simultaneously.

I have pursued all of this work *in place*, putting theory in mutually transformative conversation with the situated realities of life in Maine—my home. This is a task riddled with tensions: between the broad, connective ethico-political work to which I am committed and the relative obscurity of the academic terms in which I am writing; between the hegemonic self-understandings of many I have spoken with and the (sometimes unintentional) counterhegemonic openings I have drawn out of our conversations; between the ethical demands for transformative vulnerability that I have posed and the daily realities of vulnerability against which so many people rightfully struggle; between the composition of theory in these pages and the work it calls for beyond any text. And yet this book could not have been a work of "pure theory," elaborating a vision of ecological livelihoods in the rarefied and unlocated space of abstract thought, since the very point is to invoke these tensions and open up the question of what might emerge from them with effort, over time. Indeed, there is no "theory of ecological livelihoods" outside the actual places in which we live, think, work, and struggle. The task is always to trace the actual, concrete contours of hegemony in a particular place, to seek the cracks that emerge there, and to experiment with languages that are already on the verge of resonance.

What, then, might emerge in Maine via an articulation of a politics of ecological livelihood? What are the ethico-political transformations that might be enabled by the concepts I have explored in this book? These are, ultimately, questions that can be answered only through engagement outside these pages, in collaboration with those already working to imagine and enact dimensions of ecological livelihood in our communities. Speculative thinking is nonetheless important, if only to provoke further questions. In closing (or, better yet, in opening *beyond*), I imagine a few key shifts that the concepts developed here might help to catalyze in Maine. I will stay close to home, revisiting the story of Rick and Theresa from the introduction and then returning to the worlds of the professionals with whom I have had such generative conversations. In an emergent assemblage of ecological livelihood and the trans-commoning of habitat, what might Rick and Theresa become? What might Maine's economic developers, social workers, and environmental advocates become?

Reprise: Rick and Theresa

I opened the book with the semi-fictional story of Rick and Theresa in northern Maine. We left them, many pages ago, subjected to the whims of an unforgiving "economy," dependent upon a "society" that marks them as a problem, and confronted by an "environment" that seems to be more a source of threat—in its very protection by outside advocates—than of sustenance. Hosts of professionals are seeking to solve the problems faced by Rick, Theresa, and so many others in their region, but they do so in the very terms that appear to have contributed to the multiple crises. The point of developing new conceptual approaches beyond the hegemonic trio is to experiment with ways of seeing, thinking, and organizing that might break some of the impasses that characterize these challenges. How do we undo the trap in which Rick, Theresa, and so many of their professional advocates find themselves? How might their stories change when recomposed through the kaleidoscopic lens of ecological livelihoods?

In the dimension of *making* a living, it turns out that Rick and Theresa's jobs are not their only sites of active sustenance production. They grow gardens, hunt for deer and moose, pick fiddlehead ferns in the spring and scavenge apples in the fall from nearby wild trees, do their own carpentry and plumbing when needed, keep the old truck running with clever tinkering, cut firewood for heating from a small woodlot, share parenting, cleaning, and cooking work, barter with friends and neighbors for many goods and services, and care for their community and the land they live on in multiple ways. Are they "poor"? In some dimensions, but certainly not others. How many of the policy professionals trying to fix them and "develop" their part of Maine have such multifaceted capabilities? This is not to deny or downplay their very real struggles, and the precarity of so much of their habitat, but it is to say that there is much more going on here—and perhaps much more that is possible—than the hegemonic narrative would render visible and valuable. A development practice that began from this diversity would look radically different from a business incentive package and a job-retraining program for Rick. What might rural Maine come to look like if we actually valued and supported the wide array of life-making practices already under way?

In the dimension of having a living *made for them* by others (allopoiesis), Rick and Theresa are undoubtedly dependent. But are they any more dependent than the social workers who interview them for their food stamps or subsidized health insurance? If the hegemonic articulation tends to highlight dependencies on social programs and elevate independence as a virtue (or even a possibility), an ecological-livelihoods frame acknowledges an immensity of (inter)dependencies that cannot be wholly accounted for: Rick and Theresa rely on the oxygen, tree growth, deer habitat, and the quiet respite produced by their local forests; on soil bacteria and worms in the garden; on a relatively stable climate system (though strange things have been happening lately . . .); and a biosocial habitat that does not given them cancer or mercury poisoning at age fifty-three. They rely on migrant laborers, many of whom are undocumented, growing and harvesting the food they buy. They rely on Theresa's mother for help with the kids; on friends and neighbors for all kinds of things; on other taxpayers to support them via social programs when times get hard; and on people in nearby and distant places whose land is mined, polluted, or stolen in order to make the phones, cars, microwaves, and televisions that they have come to want or need. The list could go on.

Two crucial openings emerge here. First, it should be clear that one cannot take sides between the goals of "economic development" on one hand and "environmental protection" on the other when standing in the full presence of interdependence. These categories appear as little more than distractions at best and acts of discursive violence at worst—severing people from a recognition and connection with that which actually sustains. What kinds of transformative alliance might be possible if these problematic articulations were dropped in favor of *engagement* with actual, shared interdependencies? What if the economic developers, social workers, and environmentalists shed their domains and met—with Rick and Theresa and their communities at the center of the conversation—to engage the question of how to defend and care for that which actually sustains us? What kinds of new commonings and trans-commonings, not to mention new identities, might emerge from such a process?

Second, the stigma and judgment associated with "dependency" must change if such dependency is no longer a matter of failure but is rather a *constitutive dimension of livelihood itself.* Isn't the CEO of the corporation who laid off Rick just as dependent as his former employees, if not more so? They are dependent on the same forests, even if many times removed from their living labor; on the same climate system, even if insurance might pay for the rebuild of their second house on the Cape; and on the same migrant farmworkers, even if their money can finance the political campaigns of wall-builders. And they may well depend on *money*, and therefore on the ongoing stability of its value and of the institutions that sustain it, to a much greater degree than do many working-class rural Mainers. What would they *do* if the banks turned into squats for climate refugees? Can they grow their own food? Hunt? Fix their own roof? How many of their neighbors do they know? Furthermore, they are dependent on government tax breaks and deregulation to meet quarterly growth projections; on the hard, low-paid labor of thousands of mill workers; on Rick's unemployment as a "necessary social cost" of the capitalist growth machine; and on friendly economists to justify all of this. Who are the parasites? Certainly not just those who buy their groceries with food stamps. Perhaps *we are all parasites* (Serres 2007), each in our own ways, and a struggle for recognition of this might change the landscape of politics in fundamental ways.

Indeed, it turns out that the people who are so commonly accused of deficiency for relying on "handouts" are some of the most active sustainers of the lives of others (alterpoiesis). Rick and Theresa are, of course, hosts to millions of nonhuman bacteria, and participate continually in the cycles of ecological metabolism. But on a more visible level: they sustain their children in myriad ways (for starters, they taught them how to use language, how to walk, and how to live among other humans); they care for Rick's elderly parents; they go to bean suppers at the local Grange to support families in need. Rick volunteers with the town's fire department, responding more actively than ever now that he has more time on his hands. Theresa drops in on a regular round of neighbors, passing on stories and advice, problem-solving daily struggles, and sharing extra zucchini. Both of them participate occasionally in the Sportsman's Alliance of Maine, which advocates for (among other things) the protection of deer and fish habitats. Once again, I could go on with examples. For all their very real hardship and need, Rick and Theresa are key nodes in a larger mesh of live-lihood that sustains far more than just them and their family. What might change if we were to more effectively recognize the depth and power of such alterpoiesis and the connections it nourishes? What if our institutional habitats were crafted to *support and care* for such relations rather than render them *invisible*? And again, what common-ings and trans-commonings might emerge from a politics capable of taking the life-sustaining work of Maine people seriously?

One thing should be clear: there is no economy, society, or environ-ment here, except and to the extent that media, researchers, policymak-ers, and other professionals mobilize forms of measurement and enforce modes of institution that render Rick and Theresa's complex relations intelligible in these terms. If we engage, instead, in terms of ecological livelihoods, a very different picture emerges, and with it a different set of possibilities and openings for transformative thought and action. Rather than a series of preconstituted divisions in which everything is already laid out and traced, we confront complex ethical-material nego-tiations among multiple beings. There are no "laws" of the market, no essential or inevitable categories into which everything fits, no pre-determined outcomes. Rick and Theresa are no longer marginal to the action; or, at least, they are not marginal in the same way—no more or less marginal than any other tiny humans in a web of constitu-tive interrelations. At the same time, Rick and Theresa are not sim-ply pregiven individuals standing amid a field of conflicting domains; rather, they emerge as such from a complex assemblage. Rick and The-resa's resentment and despair have institutional, cultural-conceptual, and emotional-affective habitats that render them into their current forms, and it is such habitat that a politics of livelihood must aim to transform—making other affects, openings, and alliances possible.

This transformation is no small task, and I have barely scratched the surface in this book of what it would entail. It is all too easy, for example, for me to write about ethical exposure, vulnerability, and becoming-present to the open and terrifying questions of ecology; I live in relative safety, in a well-made house, on fertile and secure (col-lective) land, in a strong community of skilled and loving people, and with access to regular, well-paid employment and a vast network of other livelihood relations that extend far beyond the place I call "home." It is easier to call for vulnerability when one's daily sustenance is not subjected to this very dynamic. Rick and Theresa, however, have no such luxury; theirs is an assemblage in immediate and palpable crisis. What does it mean to ask them to step into a space of even more vulnerability, to become further exposed to the ecologies that make (or unmake) them? Should it be surprising if they were to retreat into the seeming-certainties of fundamentalist Christianity, or to vote for politicians dedicated to spreading the politics of resentment, fueling white supremacy, and dismantling social redistribution systems in the name of "opportunity" and "personal responsibility"? Perhaps more important for the ethico-political task that confronts us, what kinds of etho-ecologies might compose enough safety and support to enable Rick, Theresa, and others to step into spaces of radical experimentation and becoming-otherwise without fear of losing the precious bit of stability they might yet hold? Nothing I have written in this book will be truly relevant without active, ongoing engagement with this question.

Transforming the Trio's Professions

What, then, of all the professionals whose work is variously aimed at developing the economy, adjusting society, and protecting the environment? If economic developers, social workers, and environmental advocates in Maine were to stop structuring their work around the categories of the hegemonic assemblage, what would they do instead? What would they *become*? In his book *Politics of Nature* (2004a), Bruno Latour proposes to redeploy the skills of particular professions (scientists, politicians, economists, and moralists) in the service of a new ontological frame of reference beyond the Nature-Culture divide. I would like to suggest something similar, but with an important difference. In his reformulation, Latour leaves the core functions and capabilities of each profession intact, only focusing them in different ways. Economists, most notably, remain devoted to the work of numerical reduction, calculation, and ordinal ranking, which Latour associates with the possibility of a *"common language* [for] those whose task is precisely to discover the *best* of the *common* worlds" (2004a, 152). Nothing of the hegemonic assemblage is actually challenged in this formulation, and ecopoiesis remains in the uncommoning grip of a myopic, Robbinsonian version of economics—a science of calculative behaviorism. Latour thus undermines his own project of opening new space for transversal negotiation by doubling down on one of the areas most in need of a radical challenge.

It should be clear that a transformation at the ontological level demands accompanying transformations in the very configuration and content of the professions themselves. One cannot, therefore, simply say that "economic developers should become *x*, social workers *y*, and environmentalists *z*," since this presumes too much alignment between the hegemonic categories and that which might emerge beyond them. Yet neither does it imply that the people whose words have animated so many pages of this book are simply *obsolete* and have nothing to contribute in a world beyond economy, society, and environment. On the contrary! It is not a matter of calling for early retirement, but of *scrambling* the institutional assemblages, mixing up the fields, redeploying and sometimes retooling skills in light of new, transversal forms of shared work. Such restructuring would undoubtedly pose staggering challenges to any aspiring organizers, but imagining its possible contours is nonetheless an urgent and useful task.

We can start with what might sound like a joke: What do (some) economic developers and (some) environmentalists have in common? Along with certain "social" professionals, they seek to foster effective strategies by which human needs are met and to cultivate multiple dimensions of healthy habitat. Whether seeking more reliable and equitable forms of employment, facilitating local production, protecting water quality, creating wild recreational spaces, reducing carbon emissions, challenging institutional white supremacy, building safer neighborhoods, or defending redistributive government programs in the face of austerity and cultural cruelty, these are all *livelihood workers*. Their work can be mapped, in part, by the various moments depicted in the circle of trans-commoning in chapter 9 (Figure 15). Some livelihood workers cultivate and defend various types of habitat, from biosocial dimensions to the emotional-affective (though we might do without those who are obsessed with the "business climate"); others might support reciprocal forms of procurement, responsible production practices, equitable transactions, ethical and nourishing forms of consumption, and the just and regenerative mobilization of surplus. Some may focus on supportive public policy and various practices of collective organization and decision-making, and others on ensuring that people have adequate access to effective mediators (skills, tools, technologies, etc.) at all levels of practice. Finally, a host of livelihood workers must do what so many economic developers are already (albeit narrowly) focused on: mapping opportunities and practices, networking, and catalyzing collective energy for the creation of new synergies. Is this not, transposed out of the hegemonic formation, the work of *trans-commoning*?

Not all livelihood developers, of course, are motivated primarily by human well-being; some are dedicated to a focus on more-than-human lives and habitats. But the crucial difference here is not between those who care about an "economy" and those who care about a nonhuman "environment," but rather *which communities or populations one is seeking to support and defend*. It is a matter of constituency, and of who is placed at the center of the circle for the purposes of commoning and trans-commoning. Some people are focused on the human populations of particular towns or regions, while others emphasize specific more-than-human communities (the Canada Lynx and its habitat relations, for example). This is what I intended in suggesting to some interviewees—amid confusion and unsettled laughter—that "human economies" might be only some livelihood configurations among others, including "deer economies" and "dog economies." If the term "economy" is to be used at all, why not use it to refer to particular, heuristic centerings of beings or communities within their wider assemblages of sustenance (Gibson-Graham and Miller 2015)? Some wildlife biologists might then be economists in the substantive sense, only focused on other species. And does "economics" then become a transdisciplinary field of *livelihood studies*?

If some people focus on humans while others focus on deer, dogs, apple trees, ticks, or particular species of fungus, how do we avoid yet another actualization of the Nature-Culture diagram and an ongoing denial of key forms of human dependence on more-than-human lives and processes? This is where another key role comes in. While some environmentalists have focused on defending human and nonhuman habitats, others take on a very different and equally crucial role: they continually remind us all that we are connected to others, enmeshed in interdependence, and must remain humbled before the complexities of our habitat relations. Did you think you could burn that coal for electricity without causing the permafrost in Siberia to melt? No such luck. At the same time, a host of people working in the former realm of the "social," often under the banner of social justice, are dedicated to similar work: they demand a radical expansion of our sense of complicity, responsibility, and solidarity. Did you think that your local food movement was unconnected to the assemblages of racism and class

oppression? Wrong. Did you think that gender comes in twos, wear-
ing pink or blue? Think again. Latour calls these workers "moralists"
(2004a, 157), but I prefer to think of them as *edge commoners* or *solidarity workers*. These are the courageous people who cause necessary
"good trouble" for all who would minimize or deny the ethical demands
of interdependence.[1] More and more such folks might leave their "environmental" and "social" organizations behind—and this is *already*
happening—to compose new alliances of all those committed to transforming habitats of violence, oppression, and degradation into habitats of liberation, healing, and flourishing.

Such transformation cannot happen, though, without at least one
more crucial role—drawn, perhaps, from the remaining ranks of "social
workers." These are the people who work in the very middle of the circle (chapter 9, Figure 15), helping others to cultivate the skills, capacities, and subjectivities necessary for the ceaseless work of *being-with*.
We might even keep the old name of "social work" for this role, since
the social can now be delinked from the force or domain of "society"
to designate *all* forms of relation (Latour 2005), especially practices
of cohabitation and conviviality. Social workers in an ecological-
livelihoods frame set themselves to the challenging but invaluable
tasks of helping people to heal from trauma and develop their capacities for imagination, hope, and connection. They work in collaboration with others to foster forms of expansive and inclusive belonging
and to build collective capacity for cooperation, mutual care, and the
nonviolent negotiation of conflict. This is not primarily about foster-
ing "independence" or "self-sufficiency," and certainly not about generating good employees for the next round of extractive job creation,
but about *cultivating forms of empowerment, safety, and connection*
that render the ethical recognition and negotiation of interdependence
ever more possible. It is about helping to compose subjectivities—
individual and collective—that are capable of embracing the work of
honest living on a wild earth.

Taken together, all of these roles point toward not only a new
configuration of institutional practice around the cultivation of life
and livelihood but also a radically different articulation of the discourse with which this book began: *sustainable development*. As I
have already suggested, "development" shifts here from the enforcement of a standardized, teleological model of the good life to an *event*

of collective creation. It has no predetermined goal or outcome, no necessary trajectory toward "growth" or "modernization" or any other ideal. Development begins with questions, asked collectively, about *need* and *desire* (De Vries 2007). What is the life we aspire to create for ourselves and with others? It is, in J. K. Gibson-Graham's words, "How 'we' (that is, all the human/nonhuman participants in the becoming world) organize our lives (or how life organizes us) to thrive in porously bounded spaces" (2011, 5).

This means, then, that development is always already about sustenance and sustainability: Who constitutes the community of necessity, desire, and care? Whom are we seeking to sustain? What must be challenged and undone in order for this sustenance to succeed? And on what scales of space and time must our thinking and action unfold in order to adequately accomplish this work? We are, once again, in the ethico-political space of commoning and uncommoning. "Sustainable development," then, if it is to avoid becoming a form of violence, must be nothing less than the institution of the *radically democratic negotiation of ecopoiesis.* It demands the active dismantling of uncommoning assemblages that undermine habitat and livelihood, and it calls forth practices of community and care that open space for new visions, desires, and possibilities to emerge. Sustainable development is the blocking of coal trains, the reoccupation and defense of common lands, the demand for dignity by all those whose lives and bodies have been devalued and targeted for violence, the cultivation of livelihood practices outside the diagram of Capital-State, the work of organizing to build grassroots power, and the mobilization of this power to move from making demands of the hegemonic assemblage to composing new assemblages beyond the grip of the hegemonic trio. Sustainable development is the radical *event* of ecological livelihoods.

An Invitation

The title of this conclusion has a double meaning that becomes clear only with some added punctuation: "becoming, otherwise. . . ." On one hand, it beckons toward myriad possible directions for transformation that are already emerging beyond the hegemonic trio of economy, society, and environment. On the other hand, it constitutes a warning. The assemblage that I have challenged in this book cannot be written

off as simply a matter of words, categories, or well-intentioned sim-
plifications. The division of the world into an economy, a society, and
an environment—however interconnected these three dimensions are
asserted to be—is both a symptom and a cause of the "slow motion
disaster" (Fitch 2011) that is contemporary capitalist modernity. The
juxtaposed graphs of rising carbon dioxide emissions and the advent
of the trio as a historical assemblage (chapter 1, Figure 5a and b) only
serve to illustrate what so many know to be the case: that the ways
we have conceptualized and organized our world over the past few
centuries have generated not only new forms of freedom and human
capacity but also unprecedented forms of destruction, violence, and
destabilization.

It is ironic, perhaps, that the commencement of a geological age
named after the planetary-scale transformations wrought by (certain)
human beings would mark the end—indeed, the impossibility—of that
very form of humanity. But the nomination of the Anthropocene is a
preemptive memorial for that which we know we must leave behind.
We can no longer live by the illusion of humanist autonomy; we can
no longer pretend that human productive and consumptive activity
stands in proud isolation from the rest of the living world; we can no
longer proceed as if aspirations for human liberation could be under-
written by the degradation of the rest of the living world from which
we emerge and to which we return. New concepts and new articulations of collective life must be composed if we are to have any chance
of living well in the coming centuries.

Here is what this book is for: adding another experiment to the
many others that are emerging, yearning, and stumbling toward new
assemblages. Can we begin to catch glimmers of what it might mean
to shift from protecting an "environment" to defending the relations
that sustain us and others? From fixing "social problems" to constructing modes of life in which both autonomy and shared vulnerability
become more and more possible? From developing an "economy" to
cultivating trans-commoning practices of ethical sustenance? Can we
begin to imagine what a conceptual, institutional, and affective habitat for such work might look like? Can we begin to teach and organize
toward such glimmers in our places? "Asking, we walk," says Subco-
mandante Marcos of the Zapatistas (Holloway 1996, 25). There are no
magic recipes here, no blueprints for change, and these ideas will matter only to the extent that they enter into new relations with others—

ideas, bodies, forces—that take them up as experimental propositions, give them new life, and transform them through collective learning and struggle. I can only hope that they might contribute one small spark to a wider, ongoing multigenerational effort to undo the diagram under which so many suffer, and to weave the threads of fugitive possibilities into a new fabric of collective healing and possibility.

ACKNOWLEDGMENTS

"To be one is to become with many," writes Donna Haraway, and a book is no exception. This project emerges from a vast web of sustenance, care, and support that extends over continents and years, which I can only begin to describe. I am immensely blessed with inspiring teachers, generous and insightful colleagues, loving and patient friends and family, and multiple extended communities of support. My work in these pages would be impossible without this nourishing habitat, this *oikos*.

First and foremost, this book comes into the world because of the mentoring, teaching, collaboration, and friendship I have been gifted by Katherine Gibson and the late Julie Graham. Julie drew me into graduate school after ten years of odd jobs, rabble-rousing, and collective homesteading, assuring me (and she was right) that one *can* be an activist and a scholar at the same time, and that theory must be *felt* and *lived* and not just thought. Katherine graciously took the torch from Julie and invited me to pursue a PhD and join more fully the community of inspiring community economies scholars imagining and enacting "other worlds." Whether insisting that I bring my ideas to life through direct connection with concrete practice or collaborating on explorations at the edges of both of our thinking, I am endlessly nourished, challenged, and inspired by her wit and wisdom.

I am particularly blessed to have found an intellectual home with the group of activist-scholars that constitutes the Community Economies Collective (CEC). Sparked by shared affinities with the work of J. K. Gibson-Graham, these generous, collaborative activist-researchers have been a nourishing oasis amid an academic culture that all too often generates isolation, exhaustion, and cynicism. I could not have pursued this path without such a collectivity, and I thank all members of the CEC—past and present—for their work to help make such a precious community come to life.

Significant portions of this book were drafted or edited at three Community Economies Theory and Writing Retreats in Bolsena, Italy (2013, 2015, and 2017), with the support of the Julie Graham Community Economies Research Fund. These gatherings were spaces not only of quiet focus but also of fertile co-thinking, and I thank my fellow retreat participants for inspiration, insight, and support within and beyond these gatherings.

Katherine Gibson, Gerda Roelvink, Stephen Healy, Bruce Braun, Romand Coles, Mick Smith, and an anonymous reviewer all patiently read and commented on full versions of some form of this book, including the dissertation from which it was born. I could not ask for a more generously engaged and appreciatively critical group of readers: their questions, insights, and challenges undoubtedly strengthened this project, and I am deeply grateful.

I thank many others who provided valuable feedback and insight on various writing fragments, ideas, and questions that have informed the book: Adam Auerbach, Elizabeth Barron, Sherie Blumenthal, Kate Boverman, Kate Brennan, Jenny Cameron, Betsy Catlin, Ben Chin, Nicola Chin, Rocky Coastlines, Bill Corlett, Jane Costlow, Kelly Dombroski, Simon Dougherty, Luke Drake, Francis Eanes, Esra Erdem, Holly Ewing, Nate Gabriel, Olivia Geiger, Rhyall Gordon, David Grinspoon, Ans Inés Heras, Ann Hill, Nell Houde, Jack Isherwood, Michael Johnson, Anna Kruzynski, Declan Kuch, Isaac Lyne, Lynn Margulis, Katharine McKinnon, Jo McNeill, William Miller, Bronwen Morgan, Oona Morrow, Janet Newbury, Anne O'Brien, Camille Parrish, Gabriel Piser, Josh Rubin, Hermann Ruiz, Craig Saddlemire, Maliha Safri, Eric Sarmiento, Matt Schlobohm, Boone Shear, Bonnie Shulman, Rob Snyder, Kevin St. Martin, Carl Straub, Davis Taylor, Gerry Walsh, Storm Waters, Jess Weir, Newell Woodworth, and all of the others I have missed. I thank my students from two semesters of "Oikos: Rethinking Economy and Ecology" (ENVR 272) at Bates College (Fall 2015 and Winter 2017) for the enthusiasm, thoughtful questions, and insightful perspectives that are undoubtedly woven into these pages.

This book would, of course, be impossible without my interviewees, who shared generously of time and thought and from whom I have learned so much. My commitment to anonymity prevents me from naming you here, but you are crucial collaborators nonetheless. I can only hope that the unconventional ends to which I have put your words and ideas in these pages might be encountered as a welcomed adventure of thought and an invitation to further conversation.

Thank you to Jason Weidemann from the University of Minnesota Press for encouraging and supporting this project at every turn, and for facilitating and distilling such valuable feedback along the way. My gratitude to Gabriel Levin's patient and thorough logistical support in the manuscript preparation process and to the rest of the staff at UMP who made this book possible. Thank you to Marilyn Campbell for her keen copyediting eye, to Neil West and the rest of his team at BN Typographics West, to Kai Evenson at Bates College for imaging assistance, and to David Drummond at Salamander Hill Design for the lucid cover design.

To the editors of the Diverse Economies for Livable Worlds book series—Katherine Gibson, Stephen Healy, Maliha Safri, and Kevin St. Martin: thank you for your vision, invitation, and enthusiastic affirmation of this project. I am honored to have this book join the series.

My thinking and writing have been sustained by multiple communities of "home": members of the Flying Fox collective house in Panania; the welcoming family of Kath, David, Lil, and Dan in Picnic Point; the Maine Earth First! crew, especially Ryan Clarke, Jimmy Freeman, Hillary Lister, Will Niels, Logan Perkins, and Emily Posner; my ever-supportive colleagues in the Bates College Environmental Studies Program; the many participants of the JED/Wild Mountain community in Greene; and an extended web of friends scattered across Maine and beyond. Thank you, in particular, to Jim and Naomi Nesbitt, Sophie Dougher, Colin Dougher, Tommy (Papa) Dougher, Whit Anicelli, Sherie Blumenthal, Gerry Walsh, Maia Rose Blumenthal-Walsh, Manis and Fanek Herrmann, Kate Brennan, Matt Schlobohm, Colin and Avery Schlobohm, Ben Chin, Craig Saddlemire, Brian Banton, Annie Doran, Alec Aman, Rebecca Froom, Ann Hill, and Seth Yentes for immeasurable patience, love, and support.

A few people deserve particular mention as contributors to this project and to my life as I have engaged with it. Kelly Dombroski, perhaps without always knowing it, has been an inspiration and guide as we have traveled a similar PhD and book-writing path. Always walking a few steps before me, and doing so with skill, grace, and generosity, Kelly has made the way so much easier and more fun to follow. Bill Corlett's teaching and friendship have shaped my life in ways for which I am ever grateful. As my undergraduate thesis advisor at Bates College, he opened my pathway into radical and practically engaged political theory, and our more recent collaborative reading and teaching of Gilles Deleuze and Félix Guattari's *A Thousand Plateaus* opened a new trajectory for my research, reflected strongly in these pages (though my "fast and loose" reading of this text, as Bill would teasingly call it, is solely my responsibility). Bonnie Shulman has been a steadfast, affirming, and energizing friend through thick and thin—a catalyst and co-conspirator in big dreams; a source of honest, loving, and precious feedback; and anchor amid churning waters. And Holly Ewing never ceases to teach me what it means to be both truly *awake* in the world—attentive to detail, nuance, and responsibility—and to meet this world with dedication, hard work, and joyful laughter. My thinking has been forever strengthened by the question I now ask myself regularly (even if I fail to answer it well): "What would Holly say about this?"

Finally, words cannot express the contributions that my families—Millers, Sheehan-Beckers, Bovermans—have made to this project. My grandparents, parents, my parents-in-love, and my sister, Lindsay, are steadfast and generous beyond measure in their love and support. My sweet son, Loren, is a brilliant star in my darkest night. My partner Kate Boverman, my favorite animal and best friend, should get an honorary doctorate plus a lifetime of back scratches for the heroic work of patience, insight, support, provocative challenge, care, and sustenance of body, mind, and heart that she has enacted to make this book—and so much more—possible. Though the words written here are mine, she is truly my coauthor.

NOTES

Introduction

1. Rick and Theresa are composite characters, based on a number of people and stories I have encountered in fieldwork and in many years living and working in Maine.

2. Plum Creek's proposed development is located in a region where poverty and unemployment rates are significantly higher than in the southern portion of the state.

3. All of this unfolded despite polls showing that Maine people opposed the plan nearly two-to-one (Critical Insights 2006).

4. This quote is from memory, as I have been unable to find a record of this advertisement.

5. For examples of articulations of solidarity economy organizing that clearly exceed economistic framings, see Arruda (2009); Mance (2010); and Miller (2010).

6. For a notable but brief and only suggestive exception, see Giddings, Hopwood, and O'Brien (2002).

7. In naming this place, it is crucial to recognize the history of colonization that has constructed the "State of Maine." The land now known as Maine has been, and continues to be, inhabited by the Wabanaki (Abenaki, Maliseet, Mi'kmaq, Passamaquoddy, and Penobscot) people and was forcibly taken and transformed into what is now called "Maine."

8. I am riffing here on Lévi-Strauss's (1966) notion that "animals are good to think."

9. On Maine's shifting land ownership and industrial configurations, see Hagan, Irland, and Whitman (2005); Colgan (2006); Acheson and Acheson (2015); and Lustig (2016).

10. They are, therefore, sites of struggle. The hope is that having such sites might offer possibilities for transformation.

11. Relative to larger states such as New York, Maine's governance structure is small, with fewer professional politicians (Maine has a "citizen" legislature in which most members work other jobs in their home communities) and a culture of

comparative informality in policymaking interaction. Grassroots activists, business lobbyists, legislators, and state officials frequently interact, communicate, and negotiate in a state capital (Augusta) populated by fewer than 20,000 people (the third-smallest in the United States).

12. I conducted forty interviews between November 2012 and December 2013. I aimed to speak with people whose organizations explicitly identify their work as pertaining to one of the three categories, whether via the organizational name or mission statement, whose work is addressed either to statewide policy and action or to regional-scale work (i.e., at the level of the county or economic development district), and who had at least five years of experience working in their particular field. This fieldwork was approved by the Western Sydney University Human Ethics Research Committee, approval number H9867. All interviewees have been anonymized via the use of pseudonyms.

1. Constitutional Geometry

1. These performative measurements appear in Maine via such sources as the Bureau of Labor Statistics' *Maine Economy at a Glance* (2014) report; the *State of Maine's Environment* report issued by the Colby College Environmental Policy Group (2010); and the Maine implementation of Harvard University's *Social Capital Community Benchmark Survey* (Maine Community Foundation 2006).

2. For examples of this kind of thinking, see Beckerman (1992); Grossman and Krueger (1995); and Hollander (2004).

3. *Oxford English Dictionary* (2008b).

4. Though the word was not entirely new, Carlyle's use was novel enough that his friend and fellow writer John Sterling critiqued it—along with other neologisms by Carlyle—as "words, so far as I know, without any authority" (qtd. in Jessop 2012, 710).

5. Another option within this problem-space, of course, has been to dismiss the existence of "society" entirely and reduce human dynamics to individual choices (Margaret Thatcher's statement that "there is no such thing" as society is a famous example). The constitutional geometry lost a term here among certain ideologues, but this only affirmed the sovereignty of the economy, which was then effectively positioned as the *only* form of human collectivity.

6. The adjective form of "society" was substituted for the noun form in this query, since the results from a "society" search are skewed by uses of that term by organizations (as in the Humane Society). The query did not include references later than 2000 due to a change in Google's treatment of the corpus that distorts results across the millennial boundary. While the overall trends displayed by this analysis are generally considered valid, numerous factors render the Google n-gram analysis suspect as a source of precise correlatable data (Pechenick, Danforth, and Dodds 2015). I use this graph primarily to dramatize that which has already been established in my earlier historical sketch.

7. *Oxford English Dictionary* (2008a).

8. This understanding is closely related to (and is, in fact, a source for) the notion of "composition" within actor-network theory as developed by Callon, Law, Latour, and others. Entities, in this view, are not conceptualized as discrete, self-contained positivities, but rather as convergences of multiple relations or "patterned networks of heterogeneous materials" (Law 1992, 391). The term "composition" has been particularly developed by Latour (2010). "We shall say of a collective," proposes Latour, referring to any kind of multiply constituted entity, "that it is *more* or *less* articulated, in every sense of the word" (Latour 2004a, 86).

9. See De Angelis (2007) on enclosures; Latour (1987) on stable references and (1990) on visuals; Stengers (2010) on obligation; and on subjectification, see, for example, Burchell, Gordon, and Miller (1991); Rose (1999); and M. Dean (2009).

10. Neither "socialization" nor "environmentalization" is widely developed as a conceptual term in the way that Çaliskan and Callon propose economization. In the case of "socialization," this is likely due to the very different way in which the term has been used in sociology to refer to processes of assimilation or integration into a particular social milieu (see, e.g., Parsons and Bales 1956; Grusec and Hastings 2008). A number of scholars have effectively pursued a process-oriented research program around "society" and "the social" under different terms (see Rose 1999; Helliwell and Hindess 1999; Rose and Miller 2008; Higgins and Larner 2010). In the case of "environmentalization," an approach has arisen in rural sociology that uses the term to trace ways in which particular forms of environmental consciousness, discourse, and politics move through social spaces and influence the shape of various struggles (see Buttel 1992; Acselrad 2010). Timothy Luke's work on "environmentality" (1995), including a brief mention of a notion of environmentalization, points toward this alternative direction for performative inquiry around "the environment."

11. While Phillips (2006) points out that "assemblage" may not be an adequate translation of *agencement*, I nonetheless follow the well-established convention for the sake of familiarity and continuity.

12. Deleuze and Guattari do not often use the term "hegemony," but I read it in their work nonetheless. One particularly clear formulation of the political assemblage I have in mind is found in Guattari (2011), when he refers to "molar power that equips, stratifies the socius and is supported by power formations, and takes on an equipmental function, implanting a Collective equipment network" (75). By "equipment" he means the broad array of tools and practices by which a given collectivity produces and maintains its life and world.

PART II

1. For a clear instance of this bifurcation, see the 2015 symposium in *Rethinking Marxism* on approaches to communism, centered on papers by Jodi Dean (2015) and Stephen Healy (2015).

2. See, for example, Fine (2003); and Mallavarapu and Prasad (2006).

3. This position is exemplified by Jodi Dean (2012).

4. Spivak's notion of "strategic essentialism" (1996) was a way to simultaneously acknowledge the dangers of essentialism while not rejecting its strategic—though always problematic—use in particular (postcolonial) contexts.

2. Forces and Domains

1. See Butler (1997) for more on this double sense of subjection and subjectification.

2. I use the term "institution" with a nod toward Foucault's notion of "institutionalization," which involves a whole array of material-semiotic practices of disciplinary normalization and the rendering-durable and obligatory of various forms of behavior (Foucault 1982, 792).

3. For indigenous Wabanaki people in Maine, this enclosure can be dated back to the time of invasion in the mid-seventeenth century; for Mainers of European descent, in began with the undoing of subsistence-oriented homesteading by the forced rents imposed by the "great proprietor" land barons and their surveyors in the early to mid nineteenth century (Taylor 1990) and continued over the course of the nineteenth and early twentieth centuries with the progressive eclipse of remaining subsistence practices by regimes of wage labor (Judd 2000). Many contemporary Maine people still practice nonmonetary, nonmarket, and noncapitalist forms of subsistence (Andrews 2014), but employment and access to money—and thus engagement with "the economy"—are nonetheless effectively obligatory for most of us.

4. See Gibson-Graham (2006c, ch. 5) for a powerful analysis of the relation between discourses of the body and "the economy."

5. This is just another way to describe what Marx calls "fetishism": "The commodity reflects the social characteristics of men's own labor as objective characteristics of the products of labor themselves, as socio-natural properties of these things. . . . It is nothing but the definite social relation between men themselves which assumes here, for them, the fantastic relation between things" (Marx 1992, 164–65). What should be clear here is that Marx's description of capitalism's fetishism is, in fact, also a description of the production "the economy" itself.

6. This is, of course, not *always* true—especially in the case of environmental activists fighting for protection of more-than-human habitats. I will highlight such work in Parts III and IV. The point for now is that a particular, hegemonic anthropocentrism can be seen to undergird certain articulations of "the environment" and to be (inadvertently, or perhaps as regretful strategic compromise) reproduced in others.

7. For salient critiques of this articulation, see Luke (1994) and Harvey (1996).

8. The role of capitalist development in ecological degradation is well established. See, for example, Harvey (1996); O'Connor (1998); Kovel (2007); and Foster, Clark, and York (2012).

9. Yet even this demand opens the question of whether various attempts in radical ecological philosophy to render "nature as a subject" (e.g., Katz 1997; Lo 1999;

Stone 2010) are not still trapped within the very same regime of subjection, playing out a certain egalitarian redistribution of subjectivity *within* this still-hegemonic regime.

10. For clear articulations of this critique, see Guha (1989); Cronon (1996); Di Chiro (1996); White (1996); Cole and Sheila (2001); and Sandler and Pezzulo (2007).

3. Enclosures and Outsides

1. "Coordination" here should be taken as a depoliticized euphemism for a dynamic much like Marx's articulation of "free labor" (1992, 272), which emerges only from myriad forms of coercion and enforced obligation.

2. Similar critiques have been made of international conservation projects that displace local and native people in the name of environmental protection (e.g., Agrawal and Redford 2009; Corson 2011; Kelly 2011).

3. As Callon writes, "In itself, the existence of externalities is not in the least outrageous. That certain people should pay for others or profit from others without bearing the associated costs is not disgusting or disturbing. Such transfers are inevitable: after all, the laws of thermodynamics teach us that you cannot have order without paying the price of chaos" (1998, 246). In a very abstract sense, perhaps, he is correct. But his move to avoid the "outrageous" dimensions of framing and overflowing is itself a framing that pushes analyses of exploitation and violence to an "outside" that renders the theory safe for many of the economists and sociologists he is presumably seeking to address. Callon's externalization therefore enables his thinking to remain untainted by the specter of Marxist class analysis and other "radical" theorizations that might help to constitute outrage at the dynamics of framing and overflowing (see Callon's repudiation of core Marxian categories in Barry and Slater 2002).

4. Numerous feminist economists and economic geographers have developed a similar argument, and my analysis is inspired by their work. See Brandt (1995); Henderson (1995); Bennholdt-Thomsen and Mies (1999); Cameron and Gibson-Graham (2003); Gibson-Graham (2006a); and Roelvink and Gibson-Graham (2009).

5. Maine's vast diversity of livelihood practice has been noted by other scholars, including St. Martin (2005); Robbins, Emery, and Rice (2008); Baumflek, Emery, and Ginger (2010); Snyder (2011); Andrews (2014); and McCourt and Perkins (2014).

6. See Adam Smith (1982, 109–13).

7. These multiple noneconomic sustenance relations and practices are in a position of constitutive exclusion not entirely unlike that of Marx's "reserve army of labor," the population of unemployed people that capitalist markets produce by discarding and yet nonetheless rely upon (Marx 1992, 781). These are practices and people often relegated to the shadows and margins of the "social," rendered into problematic sites for intervention while all the while remaining essential for the functioning of that which ignores, undermines, uses, drains, and disciplines them.

We can see here, once again, the "asymmetrical reciprocity" (see chapter 2) enacted between the economic and the social.

8. I do not, however, link my notion of abjection to a whole psychoanalytic assemblage, and reference to Kristeva should be taken as merely suggestive. I mobilize abjection here in a broad sense as the excluded surplus or excess which haunts the edges of that which has constituted it and which it, in turn, constitutes (see, e.g., Corlett 1998; Endnotes 2013).

9. This is one lesson of the powerful film *Snowpiercer* (2013). Thanks to Boone Shear for leading me here.

10. See Morton (2010) for a critique of this purified image of ecology.

4. A Diagram of Power

1. One might say, therefore, that a triple-axis, abstract ontologizing machine fractures and reconsolidates multiplicities into the categories of the economic, the social, and the environmental and "projects" this into actuality in Maine. The limitation of this prism figure, of course, is the danger of viewing it as a structure. It is actually the case that the prism itself has no existence apart from the light it refracts. *The refraction itself brings the prism into being.*

2. My use of the notion of diagram is additionally inspired by Vinay Gidwani's (2008) work on the diagram of "development."

3. I capitalize the five terms of this diagram as a way to clarify their sense as abstract "virtual" nodes. This will be particularly important with regard to the abstract State as distinct from particular, actualized governmental institutions we might call "the state."

4. Maine's GDP in 2012 (at the time of the ecosystem valuation study by Troy) was $53.7 billion, of which $15.9 billion was made up of the finance, real estate, and professional service sectors (Bureau of Economic Analysis 2013).

5. For a similar view, see Lazzarato (2012).

6. This slippage is also noted by Gibson-Graham (2006c, 89), who notes the "difficult and elusive" disjunction between Deleuze and Guattari's seemingly total "worldwide capitalist axiomatic" and their commitment to radical undecidability and "the becoming of everybody/everything" (Deleuze and Guattari 1987, 473) outside the domain of Capital.

7. Capital is quite often derivative and parasitic rather than self-composed and creative; as Marx (1992) noted so clearly relative to the productive power of co-operation, Capital loves to take credit for that which it could never achieve.

8. If Capital is constituted as "self-valorizing value" (Marx 1992; De Angelis 2007, 39), a force that takes us up into its clutches, transforms us, and even (partially) produces "us" in various radically differentiated forms, this is not because it has a godlike subjectivity and discrete agency of its own. It is because a wholly contingent, path-dependent historical web of articulations has generated and sustained a "habit" (Latour 2004a, 86) that we can now call Capital. Habits have no essential trajectory and can be broken, though sometimes not without immense difficulty.

9. "The State is not defined by the existence of chiefs; it is defined by the perpetuation or conservation of organs of power. The concern of the State is to conserve" (Deleuze and Guattari 1987, 357).

10. "From its birth," says Deleuze in an interview, "capitalism has been connected with a savage repression. It very quickly acquired its organization and State apparatus. Did capitalism entail the dissolution of previous codes and powers? Absolutely. But it had already set up the gears of its power, including its State power, in the fissures of previous regimes" (Deleuze 2004, 268).

11. The actual (and hegemonic) distinction between "market" and "state," and the politics of oscillation that play out around it only serve to obscure the role of the State in constituting markets and market dynamics, and the complicity of various collections of capitalists in shaping policy.

12. Mathematically, 8 elements have 40,320 possible combinations!

PART III

1. Thanks to Kevin St. Martin (pers. comm. 2017) for pointing out the way in which Latour's term "composition" invokes the process-oriented sense of "assemblage" while also indicating an *intention*—as when a composer produces music. Composition, then, helps to amplify the role of discourse, research, and purposeful action in making (or unmaking) assemblages.

2. This is an important dimension of performativity: the sense in which one cannot rely on intention to successfully generate a particular, pre-imagined outcome. As MacKenzie (2007) has shown with reference to economics, performativity comes in a variety of forms and includes "counterperformativity" in which a particular discourse generates effects that render the world *less* in line with its purported description.

5. Cracks in the Assemblage

1. On the surface this might seem like a distinction between what is *said* and what is *done* ("They say they're dividing, but they're actually mixing"), but in fact purification and translation are said and done *at the same time*. It is only their co-existence that is effectively denied (Latour 1993, 40).

2. Latour clearly acknowledges this shift in his more recent work (see, especially, Latour 2017).

3. This is evidenced by Shellenberger and Nordhaus's "post-environmentalism" (2009), which embraces the dissolution of a nature/culture binary in favor of a deeply anthropocentric, procapitalist, Promethean developmentalism that sits quite comfortably with wider trends to "reconcile" the economy-environment tension by privatizing, monetizing, and commodifying ecological relations.

4. This is the whole stream of economics that has taken Lionel Robbins's famous definition of the discipline as its foundational credo: "Economics is the science which studies human behaviour as a relationship between ends and scarce means which have alternative uses" (Robbins 1932, 15).

6. Multiplying Articulations

1. David Graeber (2011), in his historical work on debt and the origins of money and credit, describes a number of such examples where economists employ crude stories to render particular power-laden and contingent relations into seemingly "natural" progressions.

2. This notion of ethics as an open question of responsibility amid complex interdependency is also shared and further elaborated by J. K. Gibson-Graham and others in the Community Economies Collective (see, e.g., Gibson-Graham 2006a; Roelvink and Gibson-Graham 2009; Miller 2013b; Hill 2014). I engage this work further in chapter 7.

3. The dialectic is such a clean and elegant model for thinking complexity, and yet I cannot help but suspect that the very structure of this model is the product of an epoch obsessed with thinking in "twos." The "dia-" may exist in philosophy books more than in any actual mess of historical change. Perhaps there is a *polylectic*.

PART IV

1. A panic may be one of the key ingredients in the emergence of fascism as a mode of security-seeking amid experiences of chaos and breakdown. This is clearly something that a revolutionary politics must avoid, even while actively seeking to undo core elements of the present web of assemblages.

2. Rosi Braidotti's (2013) notion of "affirmative politics" clarifies the strategy of "pushing that which is falling" as more than mere destruction, and as active creation. The collapse of modernity's categorical distinctions—symptomatic of a wider crisis of humanism—is an opportunity to be seized: "Instead of falling back on the sedimented habits of thought that the humanist past has institutionalized," she suggests, "the posthuman predicament encourages us to undertake a leap forward into the complexities and paradoxes of our times" (2013, 54).

3. I am paraphrasing Deleuze and Guattari's "recipe" for transformative experimentation: "This is how it should be done: Lodge yourself on a stratum, experiment with the opportunities it offers, find an advantageous place on it, find potential movements of deterritorialization, possible lines of flight, experience them, produce flow conjunctions here and there, try out continuums of intensities segment by segment, have a small plot of new land at all times" (1987, 161).

7. Ecopoiesis

1. The term "ecopoiesis" has also been used in ecological literary theory to refer to the imaginative disclosure of the more-than-human world through writing (Bate 2000; Rigby 2004).

2. Unlike Moore, however, I have no allegiance to a "dialectic" within which "species and environment" would stand as "the ontological pivot . . . of historical change" (2015, 35), since even this attempt at blurring lines remains wedded to the

reproduction of a distinction that appears to preexist its material-semiotic articulation as such. Ecopoiesis is not a dialectic of anything with anything else, but the very process from which things that come to relate (including coproduced binaries that can be modeled in terms of dialectics) emerge. Furthermore, where Moore focuses on the ways in which capitalism emerges from and constitutes a particular, problematic mode of life-making, I am interested in amplifying some of the many ways in which ecopoiesis *escapes* the dynamics of Capital and its reproduction.

3. Beth Dempster (2007) has offered an important challenge and supplement to Maturana and Varela's concept of autopoiesis that resonates significantly with my project here. Complex systems, she argues, are dynamic and agential well beyond the boundaries of the auto. What she calls "sympoiesis"—literally, collective creation—is intended to name a contrasting system dynamic. Where autopoiesis names an organizational closure (the "organism") that is conserved via a selectively open flow, sympoiesis refers to systems that are "organizationally ajar and boundaryless" (Dempster 2007, 103), composed of multiple, relatively fluid elements in ever-changing relations, which cannot be captured by any clear distinction between a "self" and an "other." Crucial here, in particular, is Dempster's challenge to the "environment" distinction present in autopoiesis theory and her rendering of open relationality as central to world-making. Ecopoiesis has a different aim, however, in that it is intended to name not a "system" dynamic at all, but rather the processes by which systematicity as such emerges.

4. I am grateful to my father, William Miller, for offering this formulation in a conversation about the ecopoiesis concept.

5. "Belonging" is a complex term, and can easily be posed in problematic forms. I intend it here in a radically open and exploratory sense that avoids any claims to universalist, essentialist, or even place-bound notions of community. Emily O'Gorman expresses this clearly: "While belonging has been taken up in ways that promote essentialist categories of inclusion and exclusion, and that disguise specific relationships, the promise of this concept is that its emphasis on fit might be usefully reimagined to provide insight into contested spaces of biocultural relationships; how they are created and contested and with what consequences for whom?" (2014, 286).

6. There is a tension in ecology between place-bound notions of habitat and those that center more on the general sustenance "needs" of organisms or populations. On one side, we have Odum's simple definition of habitat as "the place where an organism lives, or the place where one would go to find it" (1971, 234). On the other hand, we have Krausman (for example) insisting that "habitat quality should be linked with demographics, not vegetative features" (1999, 89), and therefore that "wherever an organism is provided with resources that allow it to survive, that is habitat" (1999, 86). I intend here to push the organism-centered definition of habitat to a more relational register (out of the zone of living beings in a world of passive resources) while retaining its insight that habitat should not be conflated with location or place.

7. One must simultaneously connect the habitat with the inhabitant as parts of a single etho-ecology while also remaining uncertain about what both might become as these relations are transformed. "Inseparability does not necessarily mean dependence," Stengers reminds us (2005b, 997). The relative autonomy that emerges from a given habitat is a force of creation that is never determined by that habitat even as it is made by/of it, and transformation of habitat relations may generate unpredictable creative (un)becomings of their inhabitants.

8. It is important to be clear that community economy extends well beyond the boundaries of the human (Roelvink and Gibson-Graham 2009; Gibson-Graham and Roelvink 2010; Gibson-Graham 2014; Hill 2014; Gibson-Graham and Miller 2015). Negotiation includes the more-than-human world, the nonhuman "others that make life possible and shape the character of life" (Roelvink and Gibson-Graham 2009, 149). Ann Hill's work, in particular, seeks to "undo our human exceptionalism as ethical actors" (2014, 222). For Hill, it is crucial that we begin to robustly explore ways of engaging ethics that shift from the conventional human subject-of-action to what she refers to as "human-nonhuman ethical assemblages" (2014, 198), or, perhaps even more suggestively, the "ethical agency of a more-than-subject" (2014, 217).

9. Jean-Luc Nancy, from whom Gibson-Graham draws, describes this difference in terms of the "socially imploded generality" (1991, 74) of capitalist relations that institute a common-being (commensurability and exchange value) over and above that which cannot be measured or compared; and the "socially exposed particularity" (1991, 74) of a community that refuses, resists, or escapes such colonization.

10. Stengers illustrates this notion with the example of animal experimentation. Rather than moralizing about this issue, she wants to ask questions about the kinds of assemblages that render certain relations immune to ethical encounter and also speculate about what new assemblages might reverse this process: "We don't know what a researcher who today affirms the legitimacy or even the necessity of experiments on animals is capable of becoming in an *oikos* that demands that he or she think 'in the presence of' the victims of his or her decision" (Stengers 2005b, 997).

11. As rich as these stories are, I am not able to describe any one of them in detail, as this would risk compromising my commitment to anonymity. This limitation does not, however, undermine my ability to make the argument I am focused on here, as it is more about the broad dynamics of negotiation than about the details of how they unfold in particular moments and sites.

12. "Freedom from labor" might also be considered a euphemism for "exploitation," in the sense that the avoidance of negotiation in the composition of life can only come from a kind of unilateral imposition or theft or/from another. In Marxian terms, the appropriation of surplus value from labor would constitute a short-circuiting of negotiation (hence the common image of the capitalist as a parasite or vampire who takes without giving). The force of negotiation remains, of course: it is then transposed into the realm of labor struggle, where powers of living labor

are mobilized to undermine, influence, overtake, or transform the capitalist refusal to negotiate at the moment of surplus production.

13. According to the *OED*, *to negotiate* is "to do business or trade; to engage in commerce," "to find a way through, round, or over," and "to succeed in dealing with," "to manage or bring about successfully" (or not). In particular, I find a playful pun-reading of the following definition quite compelling in light of recent attempts to rematerialize social theory: "To communicate or confer (*with* another or others) for the purpose of arranging some matter" (*Oxford English Dictionary* 2008c).

8. Ecological Livelihoods

1. This is gleaned from etymologies of the word, sourced from the *Oxford English Dictionary* and the *Online Etymology Dictionary* (http://www.etymon line.com/index.php?term=livelihood).

2. It is important to note the significant controversy surrounding Polanyi's notion of embeddedness. While some readings of *The Great Transformation* (in particular) suggest that the market economy was *actually* disembedded from society (e.g., Braudel 1983), others propose a more nuanced reading in which an impossible disembedding is nonetheless proposed by economic theory and thus dangerously enacted in practice (Block 2001). Fred Block (2003) proposes that Polanyi's notion of embeddedness developed over time and was not fully fleshed out at the time of writing *The Great Transformation*. In later work (e.g., Polanyi 1992), he is much clearer about the "always embedded market economy" (Block 2003, 276). Nonetheless, there can be little doubt that the distinction (and connection) between domains of "economy" and "society" remains operative in any form of this theorization.

3. In a later work, Scoones explains this language in terms of a strategy to remain connected with, and legitimate in the eyes of, the discipline of economics: "In the notionally trans-disciplinary subject area of development, making sense to economists is a must. . . . In particular, the focus on 'capitals' and the 'asset pentagon' kept the discussion firmly in the territory of economic analysis" (2009, 176–77). While the strategy is somewhat understandable given the hegemonic power of economics, the choice is nonetheless disappointing in its re-performance of a discourse that has worked to undermine the viability of so many livelihoods and habitats.

4. See, for example, DFiD (2001); Hussein (2002); Hamilton-Peach and Townsley (2004); Khanya-AICDD (2006); and Serrat (2008). Chambers (2005) has noted the profoundly depoliticizing effects of this trend toward individualization of livelihoods.

5. Examples of public positions taken on this bill can be found on the Maine State Legislature's website, https://legislature.maine.gov.

6. Richard Judd's (2000) working-class history of conservation in New England describes the long process by which subsistence practices in Maine were shifted from mainstream modes of life toward something demanding escape: who would not want to leave behind an uncertain life increasingly seen as "a residue of

backcountry indolence dragging down [Maine's] rigorous industrial economy" (2000, 136)? Even if we view such a shift in critical terms (and rightly we should), we must nonetheless acknowledge the real limits of advocating in Maine for a politics of "subsistence."

7. With a nod to Jacques Derrida (1998). See also the work of Simon Critchley (2007) on the impossible (yet unavoidable) demands of ethical interrelation.

8. I use the term "singularity" as an alternative to terms such as "individual," which presume the boundaries of the figure from the outset. Following Nancy (1991), "singularity" names an entity that is neither necessarily an individual nor a group (though it can also be either or both).

9. One might argue that many autotrophs, too, require use of the life-force and bodies of others—as, for example, when plant roots take in nutrients released from decomposition processes.

10. This is to say, following Deleuze and Guattari, that representations of unity, systematicity, or determination do not in fact *represent*. The transcendent object or process they claim to capture is only one more effect (or *affect*) within immanence itself, one more component or affect added on. "Transcendence is always a product of immanence," writes Deleuze (2001, 31). It is, in fact, a question of power and struggle: "The notion of unity . . . appears only when there is a power takeover in the multiplicity by the signifier or a corresponding subjectification " (Deleuze and Guattari 1987, 8). This formulation is close to Latour's notion—likely developed with unacknowledged debt to Deleuze and Guattari—that "the macro is neither 'above' nor 'below' the interactions, but added to them as another of their connections, feeding them and feeding off of them" (2005, 177).

9. Tools for a Politics of Ecological Livelihood

1. See http://maine.coop/; http://www.ecologybasedeconomy.org/; and http://www.mainefoodcouncils.net/.

2. See Community Economies website, http://www.communityeconomies.org.

3. To be precise, there may be allopoiesis without autopoiesis, as when particular relations of mass and gravity compose a durable body of rock in space, but this does not work the other way around. All autopoietic entities are also, at the same time, allopoietic.

4. A similar, though less conceptually developed, proposal for rethinking ecosystem services is made by Turnhout et al. (2013).

5. As the prayer goes: "God, give us grace to accept with serenity the things that cannot be changed, courage to change the things that should be changed, and the wisdom to distinguish the one from the other." I would only add that courage must include the fortitude to relentlessly experiment with—and participate in transforming—the *line* between that which can and cannot be changed.

6. Latour articulates a similar notion of habit and its relation to habitat in his *Modes of Existence* project: "We can say of habit that in effect it makes the world *habitable*, that is, susceptible to an *ethos*, to an ethology" (2013, 268).

7. This question, and my work on habitat in general, is inspired by Gibson, Cahill, and McKay's (2010) elaboration of Jane Jacobs's (2001) notion of "habitat maintenance."

8. I map human habitat here based on the specificities of human relationalities as I understand them. This does not preclude a different schema relevant to other species.

9. I use the term "biosocial," despite its limitations as a hybrid of two conventional binaries, in the sense of Ingold and Palsson (2013): "Our claim is not that the biological and the social are complementary, or that they pertain respectively to the level of discrete individuals and to that of the wider groupings into which they are incorporated, but that there is no division between them. . . . At every level of resolution we find the same complexity, the same intertwining of threads, the same metabolic exchange. Like the rope, the becoming is biological all the way up, and social all the way down" (Ingold 2013, 9). The term "geosocial" is intended with similar implications, referring to "forces that are both coupled to the earth and its various stratifications, and internalized or imbricated within social formations" (Yusoff 2017, 109). See also Clark and Yusoff (2017).

10. See, for example, Dolsak and Ostrom (2003); Barnes (2006); Bollier and Helfrich (2012); Gibson-Graham, Cameron, and Healy (2013); Bollier (2014); and Amin and Howell (2016).

11. A similar point about avoiding the opposition of commons and enclosure is made by David Harvey (2012, 70).

12. Two points about the term "uncommons": First, Peter Linebaugh uses the term "discommoning" to refer to the dismantling of commons (2008, 49), and thus as a synonym for enclosure. While this is surely an example of uncommoning in action, it does not exhaust the possible field of action that uncommoning refers to. Many relations can be said to involve uncommoning without any explicit moment of privatization or expropriation; in this sense, uncommoning is a mode of *institution* rather than the name of its undoing. Second, the term "uncommoning" has been used by Blaser and de la Cadena (2017), among others, to refer to something closer to what I have called the abject or even constitutive outside (chapter 3), a "condition that disrupts (yet does not replace) the idea of 'the world' as shared ground" (2017, 186). I am developing the term in a different, but not antithetical, direction.

13. We could speak, then, of *commoning enclosures* and *uncommoning enclosures*.

14. Thanks to Mick Smith for raising this critical issue and prompting further (even if not yet enough!) thinking.

15. For a detailed account of this experience, see Snyder and St. Martin (2015).

16. While our concepts are closely allied, De Angelis's term "boundary commoning" does not clearly express the idea he has so robustly developed—namely, that commoning must be sustained by practices that connect commons and thus construct commons ecologies. "Boundary" reminds me of division, while "trans" gets at the movement of connection across different practices. I suspect that

De Angelis's choice of terms is related to his reliance on systems theory, in which the language of boundary is central.

17. I have worked for a number of years to develop conceptual frameworks in support of solidarity economy (SE) organizing (Miller 2006, 2010, 2013b), and I remain committed to this work. But what happens when the term "economy" and its associated divisions are challenged? This question, as I noted in the introduction, was a starting point for this book project. I propose here that "solidarity economics" can be transposed into the key of ecological livelihoods through the notion of trans-commoning, combined with a robust framework for visualizing actual and potential connections across commoning domains. This is not to say that solidarity economy organizers should necessarily change the terms within which they are working—this must be a situated, strategic choice—but it is to suggest that SE *practice* does not require the language of "economy" at its foundation.

10. Ontopolitical Coordinates

1. It is from Oscar (interview) that I derive my term for this coordinate, though I also intend it to generate some resonance (even if wholly undeveloped here) with notions of "constituent power" in the work of some autonomist Marxists (e.g., Negri 1999; Shukaitis and Graeber 2007).

2. These are common practices of valuation in environmental economics. See, for example, Garrod and Willis (1999) and Freeman (2003).

3. For Max-Neef, the distinction is phrased in terms of "needs" and "satisfiers."

4. For a further elaboration of this argument, see Miller (2013a). I do not intend for this critique to extend to all possible versions of Marxist notions of "necessary labor," since I recognize that some strains of Marxism constrain this concept to a particular situation—namely, the accounting required to render capitalist surplus extraction visible. Following Diane Elson (1979), I believe that Marx's value theory is best understood as a claim applicable only to capitalist assemblages. The necessary/surplus distinction can be seen as a *particular articulation* of human labor in a context in which livelihood has been restricted by the dominance of money mediation; in which a wage serves to provide the means to secure this livelihood; and in which the community of necessity has been restricted to individuals and families by particular ideological and kinship articulations. Application of the concept beyond this situation risks overgeneralization and overextension of a historically specific formulation.

5. I am referring here to the mainstream economic notions of consumer and producer surplus.

Conclusion

1. "Good trouble" is a phrase from congressman and civil rights activist John Lewis. See Mettler (2016).

BIBLIOGRAPHY

Acheson, Ann W. 2007. "Poverty in Maine." *Maine Policy Review* 16 (1): 12–29.

Acheson, James M., and Ann W. Acheson. 2015. "Cycles of Industrial Change in Maine." In *The Anthropology of Postindustrialism: Ethnographies of Disconnection*, edited by Ismael Vaccaro, Krista Harper, and Seth Murray. New York: Routledge.

Acselrad, Henri. 2010. "The 'Environmentalization' of Social Struggles: The Environmental Justice Movement in Brazil." *Estudos Avançados* 24 (68): 103–19.

Agrawal, Arun, and Kent Redford. 2009. "Conservation and Displacement: An Overview." *Conservation and Society* 7 (1): 1–10.

Akenji, Lewis. 2014. "Consumer Scapegoatism and Limits to Green Consumerism." *Journal of Cleaner Production* 63 (January): 13–23.

Alfredsson, E. C. 2004. "'Green' Consumption—No Solution for Climate Change." *Energy* 29 (4): 513–24.

Amin, Ash. 2005. "Local Community on Trial." *Economy and Society* 34 (4): 612–33.

Amin, Ash, and Philip Howell, eds. 2016. *Recovering the Commons*. London: Routledge.

Anderson, Benedict. 2006. *Imagined Communities: Reflections on the Origin and Spread of Nationalism*. London: Verso.

Anderson, Mark W. 1997. "Two Pigs from Maine." *Maine Scholar: A Journal of Ideas and Public Affairs* 10: 203–15.

Andrews, Marguerite L. 2014. "Contested Conservation of the Snowmobile Commons: Private Land, Public Rights, and Rural Livelihoods in Maine's Social Wilderness." PhD diss., Rutgers University, New Brunswick.

Argyrou, Vassos. 2005. *The Logic of Environmentalism: Anthropology, Ecology, and Poscoloniality*. New York: Berghahn Books.

Arruda, Marcos, ed. 2009. *A Non-Patriarchal Economy Is Possible: Looking at Solidarity Economy from Different Cultural Facets*. Rio de Janeiro: ALOE.

Asdal, Kristen. 2008. "Enacting Things through Numbers: Taking Nature into Account/ing." *Geoforum* 39 (1): 123–32.

Auerbach, Adam. 2018. "A Century of National Park Conflict: Class, Geography, and the Changing Values of Conservation Discourse in Maine." *Maine History* 52 (1): 76–108.

Austin, J. L. 1975. *How to Do Things with Words*. Cambridge, Mass.: Harvard University Press.

Barnes, Peter. 2006. *Capitalism 3.0: A Guide to Reclaiming the Commons*. San Francisco: Berrett-Koehler Publishers.

Barringer, Richard. 2004. "Maine Transformed: An Introduction." In *Changing Maine, 1960–2010*, edited by Richard Barringer. Gardiner, Maine: Tilbury House.

Barron, Elizabeth. 2015. "Situating Wild Product Gathering in a Diverse Economy: Negotiating Ethical Interactions with Natural Resources." In *Making Other Worlds Possible: Performing Diverse Economies*, edited by Gerda Roelvink, Kevin St. Martin, and J. K. Gibson-Graham. Minneapolis: University of Minnesota Press.

Barry, Andrew, and Don Slater. 2002. "Technology, Politics, and the Market: An Interview with Michel Callon." *Economy and Society* 31 (2): 285–306.

Bataille, Georges. 1985. *Visions of Excess: Selected Writings, 1927–1939*. Translated by Allan Stoeckl, Carl R. Lovitt, and Donald M. Leslie Jr. Minneapolis: University of Minnesota Press.

Bate, Jonathan. 2000. *The Song of the Earth*. London: Picador.

Baumflek, Michelle J., Marla R. Emery, and Clare Ginger. 2010. "Culturally and Economically Important Nontimber Forest Products of Northern Maine." General Technical Report NRS-68. Newtown Square, Pa.: U.S. Forest Service.

Bebbington, Anthony. 1999. "Capitals and Capabilities: A Framework for Analysing Peasant Viability, Rural Livelihoods, and Poverty." *World Development* 27 (12): 2021–44.

Beck, Ulrich. 2001. "Interview with Ulrich Beck." *Journal of Consumer Culture* 1 (2): 261–77.

Beckerman, Wilfred. 1992. "Economic Growth and the Environment: Whose Growth? Whose Environment?" *World Development* 20 (4): 481–96.

Bennett, Jane. 2010. *Vibrant Matter: A Political Ecology of Things*. Durham, N.C.: Duke University Press.

Bennholdt-Thomsen, Veronica, and Maria Mies. 1999. *The Subsistence Perspective: Beyond the Globalised Economy*. London: Zed Books.

Berlik, Mary M., David B. Kittredge, and David R. Foster. 2002. "The Illusion of Preservation: A Global Environmental Argument for the Local Production of Natural Resources." *Journal of Biogeography* 29 (10–11): 1557–68.

Besteman, Catherine. 2016. *Making Refuge: Somali Bantu Refugees and Lewiston, Maine*. Durham, N.C.: Duke University Press.

Blaser, Mario, and Marisol de la Cadena. 2017. "The Uncommons: An Introduction." *Anthropologica* 59: 185–93.

Blaug, Mark. 1997. *Economic Theory in Retrospect*. Cambridge: Cambridge University Press.

Block, Fred. 2001. "Introduction." In *The Great Transformation*, by Karl Polanyi. Boston: Beacon Press.

Block, Fred. 2003. "Karl Polanyi and the Writing of the Great Transformation." *Theory and Society* 32 (3): 275–306.

Boden, T., R. Andres, and G. Marland. 2017. "Global, Regional, and National Fossil-Fuel CO2 Emissions." Oak Ridge National Laboratory, Oak Ridge, Tenn.

Bollier, David. 2014. *Think Like a Commoner: A Short Introduction to the Life of the Commons*. Gabriola Island, B.C.: New Society Publishers.

Bollier, David, and Silke Helfrich, eds. 2012. *The Wealth of the Commons*. Amherst, Mass.: Levellers Press.

Bowley, Diana. 2007. "Panel to Speak Up on Plum Creek." *Bangor Daily News*, August 15.

Braidotti, Rosi. 2006. *Transpositions: On Nomadic Ethics*. Cambridge: Polity.

Braidotti, Rosi. 2013. *The Posthuman*. New York: John Wiley & Sons.

Brandt, Barbara. 1995. *Whole Life Economics*. Philadelphia: New Society Publishers.

Braudel, Fernand. 1983. *Civilization and Capitalism, 15th–18th Century*, Vol. 2: *The Wheels of Commerce*. Translated by Sian Reynolds. London: William Collins Sons.

Braun, Bruce. 2002. *The Intemperate Rainforest: Nature, Culture, and Power on Canada's West Coast*. Minneapolis: University of Minnesota Press.

Braun, Bruce, and Noel Castree, eds. 1998. *Remaking Reality: Nature at the Millennium*. New York: Routledge.

Brocklesby, Mary Ann, and Eleanor Fisher. 2003. "Community Development in Sustainable Livelihoods Approaches: An Introduction." *Community Development Journal* 38 (3): 185–98.

Brookings Institution. 2006. *Charting Maine's Future: An Action Plan for Promoting Sustainable Prosperity and Quality Places*. Washington, D.C.: Brookings Institution Metropolitan Policy Program.

Buchanan, Brett. 2008. *Onto-Ethologies: The Animal Environments of Uexkull, Heidegger, Merleau-Ponty, and Deleuze*. Albany: State University of New York Press.

Burchell, Graham, Colin Gordon, and Peter Miller, eds. 1991. *The Foucault Effect: Studies in Governmentality*. Chicago: University of Chicago Press.

Bureau of Economic Analysis. 2013. "News Release: GDP by State." June 6.

Bureau of Labor Statistics. 2014. *Maine Economy at a Glance*. United States Department of Labor, Bureau of Labor Statistics, April 11. https://www.bls.gov/eag/eag.me.htm.

Butler, Judith. 1992. "Contingent Foundations: Feminism and the Question of 'Postmodernism.'" In *Feminists Theorize the Political*, edited by Judith Butler and Joan W. Scott. New York: Routledge.

Butler, Judith. 1993. *Bodies That Matter: On the Discursive Limits of "Sex."* New York: Routledge.

Butler, Judith. 1997. *The Psychic Life of Power: Theories in Subjection*. Stanford, Calif.: Stanford University Press.

Buttel, Frederick. 1992. "Environmentalization: Origins, Processes, and Implications for Rural Social Change." *Rural Sociology* 57 (1): 1–27.

Çaliskan, Koray, and Michel Callon. 2009. "Economization, Part 1: Shifting Attention from the Economy towards Processes of Economization." *Economy and Society* 38 (3): 369–98.

Çaliskan, Koray, and Michel Callon. 2010. "Economization, Part 2: A Research Programme for the Study of Markets." *Economy and Society* 39 (1): 1–32.

Callon, Michel. 1998. "An Essay on Framing and Overflowing: Economic Externalities Revisited by Sociology." In *The Laws of the Markets*, edited by Michel Callon. London: Blackwell Publishers.

Callon, Michel. 2005. "Why Virtualism Paves the Way to Political Impotence: A Reply to Daniel Miller's Critique of 'The Laws of the Markets.'" *Economic Sociology: European Electronic Newsletter* 6 (2): 3–20.

Cameron, Jenny, and J. K. Gibson-Graham. 2003. "Feminising the Economy: Metaphors, Strategies, Politics." *Gender, Place & Culture* 10 (2): 145–57.

Camoin Associates. 2012. "Maine Innovation Index." Augusta: Maine Department of Community and Economic Development.

Carley, Kevin. 2007. "Experts Agree: Plum Creek's Plan for Moosehead Will Adversely Affect Wildlife and Wildlife Habitat." Augusta: Maine Audubon Society.

Caron, Alan. 2015. "Analysis: Maine's New Economy Requires New Attitude." *Portland Press Herald* (blog), December 6.

Carson, Rachel. 1962. *Silent Spring*. New York: Crest.

Castel, Robert. 1991. "From Dangerousness to Risk." In *The Foucault Effect: Studies in Governmentality*, edited by Graham Burchell, Colin Gordon, and Peter Miller. Chicago: University of Chicago Press.

Castoriadis, Cornelius. 1998. *The Imaginary Institution of Society*. Translated by Kathleen Blamey. Cambridge, Mass.: MIT Press.

Cervone, Ed. 2012. "Making Maine Work: Investment in Young Children = Real Economic Development." Augusta: Maine Development Foundation and Maine State Chamber of Commerce.

Chambers, Robert. 2005. *Ideas for Development*. London: Earthscan.

Chambers, Robert, and Gordon Conway. 1991. "Sustainable Rural Livelihoods: Practical Concepts for the 21st Century." IDS Working Paper 296. Brighton, U.K.: Institute of Development Studies.

Clair, James A., Gradon R. Haehnel, Joel D. Johnson, J. Scott Moody, and Eric N. Stinneford. 2013. "Report of the Consensus Economic Forecasting Commission, November 1, 2013." Augusta, Maine: Consensus Economic Forecasting Commission.

Clark, Nigel, and Kathryn Yusoff. 2017. "Geosocial Formations in the Anthropocene." *Theory, Culture & Society* 34 (2–3): 3–23.

Coastal Enterprises. 2009. "Coastal Enterprises, Inc.: Triple Bottom Line or '3E Investing' Profile." Wiscasset, Maine: Coastal Enterprises.

Colby College Environmental Policy Group. 2010. "The State of Maine's Environment 2010." Waterville, Maine: Colby College.

Cole, Luke W., and Sheila R. Foster. 2001. *From the Ground Up: Environmental Racism and the Rise of the Environmental Justice Movement*. New York: New York University Press.

Colgan, Charles S. 2006. "The Maine Economy: Yesterday, Today and Tomorrow." Background paper for *Charting Maine's Future: An Action Plan for Promoting Sustainable Prosperity and Quality Places*. Washington, D.C.: Brookings Institution Metropolitan Policy Program.

Colgan, Charles S. 2007. "Estimated Economic Impacts from Development Associated with the Proposed Rezoning of Lands Owned by Plum Creek Timber in the Moosehead Lake Region." Portland: Center for Business and Economic Research, University of Southern Maine.

Common, Michael, and Sigrid Stagl. 2005. *Ecological Economics: An Introduction*. Cambridge: Cambridge University Press.

Connolly, William E. 1995. *The Ethos of Pluralization*. Minneapolis: University of Minnesota Press.

Connolly, William E. 2002. *Identity/Difference: Democratic Negotiations of Political Paradox*. Minneapolis: University of Minnesota Press.

Corlett, William. 1998. *Class Action: Reading Labor, Theory, and Value*. Ithaca, N.Y.: Cornell University Press.

Corson, Catherine. 2011. "Territorialization, Enclosure, and Neoliberalism: Non-State Influence in Struggles Over Madagascar's Forests." *Journal of Peasant Studies* 38 (4): 703–26.

Critchley, Simon. 2007. *Infinitely Demanding: Ethics of Commitment, Politics of Resistance*. London: Verso.

Critical Insights. 2006. "Natural Resources Council of Maine Attitudes toward the Plum Creek Development Summary Report." Portland, Maine: Critical Insights.

Cronon, William. 1996. "The Trouble with Wilderness; or, Getting Back to the Wrong Nature." *Environmental History* 1 (1): 7–28.

Crutzen, Paul J. 2002. "The 'Anthropocene.'" *Journal de Physique IV (Proceedings)* 12 (10): 1–5.

Dale, Gareth. 2010. *Karl Polanyi: The Limits of the Market*. London: Polity Press.

Daly, Herman, and Joshua Farley. 2010. *Ecological Economics: Principles and Applications*. Washington, D.C.: Island Press.

Davis, Anthony. 1991. "Insidious Rationalities: The Institutionalisation of Small Boat Fishing and the Rise of the Rapacious Fisher." *Maritime Anthropological Studies* 4 (1): 13–31.

Dean, Jodi. 2012. *The Communist Horizon*. London: Verso.

Dean, Jodi. 2015. "The Party and Communist Solidarity." *Rethinking Marxism* 27 (3): 332–42.

Dean, Mitchell. 2009. *Governmentality: Power and Rule in Modern Society*. London: Sage.

De Angelis, Massimo. 2001. "Marx and Primitive Accumulation: The Continuous Character of Capital's 'Enclosures.'" *The Commoner* 2: 1–22.

De Angelis, Massimo. 2003. "Reflections on Alternatives, Commons, and Communities." *The Commoner* 6: 1–14.

De Angelis, Massimo. 2007. *The Beginning of History: Value Struggles and Global Capital*. London: Pluto Press.

De Angelis, Massimo. 2010. "The Production of Commons and the 'Explosion' of the Middle Class." *Antipode* 42 (4): 954–77.

De Angelis, Massimo. 2017. *Omnia Sunt Communia: On the Commons and the Transformation to Postcapitalism*. London: Zed Books.

Deely, John. 2004. "Semiotics and Jakob von Uexküll's Concept of Umwelt." *Sign Systems Studies* 32 (1/2): 11–34.

De Haan, Leo, and Annelies Zoomers. 2005. "Exploring the Frontier of Livelihoods Research." *Development and Change* 36 (1): 27–47.

De Landa, Manuel. 2006. *A New Philosophy of Society: Assemblage Theory and Social Complexity*. London: Continuum.

Deleuze, Gilles. 1988. *Foucault*. Translated by Sean Hand. Minneapolis: University of Minnesota Press.

Deleuze, Gilles. 1990. *Expressionism in Philosophy: Spinoza*. Translated by Martin Joughin. New York: Zone Books.

Deleuze, Gilles. 1994. *Difference and Repetition*. Translated by Paul Patton. New York: Columbia University Press.

Deleuze, Gilles. 2001. *Pure Immanence: Essays on a Life*. Translated by Ann Boyman. New York: Zone Books.

Deleuze, Gilles. 2004. *Desert Islands and Other Texts (1953–1974)*. Translated by Michael Taormina. New York: Semiotex(e).

Deleuze, Gilles, and Félix Guattari. 1983. *Anti-Oedipus: Capitalism and Schizophrenia*. Translated by Robert Hurley, Mark Seem, and Helen R. Lane. Minneapolis: University of Minnesota Press.

Deleuze, Gilles, and Félix Guattari. 1987. *A Thousand Plateaus: Capitalism and Schizophrenia*. Translated by Brian Massumi. Minneapolis: University of Minnesota Press.

Deleuze, Gilles, and Félix Guattari. 1994. *What Is Philosophy?* Translated by Hugh Tomlinson and Graham Burchell. New York: Columbia University Press.

Deleuze, Gilles, and Claire Parnet. 2007. *Dialogues II*. Translated by Hugh Tomlinson and Barbara Habberjam. New York: Columbia University Press.

DeMartino, George. 2003. "Realizing Class Justice." *Rethinking Marxism* 15 (1): 1–31.

Dempster, Beth. 2007. "Boundarylessness: Introducing a Systems Heuristic for Conceptualizing Complexity." In *Nature's Edge: Boundary Explorations in Ecological Theory and Practice*, edited by Charles S. Brown and Ted Toadvine. Albany: State University of New York Press.

Derrida, Jacques. 1998. *Of Grammatology*. Translated by Gayatri Chakravorty Spivak. Baltimore: Johns Hopkins University Press.

Despret, Vinciane. 2016. *What Would Animals Say If We Asked the Right Questions?* Minneapolis: University of Minnesota Press.

De Vries, Pieter. 2007. "Don't Compromise Your Desire for Development! A Lacanian/Deleuzian Rethinking of the Anti-Politics Machine." *Third World Quarterly* 28 (1): 25–43.

DFiD. 2001. "Sustainable Livelihoods Introduction Overview 1.1." London: Department for International Development (DFiD).

Di Chiro, Giovanna. 1996. "Nature as Community: The Convergence of Environment and Social Justice." In *Uncommon Ground: Rethinking the Human Place in Nature*, edited by William Cronon. New York: W. W. Norton & Company.

Didisheim, Pete, and Terry De Wan. 2006. "A Vision for the Moosehead Lake Region: Building Community, Conserving Natural Resources, Protecting Maine's Heritage and Future." Augusta: Natural Resources Council of Maine.

Dobson, Andrew. 1990. *Green Political Thought*. London: Routledge.

Docherty, Bonnie. 2000. "Maine's North Woods: Environmental Justice and the National Park Proposal." *Harvard Environmental Law Review* 24: 537–61.

Dolsak, Nives, and Elinor Ostrom, eds. 2003. *The Commons In the New Millennium: Challenges and Adaptations*. Cambridge, Mass.: MIT Press.

Duhigg, Charles. 2012. "Toxic Water: Find Water Polluters Near You." *New York Times* (blog), May 22. http://projects.nytimes.com/toxic-waters/polluters/maine.

Elkington, John. 1998. *Cannibals with Forks: The Triple Bottom Line of 21st Century Business*. Philadelphia: New Society Publishers.

Elson, Diane. 1979. "The Value Theory of Labour." In *Value: The Representation of Labour in Capitalism*, edited by Diane Elson. London: Humanities Press International.

Endnotes. 2013. "Logic of Gender: On the Separation of Spheres and the Process of Abjection." *Endnotes*, no. 3. http://endnotes.org.uk/en/endnotes-the-logic-of-gender.

Environment Maine. 2014. Environmentmaine.org.

Escobar, Arturo. 2009. "Other Worlds Are (Already) Possible: Self-Organisation, Complexity, and Post-Capitalist Cultures." In *The World Social Forum: Challenging Empires*, edited by Jai Sen and Peter Waterman. Montreal: Black Rose Books.

Escobar, Arturo. 2012. *Encountering Development: The Making and Unmaking of the Third World*. Princeton, N.J.: Princeton University Press.

Esteva, Gustavo. 1992. "Development." In *The Development Dictionary: A Guide to Knowledge as Power*, edited by Wolfgang Sachs. London: Zed Books.

Esteva, Gustavo. 2010. "From the Bottom-Up: New Institutional Arrangements in Latin America." *Development* 53 (1): 64–69.

Esteva, Gustavo, and Madhu Suri Prakash. 1998. *Grassroots Post-Modernism: Remaking the Soil of Cultures*. London: Zed Books.

Evernden, Neil. 1988. "The Environmentalist's Dilemma." *The Trumpeter* 5 (1): 2–6.

Evernden, Neil. 1992. *The Social Creation of Nature*. Baltimore: Johns Hopkins University Press.

Farina, Almo. 2011. "A Biosemiotic Perspective of the Resource Criterion: Toward a General Theory of Resources." *Biosemiotics* 5 (1): 17–32.

Federici, Silvia. 2012. *Revolution at Point Zero: Housework, Reproduction, and Feminist Struggle.* Oakland, Calif.: PM Press.

Fichtner, Donna. 2007. "Prefiled Testimony of Donna Fichtner." Plum Creek Maine Timberlands LLC Concept Plan Rezoning Petition ZP707. Augusta: Land Use Regulation Commission.

Fine, Ben. 2003. "Callonistics: A Disentanglement." *Economy and Society* 32 (3): 478–84.

Fine, Ben. 2010. *Theories of Social Capital: Researchers Behaving Badly.* London: Pluto Press.

Fischer-Kowalski, Marina, and Helmut Haberl. 1998. "Sustainable Development: Socio-Economic Metabolism and Colonization of Nature." *International Social Science Journal* 50 (158): 573–87.

Fish, Scott. 2006. "What about Plum Creek?" *All Maine Matters* (blog), January.

Fitch, Eric J. 2011. "Slow Motion Disaster: The Big Picture of Converging Effects of Climate Change, Sea Level Rise, and Fossil Fuel Depletion on the Viability of Human Habitat of Oceania and the Coastal Margin of the Pacific Rim." *Water Resources IMPACT* 13 (2): 13–16.

Folbre, Nancy. 2001. *The Invisible Heart: Economics and Family Values.* New York: New Press.

Foster, John Bellamy, Brett Clark, and Richard York. 2012. *The Ecological Rift: Capitalism's War on the Earth.* New York: Monthly Review Press.

Foucault, Michel. 1977. *Discipline and Punish: The Birth of the Prison.* Translated by Alan Sheridan. New York: Vintage Books.

Foucault, Michel. 1982. "The Subject and Power." *Critical Inquiry* 8 (4): 777–95.

Foucault, Michel. 1984. *The Foucault Reader.* Edited by Paul Rabinow. New York: Vintage.

Foucault, Michel. 1988. *Politics, Philosophy, Culture: Interviews and Other Writings, 1977–1984.* Edited by Lawrence D. Kritzman. New York: Routledge.

Foucault, Michel. 2001. *Fearless Speech.* Edited by Joseph Pearson. Los Angeles: Semiotext(e).

Foucault, Michel. 2007a. *Security, Territory, Population: Lectures at the Collège de France, 1977–78.* Edited by Michel Senellart. Translated by Graham Burchell. New York: Palgrave Macmillan.

Foucault, Michel. 2007b. *The Archaeology of Knowledge.* Translated by A. M. Sheridan Smith. New York: Pantheon Books.

Foucault, Michel. 2010a. *The Birth of Biopolitics: Lectures at the Collège de France, 1978–1979.* Edited by Michel Senellart. Translated by Graham Burchell. New York: Palgrave Macmillan.

Foucault, Michel. 2010b. *The Government of Self and Others: Lectures at the Collège de France, 1982–1983.* Edited by Michel Senellart. Translated by Graham Burchell. New York: Palgrave Macmillan.

Freeman, A. Myrick. 2003. *The Measurement of Environmental and Resource Values: Theory and Methods*. Washington, D.C.: Resources for the Future.

Garrod, Guy, and Kenneth George Willis. 1999. *Economic Valuation of the Environment: Methods and Case Studies*. Northampton, Mass.: Edward Elgar.

Gawler, Susan, and Andrew Cutko. 2010. *Natural Landscapes of Maine: A Guide to Natural Communities and Ecosystems*. Augusta: Maine Natural Areas Program.

Gibson, Katherine, Amanda Cahill, and Deirdre McKay. 2010. "Rethinking the Dynamics of Rural Transformation: Performing Different Development Pathways in a Philippine Municipality." *Transactions of the Institute of British Geographers* 35 (2): 237–55.

Gibson-Graham, J. K. 2002. "Beyond Global vs. Local: Economic Politics Outside the Binary Frame." In *Geographies of Power: Placing Scale*, edited by Andrew Herod and Melissa W. Wright. Oxford: Blackwell.

Gibson-Graham, J. K. 2005. "Traversing the Fantasy of Sufficiency." *Singapore Journal of Tropical Geography* 26 (2): 119–26.

Gibson-Graham, J. K. 2006a. *A Postcapitalist Politics*. Minneapolis: University of Minnesota Press.

Gibson-Graham, J. K. 2006b. "Introduction to the New Edition: Ten Years On." In *The End of Capitalism (As We Knew It): A Feminist Critique of Political Economy*. 2nd ed. Minneapolis: University of Minnesota Press.

Gibson-Graham, J. K. 2006c. *The End of Capitalism (As We Knew It): A Feminist Critique of Political Economy*. 2nd ed. Minneapolis: University of Minnesota Press.

Gibson-Graham, J. K. 2008. "Diverse Economies: Performative Practices for Other Worlds." *Progress in Human Geography* 32 (5): 1–20.

Gibson-Graham, J. K. 2011. "A Feminist Project of Belonging for the Anthropocene." *Gender, Place, and Culture* 18 (1): 1–21.

Gibson-Graham, J. K. 2014. "Being the Revolution; or, How to Live in a 'More-Than-Capitalist' World Threatened with Extinction." *Rethinking Marxism* 26 (1): 76–94.

Gibson-Graham, J. K., Jenny Cameron, and Stephen Healy. 2013. *Take Back the Economy: An Ethical Guide for Transforming Our Communities*. Minneapolis: University of Minnesota Press.

Gibson-Graham, J. K., Jenny Cameron, and Stephen Healy. 2016. "Commoning as Postcapitalist Politics." In *Recovering the Commons*, edited by Ash Amin and Philip Howell. London: Routledge.

Gibson-Graham, J. K., and Ethan Miller. 2015. "Economy as Ecological Livelihood." In *Manifesto for Living in the Anthropocene*, edited by Katherine Gibson, Deborah Bird Rose, and Ruth Fincher. Brooklyn, N.Y.: Punctum Books.

Gibson-Graham, J. K., Stephen Resnick, and Richard Wolff. 2001. *Re/Presenting Class: Essays in Postmodern Marxism*. Durham, N.C.: Duke University Press.

Gibson-Graham, J. K., and Gerda Roelvink. 2010. "An Economic Ethics for the Anthropocene." *Antipode* 41 (s1): 320–46.

Giddings, Bob, Bill Hopwood, and Geoff O'Brien. 2002. "Environment, Economy, and Society: Fitting Them Together into Sustainable Development." *Sustainable Development* 10 (4): 187–96.

Gidwani, Vinay. 2008. *Capital, Interrupted: Agrarian Development and the Politics of Work in India*. Minneapolis: University of Minnesota Press.

Gierke, Otto Friedrich von. 1957. *Natural Law and the Theory of Society 1500 to 1800*. Translated by Ernest Barker. Boston: Beacon Press.

Gilbert, Scott F. 2013. "Symbiosis as the Way of Eukaryotic Life: The Dependent Co-origination of the Body." *Journal of Biosciences* 38 (4): 1–9.

Gilbert, Scott F., Jan Sapp, and Alfred I. Tauber. 2012. "A Symbiotic View of Life: We Have Never Been Individuals." *Quarterly Review of Biology* 87 (4): 325–41.

Ginn, Cliff, and Rob Brown. 2009. "Green Jobs, Green Savings: Developing Maine's Economy by Securing Our Energy Future." Augusta: Opportunity Maine.

Gluckman, Nell. 2014. "Lepage Says Cost of Energy Keeps Wages Low, Drives Business from Maine." *Bangor Daily News* (blog), September 14.

Goffman, Erving. 1986. *Frame Analysis: An Essay on the Organization of Experience*. Boston: Northeastern University Press.

Goodall, Seth. 2011. "Environment Not Separate from Economy." *Maine State Senate Weekly Radio Address* (blog), February 4.

Governor's Council on Maine's Quality of Place. 2007. "People, Place, and Prosperity: 1st Report of the Governor's Council on Maine's Quality of Place." Augusta: Maine State Planning Office.

Graeber, David. 2011. *Debt: The First 5,000 Years*. Brooklyn, N.Y.: Melville House.

Granovetter, Mark. 1985. "Economic Action and Social Structure: The Problem of Embeddedness." *American Journal of Sociology* 91 (3): 481–510.

Grinspoon, David. 2016. *Earth in Human Hands: Shaping Our Planet's Future*. New York: Grand Central Publishing.

Grossman, Gene M., and Alan B. Krueger. 1995. "Economic Growth and the Environment." *Quarterly Journal of Economics* 110 (2): 353–77.

Grosz, Elizabeth. 2005. *Time Travels: Feminism, Nature, Power*. Crows Nest, NSW, Australia: Allen & Unwin.

Grosz, Elizabeth. 2013. "Habit Today: Ravaisson, Bergson, Deleuze, and Us." *Body & Society* 19 (2/3): 217–39.

GrowSmart Maine. 2012. *Charting Maine's Future: Making Headway*. Augusta: GrowSmart Maine.

Grusec, Joan E., and Paul D. Hastings. 2008. *Handbook of Socialization: Theory and Research*. New York: Guilford Press.

Guattari, Félix. 1996. *The Guattari Reader*. Edited by Gary Genosko. Oxford: Wiley-Blackwell.

Guattari, Félix. 2008. *Chaosophy: Texts and Interviews 1972–1977*. Edited by Sylvère Lotringer. Los Angeles: Semiotext(e).

Guattari, Félix. 2011. *Lines of Flight: For Another World*. Translated by Andrew Goffey. London: Bloomsbury Academic.

Gudeman, Stephen. 2008. *Economy's Tension: The Dialectics of Community and Market*. New York: Berghahn Books.

Gudeman, Stephen, and Alberto Rivera. 1990. *Conversations in Colombia: The Domestic Economy in Life and Text*. Cambridge: Cambridge University Press.

Guha, Ramachandra. 1989. "Radical Environmentalism and Wilderness Preservation: A Third World Critique." *Environmental Ethics* 11 (1): 71–83.

Hackett, Steven C. 2006. *Environmental and Natural Resources Economics: Theory, Policy, and the Sustainable Society*. Armonk, N.Y.: M. E. Sharpe.

Hagan, John M., Lloyd C. Irland, and Andrew A. Whitman. 2005. "Changing Timberland Ownership in the Northern Forest and Implications for Biodiversity." MCCS-FCP-2005–1. Forest Conservation Program Report. Brunswick, Maine: Manomet Center for Conservation Sciences.

Halperin, Rhoda. 1994. *Cultural Economies Past and Present*. Austin: University of Texas Press.

Hamilton-Peach, Julian, and Philip Townsley. 2004. "An IFAD Sustainable Livelihoods Framework." Rome: International Fund for Agricultural Development (IFAD).

Haraway, Donna. 1991. *Simians, Cyborgs, and Women: The Reinvention of Nature*. New York: Routledge.

Haraway, Donna. 2008. *When Species Meet*. Minneapolis: University of Minnesota Press.

Haraway, Donna. 2016. *Staying with the Trouble: Making Kin in the Chthulucene*. Durham, N.C.: Duke University Press.

Harding, Stephan. 2006. *Animate Earth: Science, Intuition, and Gaia*. White River Junction, Vt.: Chelsea Green Publishing.

Hardt, Michael. 2010. "The Militancy of Theory." *South Atlantic Quarterly* 110 (1): 19–35.

Hardt, Michael, and Antonio Negri. 2004. *Multitude: War and Democracy in the Age of Empire*. New York: Penguin.

Hardt, Michael, and Antonio Negri. 2009. *Commonwealth*. Cambridge, Mass.: Harvard University Press.

Harvey, David. 1996. *Justice, Nature, and the Geography of Difference*. London: Blackwell Publishers.

Harvey, David. 2003. *The New Imperialism*. Oxford: Oxford University Press.

Harvey, David. 2012. *Rebel Cities: From the Right to the City to the Urban Revolution*. London: Verso.

Harvie, David, Gary Slater, Bruce Philp, and Dan Wheatley. 2009. "Economic Well-Being and British Regions: The Problem with GDP per Capita." *Review of Social Economy* 67 (4): 483–505.

Haynes, Robert. 1990. "Ecopoiesis: Playing God on Mars." In *Moral Expertise: Studies in Practical and Professional Ethics*, edited by Don Macniven. New York: Routledge.

Healey, Patsy, and Tim Shaw. 1994. "Changing Meanings of 'Environment' in the British Planning System." *Transactions of the Institute of British Geographers* 19 (4): 425–38.

Healy, Stephen. 2015. "Communism as a Mode of Life." *Rethinking Marxism* 27 (3): 343–56.

Helliwell, Christine, and Barry Hindess. 1999. "'Culture,' 'Society,' and the Figure of Man." *History of the Human Sciences* 12 (4): 1–20.

Henderson, Hazel. 1995. *Paradigms in Progress: Life beyond Economics*. San Francisco: Berrett-Koehler Publishers.

Henry, Ben, and Allyson Fredricksen. 2014. "Equity in the Balance: How a Living Wage Would Help Women and People of Color Make Ends Meet." Seattle, Wash.: Alliance for a Just Society.

Higgins, Vaughan, and Wendy Larner, eds. 2010. *Calculating the Social: Standards and the Reconfiguration of Governing*. New York: Palgrave Macmillan.

Hill, Ann. 2014. "Growing Community Food Economies in the Philippines." PhD diss., Canberra: Australian National University.

Hoey, Dennis. 2014. "Lepage to Offer Plan to Expand Maine's 'War on Drugs.'" *Portland Press Herald* (blog), March 11.

Hoffmeyer, Jesper. 1996. *Signs of Meaning in the Universe*. Bloomington: Indiana University Press.

Hollander, Jack M. 2004. *The Real Environmental Crisis: Why Poverty, Not Affluence, Is the Environment's Number One Enemy*. Berkeley: University of California Press.

Holling, C. S. 2004. "From Complex Regions to Complex Worlds." *Ecology and Society* 9 (1): 11.

Holloway, John. 1996. "The Concept of Power and the Zapatistas." *Common Sense*, no. 19: 20–27.

Holstein, James A., and Jaber F. Gubrium. 2003. "Active Interviewing." In *Postmodern Interviewing*, edited by Jaber F. Gubrium and James A. Holstein. Thousand Oaks, Calif.: Sage.

Hussein, Karim. 2002. "Livelihoods Approaches Compared." London: Department for International Development (DFiD).

Hyde, Lewis. 2010. *Common as Air: Revolution, Art, and Ownership*. New York: Farrar, Straus and Giroux.

Illich, Ivan. 1992. "Needs." In *The Development Dictionary: A Guide to Knowledge as Power*, edited by Wolfgang Sachs. London: Zed Books.

Independent Sector. 2016. "The Value of Volunteer Time." http://www.independentsector.org/resource/the-value-of-volunteer-time/.

Ingold, Tim. 1993. "Globes and Spheres: The Topology of Environmentalism." In *Environmentalism: The View from Anthropology*, edited by Kay Milton. New York: Routledge.

Ingold, Tim. 2009. "Point, Line, and Counterpoint: From Environment to Fluid Space." In *Neurobiology of "Umwelt": How Living Beings Perceive the World*, edited by A. Berthoz and Yves Christen. London: Springer.

Ingold, Tim. 2013. "Prospect." In *Biosocial Becomings: Integrating Social and Biological Anthropology*, edited by Tim Ingold and Gisli Palsson. Cambridge: Cambridge University Press.

Ingold, Tim, and Gisli Palsson, eds. 2013. *Biosocial Becomings: Integrating Social and Biological Anthropology*. Cambridge: Cambridge University Press.

Jackson, Sue, and Lisa R. Palmer. 2014. "Reconceptualizing Ecosystem Services: Possibilities for Cultivating and Valuing the Ethics and Practices of Care." *Progress in Human Geography* 39 (2): 122–45.

Jacobs, Jane. 2001. *The Nature of Economies*. New York: Vintage.

Jensen, Casper, and Peter Lauritsen. 2005. "Connection: Bypassing the Power-Knowledge Nexus." *Qualitative Research* 5 (1): 59–77.

Jessop, Ralph. 2012. "Coinage of the Term Environment: A Word without Authority and Carlyle's Displacement of the Mechanical Metaphor." *Literature Compass* 9 (11): 708–20.

Judd, Richard W. 2000. *Common Lands, Common People: The Origins of Conservation in Northern New England*. Cambridge, Mass.: Harvard University Press.

Judd, Richard W., and Christopher S. Beach. 2003. *Natural States: The Environmental Imagination in Maine, Oregon, and the Nation*. Washington, D.C.: Resources for the Future.

Katz, Eric. 1997. *Nature as Subject: Human Obligation and Natural Community*. New York: Rowman & Littlefield.

Kearney, Michael. 2006. "Habitat, Environment, and Niche: What Are We Modelling?" *Oikos* 115 (1): 186–91.

Kellett, Michael, and Jym St. Pierre. 1996. "Gateway to a Healthy Economy: The Proposed Maine Woods National Park and Preserve and the Future of the Moosehead Region of Maine." Augusta: RESTORE the North Woods.

Kelley, Carol. 2010. *Investing in Maine's Environment: A Trail Map to Prosperity*. Augusta: Maine Conservation Voters Education Fund and Environmental Priorities Coalition.

Kelly, Alice B. 2011. "Conservation Practice as Primitive Accumulation." *Journal of Peasant Studies* 38 (4): 683–701.

Keynes, John Maynard. 1936. *The General Theory of Employment, Interest, and Money*. New York: Harcourt, Brace & Company.

Khanya-AICDD. 2006. "Concept Paper on Understanding and Applying the Sustainable Livelihoods Analysis (SLA)." Johannesburg, South Africa: Khanya-AICDD.

Kircheis, Fred. 2014. "History Shows Mining's Consequences: Rules to Protect Maine's Environment Are Insufficient." *Bangor Daily News* (blog), March 26.

Klein, Naomi. 2014. *This Changes Everything: Capitalism vs. the Climate*. New York: Simon and Schuster.

Koenig, Seth. 2013. "Is Maine's Population Too Old and White to Be Sustainable?" *Bangor Daily News* (blog), June 13.

Koopman, Colin. 2013. *Genealogy as Critique: Foucault and the Problems of Modernity*. Bloomington: Indiana University Press.

Kovel, Joel. 2007. *The Enemy of Nature: The End of Capitalism or the End of the World?* London: Zed Books.

Krausman, Paul R. 1999. "Some Basic Principles of Habitat Use." *Idaho Forest, Wildlife & Range Experimental Station Bulletin*, no. 70: 85–90.

Kristeva, Julia. 1982. *Powers of Horror: An Essay on Abjection*. Translated by Leon Roudiez. New York: Columbia University Press.

Laclau, Ernesto. 2005. *On Populist Reason*. London: Verso.

Laclau, Ernesto, and Chantal Mouffe. 2001. *Hegemony and Socialist Strategy: Towards a Radical Democratic Politics*. London: Verso.

Landefeld, Steven J., Eugene P. Seskin, and Barbara M. Fraumeni. 2008. "Taking the Pulse of the Economy: Measuring GDP." *Journal of Economic Perspectives* 22 (2): 193–216.

Lansky, Mitch. 2003. "Not Wilderness." In *On Wilderness: Voices from Maine*, edited by Phyllis Austin, Dean Bennett, and Robert Kimber. Gardiner, Maine: Tilbury House.

Latouche, Serge. 1993. *In the Wake of the Affluent Society: An Exploration of Post-Development*. London: Zed Books.

Latour, Bruno. 1987. *Science in Action: How to Follow Scientists and Engineers through Society*. Cambridge, Mass.: Harvard University Press.

Latour, Bruno. 1988. *The Pasteurization of France*. Cambridge, Mass.: Harvard University Press.

Latour, Bruno. 1990. "Visualisation and Cognition: Drawing Things Together." In *Representation in Scientific Practice*, edited by Michael Lynch and Steve Woolgar. Cambridge, Mass.: MIT Press.

Latour, Bruno. 1993. *We Have Never Been Modern*. Translated by Catherine Porter. Cambridge, Mass.: Harvard University Press.

Latour, Bruno. 1998. "To Modernise or Ecologise? That Is the Question." In *Remaking Reality: Nature at the Millennium*, edited by Bruce Braun and Noel Castree, translated by Charis Cussins. New York: Routledge.

Latour, Bruno. 1999. *Pandora's Hope: Essays on the Reality of Science Studies*. Cambridge, Mass.: Harvard University Press.

Latour, Bruno. 2004a. *Politics of Nature: How to Bring the Sciences into Democracy*. Translated by Catherine Porter. Cambridge, Mass.: Harvard University Press.

Latour, Bruno. 2004b. "Why Has Critique Run Out of Steam? From Matters of Fact to Matters of Concern." *Critical Inquiry* 30 (2): 225–48.

Latour, Bruno. 2005. *Reassembling the Social: An Introduction to Actor-Network-Theory*. New York: Oxford University Press.

Latour, Bruno. 2010. "An Attempt at a 'Compositionist Manifesto.'" *New Literary History* 41 (3): 471–90.

Latour, Bruno. 2013. *An Inquiry into Modes of Existence: An Anthropology of the Moderns*. Translated by Catherine Porter. Cambridge, Mass.: Harvard University Press.

Latour, Bruno. 2017. *Facing Gaia: Eight Lectures on the New Climatic Regime*. Cambridge: Polity Press.

Law, John. 1992. "Notes on the Theory of the Actor-Network: Ordering, Strategy, and Heterogeneity." *Systemic Practice and Action Research* 5 (4): 379–93.

Law, John. 2004. *After Method: Mess in Social Science Research*. New York: Routledge.

Law, John. 2009. "Actor Network Theory and Material Semiotics." In *The Blackwell Companion to Social Theory*, edited by Bryan S. Turner. London: Wiley-Blackwell.

Lawn, Philip. 2001. *Toward Sustainable Development: An Ecological Economics Approach*. Boca Raton, Fla.: Lewis Press.

Lawton, Charles T. 2008. *Maine's Bottom Line: Facing the 21st Century*. Portland, Maine: Arthur McAllister Publishers.

Lazzarato, Maurizio. 2012. *The Making of the Indebted Man*. Translated by Joshua David Jordan. Los Angeles: Semiotext(e).

Lemke, Thomas. 2002. "Foucault, Governmentality, and Critique." *Rethinking Marxism* 14 (3): 49–64.

LePage, Paul. 2013. "Paying Hospitals Is the Right Thing to Do, and Maine's Economy Demands It." *Twin City Times*, January 24.

LePage, Paul. 2014a. "2014 State of the State Address." Paper presented at the Governor's Annual State of the State Address to the Maine State Legislature, Augusta, February 4.

LePage, Paul. 2014b. "Illegal Aliens Should Not Get General Assistance." *Governor Paul LePage's Weekly Radio Address*. Augusta, Maine. http://statedocs.maine.gov/ogvn_audio/7/.

Lestel, Dominique. 2014. "Toward an Ethnography of Animal Worlds." *Angelaki* 19 (3): 75–89.

Lévi-Strauss, Claude. 1966. *The Savage Mind*. Translated by George Weidenfeld. London: Weidenfeld and Nicholson.

Lewis, Michael Anthony, and Karl Widerquist. 2013. *Economics for Social Workers: The Application of Economic Theory to Social Policy and the Human Services*. New York: Columbia University Press.

Linebaugh, Peter. 2008. *The Magna Carta Manifesto: Commons and Liberties for All*. Berkeley: University of California Press.

Lo, Yeuk-Sze. 1999. "Natural and Artifactual: Restored Nature as Subject." *Environmental Ethics* 21 (3): 247–66.

Lovelock, James. 1987. "The Ecopoiesis of Daisyworld." In *Origin and Evolution of the Universe: Evidence for Design?*, edited by John M. Robson. Montreal: McGill-Queen's University Press.

Lowrey, Kestryl. 2008. "Dead to the World: Embodied Gender Transgression and the Loss of Humanity." *E.Topia* (October).

Luke, Timothy W. 1994. "Worldwatching at the Limits of Growth." *Capitalism Nature Socialism* 5 (2): 43–63.

Luke, Timothy W. 1995. "On Environmentality: Geo-Power and Eco-Knowledge in the Discourses of Contemporary Environmentalism." *Cultural Critique*, no. 31: 57–81.

Luke, Timothy W. 1996. "Generating Green Governmentality: A Cultural Critique of Environmental Studies as a Power/Knowledge Formation." http://www.cddc.vt.edu/tim/tims/Tim514a.pdf.

Lustig, Adanya. 2016. "A Rift in the Woods." *Bangor Daily News*, December 1.

Lyotard, Jean-François. 1993. "Oikos." In *Political Writings*, translated by Bill Readings and Kevin Paul Geiman. Minneapolis: University of Minnesota Press.

MacDougall, Pauleena. 2004. *The Penobscot Dance of Resistance: Tradition in the History of a People*. Durham: University of New Hampshire Press.

MacKenzie, Donald. 2007. "Is Economics Performative? Option Theory and the Construction of Derivatives Markets." In *Do Economists Make Markets?: On the Performativity of Economics*, edited by Donald MacKenzie, Fabian Muniesa, and Lucia Siu. Princeton, N.J.: Princeton University Press.

MacKenzie, Donald, Fabian Muniesa, and Lucia Siu, eds. 2007. *Do Economists Make Markets?: On the Performativity of Economics*. Princeton, N.J.: Princeton University Press.

Macnaghten, Phil, and John Urry. 1998. *Contested Natures*. London: Sage.

Maine Alliance and Maine Chamber of Commerce and Industry. 1994. "Charting Maine's Economic Future." Augusta: Maine Alliance and Maine Chamber of Commerce and Industry.

Maine Audubon Society. 1996. "Valuing the Nature of Maine: A Bibliography." Augusta: Maine Audubon Society.

MaineBiz. 2013. "Maine's Economy at a Glance." *MaineBiz*, May 6. http://www.mainebiz.biz.

Maine Community Foundation. 2006. "Social Capital: Cultivating Community Connections in Maine." Ellsworth: Maine Community Foundation.

Maine DACF. 2014. "About DACF." *Maine Department of Agriculture, Conservation, and Forestry* (blog). http://www.maine.gov/dacf/.

Maine Land Trust Network. 2005. "The Public Benefits of Conserved Lands." Topsham: Maine Coast Heritage Trust.

Maine Rivers. 2014. "Pollution." http://mainerivers.org/pollution.htm.

Mallavarapu, Srikanth, and Amit Prasad. 2006. "Facts, Fetishes, and the Parliament of Things: Is There Any Space for Critique?" *Social Epistemology* 20 (2): 185–99.

Mance, Euclides. 2010. "Solidarity Economics." In *What Would It Mean to Win?*, edited by Turbulence Collective. Oakland, Calif.: PM Press.

Margulis, Lynn. 1999. *Symbiotic Planet: A New Look at Evolution*. New York: Basic Books.

Marx, Karl. 1964. *Economic and Philosophical Manuscripts of 1844*. Translated by Martin Milligan. New York: International Publishers.

Marx, Karl. 1975. *Early Writings*. Translated by Rodger Livingstone and Gregor Benton. New York: Penguin.

Marx, Karl. 1992. *Capital*, Vol. 1: *A Critique of Political Economy*. Translated by Ben Fowkes. New York: Penguin.

Marx, Karl, and Friedrich Engels. 1970. *The German Ideology*. London: International Publishers.

Marx, Karl, and Friedrich Engels. 2012. *The Communist Manifesto: A Modern Edition*. Translated by Samuel Moore in cooperation with Friedrich Engels. London: Verso.

Maslow, Abraham. 1943. "A Theory of Human Motivation." *Psychological Review* 50 (4): 370–96.

Massey, Doreen. 2004. "Geographies of Responsibility." *Geografiska Annaler: Series B, Human Geography* 86 (1): 5–18.

Massey, Doreen. 2005. *For Space*. London: Sage.

Massumi, Brian. 1996. *A User's Guide to Capitalism and Schizophrenia: Deviations from Deleuze and Guattari*. Cambridge, Mass.: MIT Press.

Maturana, Humberto, and Francisco Varela. 1980. *Autopoiesis and Cognition: The Realization of the Living*. Boston: D. Reidel Publishing Company.

Max-Neef, Manfred. 1991. *Human Scale Development: Conception, Application, and Further Reflections*. London: Zed Books.

Max-Neef, Manfred. 1992. "Development and Human Needs." In *Real-Life Economics: Understanding Wealth Creation*, edited by Paul Ekins and Manfred Max-Neef. London: Routledge.

McCourt, Matthew, and Gabriel Perkins. 2014. "Taking Care to Take Back." *Social & Cultural Geography* 15 (8): 983–85.

McMurtry, John. 1998. *Unequal Freedoms: The Global Market as an Ethical System*. West Hartford, Conn.: Kumarian Press.

Mdee, Anna. 2002. "Sustainable Livelihoods Approaches—Can They Transform Development?" Research Paper 2. University of Bradford, U.K.: Bradford Centre for International Development.

MEGC (Maine Economic Growth Council). 2013. *Measures of Growth in Focus*. Augusta: Maine Economic Growth Council.

Mettler, Katie. 2016. "'Good Trouble': How John Lewis Fuses New and Old Tactics to Teach about Civil Disobedience." *Washington Post*, June 23.

Michaud, Mike. 2014. "Maine Made: A Business and Investment Plan to Capitalize on Maine's Advantages." Portland: Michaud for Governor 2014.

Miller, Ethan. 2006. "Other Economies Are Possible: Organizing toward an Economy of Cooperation and Solidarity." *Dollars and Sense*, July.

Miller, Ethan. 2010. "Solidarity Economy: Key Issues and Questions." In *Solidarity Economy I: Building Alternatives for People and Planet*, edited by Emily Kawano, Tom Masterson, and Jonathan Teller-Ellsberg. Amherst, Mass.: Center for Popular Economics.

Miller, Ethan. 2013a. "Surplus of Surplus: From Accounting Convention to Ethical Coordinates." Paper presented to the Rethinking Marxism Gala, University of Massachusetts Amherst, September 2. http://www.communityeconomies.org/node/267.

Miller, Ethan. 2013b. "Community Economy: Ontology, Ethics, and Politics for Radically Democratic Economic Organizing." *Rethinking Marxism* 25 (4): 518–33.

Mills, Peter. 2004. "Maine Tax Policy: Lessons from the Domesday Book." In *Changing Maine, 1960–2010*, edited by Richard Barringer. Portland: University of Southern Maine.

Mitchell, Timothy. 1998. "Fixing the Economy." *Cultural Studies* 12 (1): 82–101.

Mitchell, Timothy. 2002. *Rule of Experts: Egypt, Techno-Politics, Modernity.* Berkeley: University of California Press.

Mitchell, Timothy. 2008. "Rethinking Economy." *Geoforum* 39 (3): 1116–21.

Mol, Annemarie. 1998. "Ontological Politics: A Word and Some Questions." *Sociological Review* 46 (S): 74–89.

Mol, Annemarie. 2002. *The Body Multiple: Ontology in Medical Practice.* Durham, N.C.: Duke University Press.

Moore, Jason W. 2015. *Capitalism in the Web of Life: Ecology and the Accumulation of Capital.* London: Verso.

Morton, Timothy. 2010. *The Ecological Thought.* Cambridge, Mass.: Harvard University Press.

Morton, Timothy. 2017. *Humankind: Solidarity with Nonhuman People.* Brooklyn, N.Y.: Verso.

NADO Research Foundation. 2011. "Mobilize Maine: Asset-based Regional Economic Development." Washington, D.C.: National Association of Development Organizations.

Nagel, Thomas. 1989. *The View from Nowhere.* Oxford: Oxford University Press.

Nancy, Jean-Luc. 1991. *The Inoperative Community.* Translated by Peter Connor, Lisa Garbus, Michael Holland, and Simona Sawhney. Minneapolis: University of Minnesota Press.

Nancy, Jean-Luc. 2000. *Being Singular Plural.* Translated by Robert D. Richardson and Anne E. O'Byrne. Stanford, Calif.: Stanford University Press.

Native Forest Network. 2008. "Post-Hearing (Not-So-Brief) Brief Regarding the Matter of Zoning Petition ZP707." Augusta, Maine: Native Forest Network.

Negri, Antonio. 1999. *Insurgencies: Constituent Power and the Modern State.* Minneapolis: University of Minnesota Press.

Nelson, Julie A. 2009a. "Between a Rock and a Soft Place: Ecological and Feminist Economics in Policy Debates." *Ecological Economics* 69 (1): 1–8.

Nelson, Julie A. 2009b. "The Study of Choice or the Study of Provisioning?: Gender and the Definition of Economics." In *Beyond Economic Man: Feminist Theory and Economics*, edited by Marianne A. Ferber and Julie A. Nelson. Chicago: University of Chicago Press.

Newman, Saul. 2001. "War on the State: Stirner and Deleuze's Anarchism." *Anarchist Studies* 9 (2): 147–64.

Neysmith, Sheila M., and Marge Reitsma-Street. 2005. "'Provisioning': Conceptualizing the Work of Women for 21st Century Social Policy." *Women's Studies International Forum* 28 (5): 381–91.

Niebuhr, Reinhold. 1987. *The Essential Reinhold Niebuhr: Selected Essays and Addresses.* Edited by Robert McAfee Brown. New Haven: Yale University Press.

Nietzsche, Friedrich. 1969. *Thus Spoke Zarathustra*. Translated by R. J. Hollingdale. London: Penguin.

Noonan, Jeff. 2006. *Democratic Society and Human Needs*. Montreal: McGill-Queen's University Press.

Norgaard, Richard. 1994. *Development Betrayed: The End of Progress and a Coevolutionary Revisioning of the Future*. New York: Routledge.

NZAID. 2006. "NZAID Sustainable Livelihoods Approach Guideline." Auckland: New Zealand International Aid and Development Agency.

O'Connell, Joseph. 1993. "Metrology: The Creation of Universality by the Circulation of Particulars." *Social Studies of Science* 23 (1): 129–73.

O'Connor, James. 1998. *Natural Causes: Essays in Ecological Marxism*. New York: Guilford Press.

Odling-Smee, F. John. 1996. "Niche Construction, Genetic Evolution, and Cultural Change." *Behavioral Processes* 35 (1/3): 195–205.

Odum, Eugene P. 1971. *Fundamentals of Ecology*. 3rd ed. New York: W. B. Saunders.

O'Gorman, Emily. 2014. "Belonging." *Environmental Humanities* 5: 283–86.

O'Hara, Frank. 2010. "Making Maine Work: Critical Investments for the Maine Economy." Augusta: Maine State Chamber of Commerce.

O'Hara, Frank. 2013. "Making Maine Work: Growing Maine's Workforce." Augusta: Maine Development Foundation and Maine State Chamber of Commerce.

Orenstein, Daniel E., and Dalit Shach-Pinsley. 2017. "A Comparative Framework for Assessing Sustainability Initiatives at the Regional Scale." *World Development* 98 (October): 245–56.

Orenstein, Henry. 1980. "Asymmetrical Reciprocity: A Contribution to the Theory of Political Legitimacy." *Current Anthropology* 21 (1): 69–91.

Osborn, W. C. 1974. *The Paper Plantation: Ralph Nader's Study Group Report on the Pulp and Paper Industry in Maine*. New York: Grossman Publishers.

Oxford English Dictionary. 2008a. "Articulation, N." *OED Online*. Oxford: Oxford University Press.

Oxford English Dictionary. 2008b. "Environment, N." *OED Online*. Oxford: Oxford University Press.

Oxford English Dictionary. 2008c. "Negotiate, V." *OED Online*. Oxford: Oxford University Press.

Pain, Rachel, and Sara Kindon. 2007. "Participatory Geographies." *Environment and Planning A* 39 (12): 2807–12.

Palmer, Kenneth T., G. Thomas Taylor, Marcus A. LiBrizzi, and Jean E. Lavigne. 2009. *Maine Politics and Government*. Lincoln: University of Nebraska Press.

Parsons, Talcott, and Robert F. Bales. 1956. *Family Socialization and Interaction Process*. New York: Routledge.

Parsons, Talcott, and Neil Smelser. 1956. *Economy and Society*. New York: Free Press.

Pease, Allen, and Wilfred Richard, eds. 1983. *Maine: Fifty Years of Change, 1940–1990*. Orono: University of Maine Press.

Pechenick, Eitan Adam, Christopher M. Danforth, and Peter Sheridan Dodds. 2015. "Characterizing the Google Books Corpus: Strong Limits to Inferences of Socio-Cultural and Linguistic Evolution." *PLOS One* 10 (10): e0137041.

Pellegrin-Rescia, Marie L., and Yair Levi. 2005. *The "Social" as Metaphor and the Case of Cooperatives*. Burlington, Vt.: Ashgate.

Perelman, Michael. 2007. "Primitive Accumulation from Feudalism to Neoliberalism." *Capitalism Nature Socialism* 18 (2): 44–61.

Perroux, François. 1950. "Economic Space: Theory and Applications." *Quarterly Journal of Economics* 64 (1): 89–104.

Perryman Group. 2008. "An Essential Resource: An Analysis of the Economic Impact of Undocumented Workers on Business Activity in the US with Estimated Effects by State and by Industry." Waco, Tex.: Perryman Group.

Phillips, J. 2006. "Agencement/Assemblage." *Theory, Culture & Society* 23 (2/3): 108–9.

Plumwood, Val. 1993. *Feminism and the Mastery of Nature*. New York: Routledge.

Plumwood, Val. 2008. "Shadow Places and the Politics of Dwelling." *Australian Humanities Review* 44: 139–50.

Polanyi, Karl. 1977. *The Livelihood of Man*. Edited by H. W. Pearson. New York: Academic Press.

Polanyi, Karl. 1992. "The Economy as Instituted Process." In *The Sociology of Economic Life*, edited by Mark Granovetter and Richard Swedberg. Boulder, Colo.: Westview Press.

Polanyi, Karl. 2001. *The Great Transformation*. Boston: Beacon Press.

Poovey, Mary. 1995. *Making a Social Body: British Cultural Formation, 1830–1864*. Chicago: University of Chicago Press.

Popke, E. Jeffrey. 2009. "The Spaces of Being-in-Common: Ethics and Social Geography." In *Handbook of Social Geographies*, edited by Susan Smith. London: Sage.

Power, Marilyn. 2004. "Social Provisioning as a Starting Point for Feminist Economics." *Feminist Economics* 10 (3): 3–19.

Puig de la Bellacasa, María. 2017. *Matters of Care: Speculative Ethics in More Than Human Worlds*. Minneapolis: University of Minnesota Press.

Rakodi, Carole. 2002. "A Livelihoods Approach: Conceptual Issues and Definitions." In *Urban Livelihoods: A People-Centred Approach to Reducing Poverty*, edited by Carole Rakodi and Tony Lloyd-Jones. London: Earthscan.

Rapport, David J. 1991. "Myths in the Foundations of Economics and Ecology." *Biological Journal of the Linnean Society* 44 (3): 185–202.

Rauschmayer, Felix, Ines Omann, and Johannes Frühmann. 2011. "Needs, Capabilities, and Quality of Life: Refocusing Sustainable Development." In *Sustainable Development: Capabilities, Needs, and Well-Being*, edited by Felix Rauschmayer, Ines Omann, and Johannes Frühmann. London: Routledge.

Reneault, Catherine Searle. 2014. "Transforming Maine's Economy: Innovation and Entrepreneurship Policy." *Maine Policy Review* 23 (1): 37–47.

Resnick, Stephen, and Richard Wolff. 2006. *New Departures in Marxian Theory*. New York: Taylor & Francis.

Rigby, Catherine E. 2004. "Earth, World, Text: On the (Im)possibility of Ecopoiesis." *New Literary History* 35 (3): 427–42.

Ritchie, Loren. 2006. "Cutting Damages Deer Livelihood." *Natural Resource Council of Maine, Issues in the News* (blog), December 10. http://www.nrcm.org/news.

Robbins, Lionel. 1932. *An Essay on the Nature and Significance of Economic Science*. London: Macmillan.

Robbins, Paul, Marla Emery, and Jennifer L. Rice. 2008. "Gathering in Thoreau's Backyard: Nontimber Forest Product Harvesting as Practice." *Area* 40 (2): 265–77.

Roelvink, Gerda. 2016. *Building Dignified Worlds: Geographies of Collective Action*. Minneapolis: University of Minnesota Press.

Roelvink, Gerda, and J. K. Gibson-Graham. 2009. "A Postcapitalist Politics of Dwelling: Ecological Humanities and Community Economies in Conversation." *Australian Humanities Review* 46: 145–58.

Rogers, Raymond A. 1998. *Solving History: The Challenge of Environmental Activism*. Montreal: Black Rose Books.

Rolde, Neil. 2004. *Unsettled Past, Unsettled Future: The Story of Maine Indians*. Gardiner, Maine: Tilbury House.

Rose, Nikolas. 1999. *Powers of Freedom: Reframing Political Thought*. Cambridge: Cambridge University Press.

Rose, Nikolas, and Peter Miller. 2008. *Governing the Present: Administering Economic, Social, and Personal Life*. Cambridge: Polity Press.

Rosenberg, Marshall B. 2003. *Nonviolent Communication: A Language of Life*. Encinitas, Calif.: PuddleDancer Press.

Ross, Rachel Talbot, and Mark Sullivan. 2014. "Maine Voices: State's Economic Disparity Discriminates Most against Minorities." *Portland Press Herald* (blog), November 30.

Rubin, Herbert J. 1988. "Shoot Anything That Flies; Claim Anything That Falls: Conversations with Economic Development Practitioners." *Economic Development Quarterly* 2 (3): 236–51.

Rukeyser, Muriel. 1968. *The Speed of Darkness*. New York: Random House.

Sachs, Wolfgang, ed. 1992. *The Development Dictionary: A Guide to Knowledge as Power*. London: Zed Books.

Sandilands, Catriona. 1993. "On 'Green' Consumerism: Environmental Privatization and 'Family Values.'" *Canadian Woman Studies* 13 (3): 45–47.

Sandler, Ronald, and Phaedra Pezzullo. 2007. *Environmental Justice and Environmentalism: The Social Justice Challenge to the Environmental Movement*. Cambridge, Mass.: MIT Press.

Schabas, Margaret. 2005. *The Natural Origins of Economics*. Chicago: University of Chicago Press.

Schumpeter, Joseph. 2003. *Capitalism, Socialism, and Democracy*. New York: Routledge.

Scoones, Ian. 1998. "Sustainable Rural Livelihoods: A Framework for Analysis." IDS Working Paper 72. Brighton, U.K.: Institute for Development Studies.

Scoones, Ian. 2009. "Livelihoods Perspectives and Rural Development." *Journal of Peasant Studies* 36 (1): 171–96.

Scott, David. 2004. *Conscripts of Modernity: The Tragedy of Colonial Enlightenment*. Durham, N.C.: Duke University Press.

Sebeok, Thomas A. 2001. *Signs: An Introduction to Semiotics*. Toronto: University of Toronto Press.

Serrat, Oliver. 2008. "The Sustainable Livelihoods Approach." Manila: Asian Development Bank.

Serres, Michel. 1995. *The Natural Contract*. Translated by Elizabeth MacArthur and William Paulson. Ann Arbor: University of Michigan Press.

Serres, Michel. 2007. *The Parasite*. Translated by Lawrence R. Schehr. Minneapolis: University of Minnesota Press.

Shanin, Teodor. 1997. "The Idea of Progress." In *The Post-Development Reader*, edited by Majid Rahnema and Victoria Bawtree. London: Zed Books.

Shellenberger, Michael, and Ted Nordhaus. 2009. *Break Through: Why We Can't Leave Saving the Planet to Environmentalists*. New York: Houghton Mifflin Harcourt.

Shukaitis, Stevphen, and David Graeber. 2007. *Constituent Imagination: Militant Investigations/Collective Theorization*. Oakland, Calif.: AK Press.

Shuman, M. H. 2007. *The Small-Mart Revolution: How Local Businesses Are Beating the Global Competition*. San Francisco: Berrett-Koehler Publishers.

Siebert, Horst. 2008. *Economics of the Environment: Theory and Policy*. Berlin: Springer-Verlag.

Smith, Adam. 1982. *The Wealth of Nations, Books 1–3*. New York: Penguin.

Smith, Andrea. 2005. *Conquest: Sexual Violence and American Indian Genocide*. Boston: South End Press.

Smith, Mick. 2013. "Ecological Community, the Sense of the World, and Senseless Extinction." *Environmental Humanities* 2 (1): 21–41.

Snowpiercer. 2013. Directed by Joon-ho Bong. New York: RADiUS-TWC. DVD.

Snyder, Robert. 2011. "Becoming Groundfishers in an Era of Depletion in the Northeastern United States." PhD diss., York University, Toronto.

Snyder, Robert, and Kevin St. Martin. 2015. "A Fishery for the Future: The Midcoast Fishermen's Association and the Work of Economic Being-in-Common." In *Making Other Worlds Possible: Performing Diverse Economies*, edited by Gerda Roelvink, Kevin St. Martin, and J. K. Gibson-Graham. Minneapolis: University of Minnesota Press.

Soper, Kate. 1995. *What Is Nature?: Culture, Politics, and the Non-Human*. London: Wiley-Blackwell.

Spalding, Ken. 2007. "Testimony of Ken Spalding Regarding ZP 707 Plum Creek Petition for Rezoning Moosehead Region." Augusta, Maine: Land Use Regulation Commission.

Spivak, Gayatri Chakravorty. 1996. "Subaltern Studies: Deconstructing Historiography." In *The Spivak Reader: Selected Works of Gayatri Chakravorty Spivak*, edited by Donna Landry and Gerald M. MacLean. New York: Routledge.

Staten, Henry. 1986. *Wittgenstein and Derrida*. Lincoln: University of Nebraska Press.

Steffen, Will, Wendy Broadgate, Lisa Deutsch, Owen Gaffney, and Cornelia Ludwig. 2015. "The Trajectory of the Anthropocene: The Great Acceleration." *Anthropocene Review* 2 (1): 81–98.

Stengers, Isabelle. 2005a. "Introductory Notes on an Ecology of Practices." *Cultural Studies Review* 11 (1): 183–96.

Stengers, Isabelle. 2005b. "The Cosmopolitical Proposal." In *Making Things Public: Atmospheres of Democracy*, edited by Bruno Latour and Peter Weibel. Cambridge, Mass.: MIT Press.

Stengers, Isabelle. 2009. "History through the Middle: Between Macro and Mesopolitics, an Interview with Brian Massumi." *INFleXions* 3 (October).

Stengers, Isabelle. 2010. *Cosmopolitics I*. Minneapolis: University of Minnesota Press.

St. Martin, Kevin. 2005. "Disrupting Enclosure in New England Fisheries." *Capitalism Nature Socialism* 16 (1): 63–80.

St. Martin, Kevin. 2009. "Toward a Cartography of the Commons: Constituting the Political and Economic Possibilities of Place." *Professional Geographer* 61 (4): 493–507.

Stone, Christopher D. 2010. *Should Trees Have Standing? Law, Morality, and the Environment*. New York: Oxford University Press.

Stone, Matthew. 2013. "Is Maine's Economy Recovering? What the Statistics Tell Us." *Bangor Daily News* (blog), September 20.

Sustainable Maine. 1996. "Sustainable Maine: Integrating Economy, Environment, and Community." Portland: Sustainable Maine.

Sweezy, Paul. 1942. *The Theory of Capitalist Development: Principles of Marxian Political Economy*. London: Dennis Dobson Limited.

Sylvain, Renée. 2002. "'Land, Water, and Truth': San Identity and Global Indigenism." *American Anthropologist* 104 (4): 1074–85.

Szerszynski, Bronislaw. 2010. "Reading and Writing the Weather: Climate Technics and the Moment of Responsibility." *Theory, Culture & Society* 27 (2/3): 9–30.

Taylor, Alan. 1990. *Liberty Men and Great Proprietors: The Revolutionary Settlement on the Maine Frontier, 1760–1820*. Chapel Hill: University of North Carolina Press.

Thistle, Scott. 2012. "Lewiston Mayor Tells Somalis to 'Leave Your Culture at the Door.'" *Bangor Daily News* (blog), September 27.

Tribe, Keith. 1978. *Land, Labor, and Economic Discourse*. London: Routledge & Keegan Paul.

Troy, Austin. 2012. "Valuing Maine's Natural Capital." Brunswick, Maine: Manomet Center for Conservation Sciences.

Turnhout, Esther, Claire Waterton, Katja Neves, and Marleen Buizer. 2013. "Rethinking Biodiversity: From Goods and Services to 'Living With.'" *Conservation Letters* 6 (3): 154–61.

Uexküll, Jakob von. 2010. *A Foray into the Worlds of Animals and Humans: With a Theory of Meaning*. Translated by Joseph D. O'Neil. Minneapolis: University of Minnesota Press.

Varela, Francisco, Humberto Maturana, and Ricardo Uribe. 1974. "Autopoiesis: The Organization of Living Systems, Its Characterization, and a Model." *Biosystems* 5 (4): 187–96.

Volk, Tyler. 2003. *Gaia's Body: Toward a Physiology of Earth*. Cambridge, Mass.: MIT Press.

Wallerstein, Immanuel. 1984. "The Development of the Concept of Development." *Sociological Theory* 2: 102–16.

Waring, Marilyn. 1988. *If Women Counted: A New Feminist Economics*. New York: Harper & Row.

Watkin, Christopher. 2007. "A Different Alterity: Jean-Luc Nancy's 'Singular Plural.'" *Paragraph* 30 (2): 50–64.

WCED. 1987a. *Food 2000: Global Policies for Sustainable Agriculture: A Report of the Advisory Panel on Food Security, Agriculture, Forestry, and Environment to the World Commission on Environment and Development*. London: Zed Books.

WCED. 1987b. *Our Common Future: The Report of the World Commission on Environment and Development*. Oxford: Oxford University Press.

Weber, Andreas. 2010. "The Book of Desire: Toward a Biological Poetics." *Biosemiotics* 3 (3): 289–87.

Weber, Max. 1994. *Political Writings*. Edited by Peter Lassman and Ronald Speirs. Cambridge: Cambridge University Press.

Weheliye, Alexander G. 2014. *Habeas Viscus: Racializing Assemblages, Biopolitics, and Black Feminist Theories of the Human*. Durham, N.C.: Duke University Press.

Whatmore, Sarah J. 1997. "Dissecting the Autonomous Self: Hybrid Cartographies for a Relational Ethics." *Environment and Planning D* 15 (1): 37–53.

White, Richard. 1996. "'Are You an Environmentalist or Do You Work for a Living?': Work and Nature." In *Uncommon Ground: Rethinking the Human Place in Nature*, edited by William Cronon. New York: W. W. Norton & Company.

Whitehead, Alfred North. 1920. *The Concept of Nature*. Cambridge: Cambridge University Press.

Wiesmeth, Hans. 2011. *Environmental Economics: Theory and Policy in Equilibrium*. Berlin: Springer-Verlag.

Williams, James. 2003. *Gilles Deleuze's Difference and Repetition: A Critical Introduction and Guide*. Edinburgh: Edinburgh University Press.

Wolf, Eric R. 1988. "Inventing Society." *American Ethnologist* 15 (4): 752–61.

Woodard, Colin. 2012. "Malaga Island: A Century of Shame." *Portland Press Herald* (blog), May 20.

Wright, Laura. 2010. *"Wilderness into Civilized Shapes": Reading the Postcolonial Environment.* Athens: University of Georgia Press.

Yusoff, Kathryn. 2013. "Geologic Life: Prehistory, Climate, Futures in the Anthropocene." *Environment and Planning D: Society and Space* 31 (5): 779–95.

Yusoff, Kathryn. 2017. "Geosocial Strata." *Theory, Culture & Society* 34 (2/3):
105–27.

Yuval-Davis, Nira. 1999. "What Is 'Transversal Politics'?" *Soundings*, no. 12: 88–
93.

INDEX

ETHAN MILLER is an activist-scholar, teacher, parent, and home-steader. He lectures in environmental studies, politics, and anthropology at Bates College and is a member of the Community Economies Collective.